Understanding the Bible
The Old Testament

Understanding the Bible

The Old Testament

edited
by John P. Bradley
and John Quinlan

GOOD WILL PUBLISHERS, INC.
Gastonia, North Carolina

Library of Congress Catalog Number: 73-92775

NIHIL OBSTAT
   Bernard L. Rosswog, O.S.B., S.T.D.
   Censor Librorum

IMPRIMATUR
   ✝ Edmund F. McCaffrey, O.S.B., Ph.D., D.D.
   Abbot-Ordinary, Diocese of Belmont Abbey Nullius

Art Editor: Kathrine B. Sanborn

ACKNOWLEDGMENTS

We wish to thank Harper and Row, Inc.
for permission to use a passage from
The Church and the Jewish People by
the late Augustin Cardinal Bea, S.J.
We also wish to thank Paulist-Newman
Press for permission to reproduce the
article *God Speaks to Us* by Hubert J.
Richards.

Printed in the United States of America

The People of God

WE ARE LIVING in an age of profound and rapid change. Nowadays this is clearly recognized as the most significant fact of our times. But a decade ago few people realized the power of the various forces of change that were already working mightily in our midst. Among those few was a man, well advanced in years, who was to become the spiritual leader of the Catholic world.

Pope John XXIII's election to the See of Peter was unexpected. Even more unexpected was his announcement, a mere ninety days after his election, that he planned to convoke an ecumenical council that would initiate an era of change and renewal in the Roman Catholic Church. Change and renewal, Pope John knew, were essential if the Church was to present the ageless gospel of Christ in a meaningful way to a world that was entering a new stage of its history.

The teaching of the Second Vatican Council, then, initiated the Church's response to the enormous challenges posed by a profoundly changing world. In the past, because of a false notion of the nature of the Church, the laity have regarded such challenges as the sole responsibility of bishops and priests. Happily, Vatican II corrected this false notion: "As sharers in the role of Christ the Priest, the Prophet, and the King, the laity have an active part to play in the life and activity of the Church. . . . The laity must be specially formed to engage in conversation with others, believers or non-believers, in order to manifest Christ's message to all men" (*Decree on the Apostolate of the Laity,* nos. 10, 31).

The laity have this role because they are the people of God. They are the Church, co-responsible with bishops and priests for Christ's mission on earth. Indeed in this age of change the laity's responsibility is of crucial importance. They are, in the words of Pope Paul VI, the Church's "bridge to the modern world." Emphasizing the importance of the laity's role in today's world, the Second Vatican Council taught that "the laity are called in a special way to make the Church present and operative in those places and circumstances where only through them can she be the salt of the earth" (*Constitution on the Church*, no. 33).

To make known Christ's message and to manifest it to others is no easy task in today's world. "A change in attitudes and in human structures frequently calls accepted values into question. This is especially true of young people. . . . As a result, parents and educators frequently experience greater difficulty day by day in discharging their tasks" (Vatican II's *Constitution on the Church in the Modern World*, no. 7).

The laity's role of being the Church's "bridge to the modern world" is indeed a difficult one. Since, however, they are called to this noble duty in virtue of their baptism and confirmation we can be sure that the spiritual helps needed for it will be generously provided. But many other forms of help will also be needed. If the laity are to make the Church present and operative in today's world, if parents and educators are to convince our young people that beneath all the changes in the world there are many realities which do not change, they must possess a sound knowledge and understanding of Christ's message.

This work was planned and built to furnish today's laity with the help needed for this task. From the outset our contributors were asked to resist the temptation to write for experts and instead to present the Christian message in a manner that today's layman would find understandable and interesting. The design and typography chosen for the volumes, and the profusion of illustrations providing the reader with an abundance of valuable visual aids, had the same goal in mind. In a word, this is a work planned and designed for the laity today, and especially for Catholic families, to assist them in their task of manifesting Christ's message in their homes and in the world around them.

It scarcely needs to be said that a large work of this kind owes its completion to many people. It is not possible to mention here everyone who shared in the considerable labor involved in producing these volumes. Particular mention must be made, however, of a few whose constant and competent cooperation was indispensable.

Our editorial advisory board—Herbert A. Musurillo, S.J., Martin Nolan, O.S.A., and James Walsh, S.J.—rendered invaluable assistance. Shirley B. Shipley designed the work and also performed a host of technical tasks too numerous to mention. Rose A. Bogan discharged with rare competence and dedication a wide range of secretarial duties that touched on every phase of the project. Kathrine B. Sanborn carried out the arduous assignments that are the lot of an art editor. Leo F. Daniels, C.O., besides compiling the indexes, no small task in a work of this scope, also contributed valuable editorial assistance. To them and to all others who cooperated in this project we express our gratitude.

J. P. B.

Preface

IT IS TRUE that the Bible is a sacred book. But to most people, alas, it is so sacred that they settle for admiring it from afar. Frequently we hear that the Bible is the best seller in history, yet few gain much from it beyond the pious satisfaction of giving it an honorable, if undisturbed, place in their homes. Surely there has never been a book owned by so many, but read and understood by so few.

The Bible has been described as the word of God in the words of men. Perhaps this description can provide us with some clues as to why it is so highly reverenced and at the same time so little appreciated for what it is.

Christians believe that the Bible is the *word of God*. That indeed is why we reverence it. But for too many, "the word of God" is an abstract phrase devoid of living, dynamic, concrete meaning. We shall come closer to the true meaning of this phrase, a meaning that grips and stirs us, if we realize that God speaks to us in the Bible. He tells us about Himself, of His personal love for each one of us, and of His plan for saving mankind. He invites us to listen to what He tells us and, with faith, to respond to His word.

Perhaps if we thought of the Bible in this living, concrete way, believing God is truly present in His word and inviting us to a lifetime's dialogue with Him, many of us would be less content to admire our Bible from afar.

The second part of our description of the Bible furnishes us with a further clue as to why it is so seldom removed from its

ix

resting place in our homes. The Bible is the written record of God's dialogue with men: it is the word of God *in the words of men.* The Bible was written by many different men over a long period of time. Though inspired by God, these men retained their own culture, their own mentality, their own limitations. They thought like men of their time and they wrote like men of their time.

Since this is so, if we are to listen with understanding to God as He speaks to us in the Bible, we must know "what meaning the sacred writer intended to express and actually expressed in particular circumstances as he used contemporary literary forms in accordance with the situation of his own time and culture" (Vatican II's *Constitution on Divine Revelation,* no. 12).

The Bible, then, though the greatest of all books, is not an easy book, especially for us who live so far removed in time and in culture from the men who wrote it. To understand the Bible we need help, and today a great deal of help is available. Thanks to the devoted labors of biblical scholars, historians, students of language, and archeologists, particularly over the last century or so, much light has been shed on the Bible and its background. Thanks also to such documents as Pius XII's encyclical letter *Divino afflante Spiritu* and Vatican II's *Constitution on Divine Revelation,* we Catholics today receive enlightened guidance through the teaching authority of the Church, an authority we accept as the authentic interpreter of the word of God.

The purpose of this book and of its companion volume dealing with the New Testament is to make more widely available the help needed for a more fruitful understanding of the Bible. God speaks in the Bible to all men, not just to theologians and other specialists. The experts who have contributed to this book are best rewarded for their labors if through them many non-experts are helped to listen with greater understanding to the word of God.

There is a further consideration touching on the need for an adequate understanding of the Bible. In its teaching the Second Vatican Council placed welcome new emphases on biblical roots.

Thus the Church now draws more deeply and extensively from the Bible in her liturgy and teaching. A better understanding of the Bible is, then, needed, if we are to gain the nourishment that the Church now offers us in her liturgy and teaching.

We are grateful to our contributors for their cooperation in the preparation of this book, and to Father Leo Daniels, C.O. and Dr. Marjorie E. Reiley for their editorial assistance.

J. P. B.

Contents

Abbreviations

The abbreviations used in Bible references are listed below according to the order in which the books appear in the Bible. In some cases (e.g., Job, John) abbreviations have not been used in this work.

THE OLD TESTAMENT

Gen.	Genesis	Eccles.	Ecclesiastes
Ex.	Exodus	Song	Song of Songs
Lev.	Leviticus	Wis.	Wisdom
Num.	Numbers	Ecclus.	Ecclesiasticus
Deut.	Deuteronomy	Is.	Isaiah
Josh.	Joshua	Jer.	Jeremiah
Judg.	Judges	Lam.	Lamentations
1 Sam.	1 Samuel	Ezek.	Ezekiel
2 Sam.	2 Samuel	Dan.	Daniel
1 Chr.	1 Chronicles	Hos.	Hosea
2 Chr.	2 Chronicles	Obad.	Obadiah
Neh.	Nehemiah	Mic.	Micah
Esth.	Esther	Hab.	Habakkuk
1 Macc.	1 Maccabees	Zeph.	Zephaniah
2 Macc.	2 Maccabees	Hag.	Haggai
Ps.	Psalms	Zech.	Zechariah
Prov.	Proverbs	Mal.	Malachi

THE NEW TESTAMENT

Matt.	Matthew	Col.	Colossians
Acts	Acts of the Apostles	1 Thess.	1 Thessalonians
Rom.	Romans	2 Thess.	2 Thessalonians
1 Cor.	1 Corinthians	1 Tim.	1 Timothy
2 Cor.	2 Corinthians	2 Tim.	2 Timothy
Gal.	Galatians	Heb.	Hebrews
Eph.	Ephesians	1 Pet.	1 Peter
Phil.	Philippians	2 Pet.	2 Peter

Rev. Revelation

How to Look Up References

Gen. 3:19 means Genesis, chapter 3, verse 19.

Josh. 24:2, 14 means Joshua, chapter 24, verse 2 and verse 14.

Is. 42:1–55:13 means Isaiah, chapter 42, verse 1 through chapter 55, verse 13.

Matt. 3:6; 21:25 means Matthew, chapter 3, verse 6, and chapter 21, verse 25 (of the same book).

Gal. 4:1f. means Galatians, chapter 4, verse 1 and the following verse; 4:1ff. means chapter 4, verse 1 and following verses.

Gen. 41:34a, 35b means Genesis, chapter 41, first part of verse 34 and the second part of verse 35.

cf. Acts 2:38 means *confer* (compare) Acts of the Apostles, chapter 2, verse 38.

The Books of the Bible

God Speaks to Us

Hubert J. Richards

When we read the Bible, God speaks to us. The Bible is, as it were, a living presence of God in our midst, which we cannot disregard, any more than we can disregard that other living presence of God in our midst—the eucharist. If, however, we are to listen with under-standing to God speaking to us in the Bible, we must have some background knowledge not only of the various books of the Bible but also of Israel's history and the culture of the men who wrote these books.

MOSES
Michelangelo

Why Read the Bible?

ONE MIGHT answer this question with the exasperating reply given by people who are asked why they climb mountains: because it is there. But perhaps the parallel is not an unhappy one. Certainly most people regard the Bible rather like a mountain. It's a very nice thing to have around as a background, but wild horses wouldn't get them to make a personal acquaintance with it. It is far too dangerous. Much wiser to admire it at a distance. What is it that makes some people discontent to keep their distance, and willing to go to the most strenuous lengths to make a closer contact with it? The answer is, because it is there, because it is what it *is*, the word of God.

One could put it this way. If this were just another holy book, we could afford to take our choice, and excuse ourselves from reading it by saying that we get more out of a prayer book or a popular magazine. But it is an article of our faith that this book is quite unique, that in some unparalleled way it is God's own word to us. Obviously this does not mean it is just a collection of divine statements: "Now understand this, there are ten commandments, nine choirs of angels, eight beatitudes, seven sacraments. . . ."

A LIVING PRESENCE OF GOD

No, God did not *dictate* His thoughts to the men He inspired. If He used these men as His instruments, He took care that they should remain thoroughly human instruments, providing their own thoughts quite freely, and expressing them in their own quite individual way. But we do still believe that each of them, in what he expressed, spoke for God, and that the net result of their work is not seventy-three individual human books, but one book which is the word of God. We believe that when we read the Bible, God speaks to us; that the Bible is, as it were, a living presence of God in our midst, which we cannot disregard, therefore, or leave to those who like that sort of thing, any more than we can make it a matter of personal preference to accept or reject that other presence of God in our midst, which is the eucharist.

AN UNATTRACTIVE STORY

It may be objected that this word of God is a very strange word. Its accent is entirely foreign to us. The French have put it forcefully enough in their saying: "The Old Testament is not for young girls." And can we seriously pretend that it *is* everyone's meat, this shabby and unedifying, this more often positively disedifying history of pride and hatred and murder and lust?

We are shocked by this story of man's constant perversion of God's plan for him. We are puzzled by its slow and uncertain beginnings. We are scandalized by the primitive and inadequate ideas the patriarchs had of God. We are mortified by the boneheaded waywardness of those descendants of theirs who made their way out of Egypt. We are revolted by the cruelty with which they identified their enemies as God's and liquidated them. We are sickened by their repeated backsliding and rejection of the prophets sent to them, by their miserable misunderstanding of the temple built for them, by the blood bath in which they were decimated before being carried into exile, by the pathetic failure of the restoration and the return to the same old ways, by the climax of all this stupidity and perverseness in their rejection of Christ. Why should we need to be dragged through all that? The answer is: because this is the history of our race.

THE HISTORY OF OUR RACE

We are only fooling ourselves if we think of the Old Testament as "them" and the New Testament as "us." There is no third party in this story, only God and the race we belong to. It is our forefathers whom God rescued from Egypt, our family who captured Jerusalem and built the temple. It is to our own people that God sent prophet after prophet, ourselves whom He has brought so slowly and so patiently from those primitive beginnings to the perfection that He finally revealed in Christ. Nor should we imagine that His education of us is finished. Do we really differ very much from these ancestors of ours? Can we read this story of God's plan being wrecked again and again by man's indifference and sin, and not see in it a pretty accurate reflection of our repeated rejection of the word which God has spoken in our own lives?

But even if we are so indifferent that we fail to see ourselves in this story, could we fail to see God there, teaching us by sheer repetition what His plan for us is? Because God has only one plan — to choose a people for Himself, to rescue them from their misery, and to lead them through suffering to the glory of His presence. What He revealed in the story of Abraham He revealed in the story of Exodus. What He did through Moses He did again through Joshua, and again through David, and Solomon, and Hezekiah, and Josiah, and the Maccabees . . . until He did it for a last time in Christ.

If anyone thinks he can get the meaning of this book by simply reading the last chapter of it, then he may as well leave the Old Testament closed. But if he feels that this story concerns him, that it is a matter of his own life and death to know as much as he possibly can of God, of what He is like, of what He does, of what He asks and what He gives, then he will want to hoard every word like a miser.

What is the Bible about?

What is it, then, that God tells us in this book? He tells us, first of all, about Himself. It is rather revealing that the title by which He is most often known in this book is "The God of our fathers, the God of Abraham and Isaac and Jacob." When we have tried to devise our own definition of God, we have seized on some *intellectual* concept and called Him a supreme spirit, existing of Him-

SEMITE WITH HIS DONKEY, *a wall painting, dated about 1900* B.C.

self, infinite in all perfections. We have spoken in abstract terms about His infinity and eternity, His omnipotence and transcendence. There is nothing as remote as that in the God we meet in the Old Testament. We meet Him in the concrete, in what He has done for our fathers, Abraham, Isaac, and Jacob.

He is the God who acts, who walks with Adam in the cool of the evening, who shuts the door of the ark to save His chosen race, who sits and talks with Abraham in the intimacy of his tent, who holds back the waters to protect His people and bring them into the land He has promised them. The Old Testament is not a series of pious speculations about God. It is the account of what God has *done*, of how He has given Himself away again and again by His patience and His pity and His love for His people, and shown Himself to be not a philosophical abstraction but a father, a shepherd, a lover, a husband, a king, and a judge.

GOD TELLS US ABOUT OURSELVES

But it is not only about Himself that God tells us here. He tells us also about ourselves. The famous story in the second book of Samuel, of the parable told by the prophet Nathan to King David after the Bathsheba affair, provides a happy example:

> Yahweh sent Nathan the prophet to David. He came to him and said: "In the same town were two men, one rich, the other poor. The rich man had flocks and herds in great abundance; the poor man had nothing but a ewe lamb, one only, a small one he had bought. This he fed, and it grew up with him and his children, eating his bread, drinking from his cup, sleeping on his breast; it was like a daughter to him. When there came a traveller to stay, the rich man refused to take one of his own flock or herd to provide for the wayfarer who had come to him. Instead he took the poor man's lamb and prepared it for his guest."
>
> David's anger flared up against the man. "As Yahweh lives," he said to Nathan, "the man who did this deserves to die. He must make fourfold restitution for the lamb, for doing such a thing and showing no compassion."
>
> Then Nathan said to David, "You are the man" [2 Sam. 12:1–7].

That final sentence, "You are the man," could stand at the end of every story in the Old Testament. All the way through, the Holy Spirit is pointing to the reader and saying, "This is *you*. This is the diary of *your* relationship to God, of the length and breadth and height and depth of God's love for *you*, and *your* failure to respond to it. This is not something you can read dispassionately, because it is an analysis of what you are, a child of God who keeps forgetting his noble origin and his glorious destiny, a sinner torn between his self-seeking and his need for the God who made him, a prodigal son who has wasted his substance and whom his Father is waiting to welcome home with tears in his eyes."

God tells us here, finally, about Christ. If we want to know Christ, it is no good confining our reading to the pages of the New Testament. We need to know something of the drama of the

Old Testament, of man's separation from God and his condemnation to death, if we are going to appreciate the free gift of salvation that God has·bestowed on us in Christ. We need to read the story of these ancestors of Christ, with all their shortcomings and sins, if we are to appreciate the wonder of Him who became one of them, and called Himself the Son of Man. We need to have savored something of the Old Testament's feeling for the majesty of God, the God who cannot be seen or imagined or even represented, if we are to appreciate the impact of the words of Him who said: "He who has seen me has seen the Father."

But we must be clear about this. It is not simply a question of appreciating the New Testament better by knowing something of what went before. The whole Old Testament is *about* Christ. And not simply because it contains some verses which foretell Him, but because the whole of it is the word of God, the same Word which was finally to be made flesh and be known to us as the person of Jesus Christ. God has not got dozens of plans which He tries out on us, one after the other. He has only one plan, one word that expresses what He is and what He wills, and that Word is Christ.

The Bible and the eucharist

Is it surprising that the great Christian writers of the first centuries saw Christ in every line of the Old Testament? Perhaps they sometimes paid less attention to the literal meaning of these lines than we do. But have we any right to criticize them when we have lagged so far behind them in seizing something that is even more essential? They like nothing better than drawing a parallel between the Bible and the eucharist, because in both we meet Christ. We are upset when people neglect the eucharist and refuse to be nourished by this food that God is holding out to them. Have we any right to be upset when we have so often turned our backs on this other food, through which God desires just as earnestly to enter into communion with us?

PASTORAL SCENE *beside the Sea of Galilee*

The Thread of Events

Without some background knowledge of Israelite history, it is not possible to understand the books of the Old Testament. The order in which they stand in the Bible is not the order in which they were written. Unless this chronological order is reconstructed, at least roughly, the books will lose half their meaning. We shall now, therefore, attempt to make such a reconstruction. The approximate dates of the events discussed are given in a chart at the end of this essay.

Since Israelite history begins with Abraham in chapter 12 of Genesis, the chapters that precede his story cannot be called GENESIS 2–3   history in the strict sense. Two of these chapters are more in the nature of a parable in which the basic truths of religion are presented in a picturesque manner: that the whole world is the creation of the one God who later revealed Himself to Israel, that it is essentially good, that man is its kingpin, that woman is his equal, that marriage is their crowning joy, that God's friendship with man was broken and will continue to be broken whenever man asserts his independence of God, that God promised that man would eventually make good the harm he had done.

The chapters that follow provide a link between these beginnings and the historical figure of Abraham. The existing traditions, legends, and folklore of Israel and Baby-GENESIS 4–11   lonia are here used and adapted to illustrate the same basic themes of sin and salvation.

A FAMILY

The traditions that have been used to tell the story of Abraham and the clan descended from him (Isaac, Jacob-Israel, the Twelve

GENESIS 12–50 Patriarchs) are more historical. They are not always consistent with each other, but their content shows them to be based on real events in Palestine in the early part of the second millenium before Christ.

Between the years 2000 and 1500 B.C., the promise of Genesis 3 was made concrete in the person of Abraham. Through his complete giving of himself to God (faith), the process whereby sin came into the world was reversed, and all nations saw the beginning of their salvation. The great promises made to him were jealously guarded by his nomadic descendants, though at this early stage they were scarcely distinguishable from their Semitic neighbors: their worship and sacrifice remained primitive, God was the God of their clan, and the patriarch was His priest.

When part of the clan (Joseph) moved to Egypt, a providential opening was given for the rest to migrate there in time of famine. In the delta area of Goshen, their nomadic way of life began to change into a semi-settled existence, though they remained proudly distinct from the non-Semitic Egyptians.

A PEOPLE

A change in Egypt's political situation threatened to enslave the clan and annihilate it. In fact it was its saving, at a time when its increased numbers already threatened its unity.

EXODUS, *Narrative parts of* NUMBERS Under Moses (about 1300 B.C.) the disorganized rabble made their escape in a series of providential happenings that they could never forget. The desert journey welded them together, and at Sinai they came to know the God who had rescued them as Yahweh, the supreme being who had condescended to enter into a covenant with them, and make them His own people.

It was at Sinai, too, that the customs which marked them off from other peoples were first regulated into a body of religious and civil law. From now, this expressed God's will for them, the word of God dwelling with them. To this they dedicated themselves. The ark in which it was placed became the throne of Yahweh, who was on the march with them.

Legislative parts of PENTATEUCH, *later further developed*

A people must have a land. After a number of unsuccessful attempts, the Israelites invaded Palestine-Canaan (about 1250 B.C.) under the leadership of Moses' lieutenant Joshua. The date was a propitious one: Egypt and Mesopotamia, for whom Canaan had long been a bone of contention, were both preoccupied with other matters. Israel's nominal control allowed the land to be portioned out provisionally among the twelve tribes.

JOSHUA

This division of forces weakened Israelite unity. Defection to the easier religion of the original Canaanite inhabitants aggravated the disunity, and some border areas were completely lost. Over a period of 200 years the tribes were occasionally rallied by God-sent liberators or "Judges," who reminded them of their purpose and of Yahweh's claims to faithfulness. The growing need for unity compelled the last of these, Samuel, to grant them a king. But he did so grudgingly: Yahweh alone was the king of this people, and a human ruler could only be His earthly representative.

JUDGES

A KINGDOM

Israel's first king, Saul, failed to live up to this ideal. Brilliantly successful in battle against the Philistines, rival claimants to the desirable property of Palestine, he nevertheless could not meet the demand for obedience and commitment to the voice of Yahweh as expressed by Samuel. In about 1000 B.C. he was rejected in favor of David, the man after Yahweh's own heart.

FIRST *and* SECOND SAMUEL

From now on, the promise by which God had tied Himself to the patriarchs and the people is to be concentrated in David and his dynasty, which inherits the title previously bestowed on Israel — the "Son of God." So the kingdom of God is established on earth. When David dies, another David will be ardently expected to complete his work. In this period of youthful optimism, the old oral traditions were written down for the first time, and Israelite literature began.

Nucleus of the PENTATEUCH

A constant tradition associates the name of David with the book

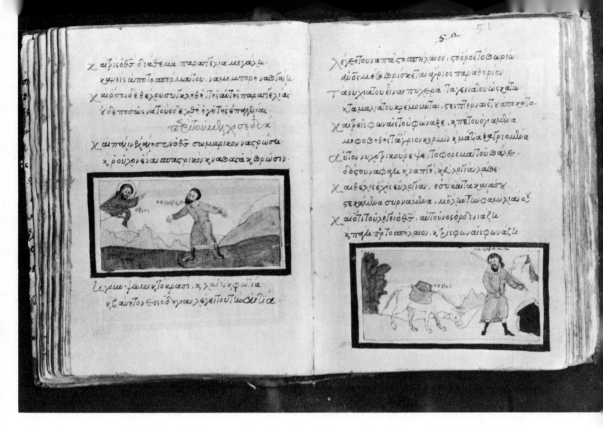

GOD TALKS TO ABRAHAM, *an illumination from a sixteenth-century manuscript in St. Catherine's Monastery at Mount Sinai*

of Psalms. Although the book was not completed until the second
century B.C., and thus reflects the whole history
of Israel, it is quite clear that it was David who
Some PSALMS
began this collection of prayers which sing to God of Israel's joys,
sorrows, and hopes.

David's reign was followed by a sad decline. His military successes, based on Saul's victories, had given Israel independence
and prosperity. Solomon's Golden Age was the
FIRST *and*
SECOND
KINGS
proof. But luxury brought decadence, and foreign alliances brought foreign religions in their
train. In 926 B.C. the more Spartan northerners, under the powerful tribe of Ephraim, rebelled and set up a rival kingdom of
Israel based on Samaria. For all its highminded idealism, this
northern kingdom was a political and religious failure. Ruled by
a series of weak kings, in rapidly changing dynasties, its religion

was soon scarcely distinguishable from that of the Canaanites. But it did produce the first prophets, those spokesmen for God who championed the religion of Sinai, made God's demands explicit, and expressed His plans for the future. Of this prophetical movement, Elijah and Elisha were the pioneers.

The successors of Elijah and Elisha developed their preaching, to bring Israel face to face with a God who was not content with lip service but demanded the service of the heart; and with a God who could love even an unfaithful Israel, because it was He who made her lovable. They foresaw and foretold Assyria's advance south to Egypt, crushing Israel in its path. Samaria fell in 722 B.C.

AMOS

HOSEA

The southern kingdom of Judah was in a more protected position, but its continual intrigue with Egypt promised that its end would eventually be the same. Prophets twice saved the kingdom from disaster.

ISAIAH 1–39

MICAH

Code of DEUTE-
RONOMY

Deuteronomic
History
JOSHUA —
JUDGES —
SAMUEL —
KINGS

About 700 B.C. King Hezekiah achieved what the prophets had always demanded, a complete self-giving in faith to Yahweh as the sole master of history, and was acclaimed as a possible messiah when this policy saved Jerusalem from the Assyrian onslaught. About 80 years later, his great-grandson Josiah took advantage of an unprecedented lull in the pressure from outside to launch a radical religious reform, based on the same prophetical ideals. A history of Israel's past, from the conquest down to the present day, was written at this time to illustrate those ideals.

JEREMIAH 1–28
NAHUM
ZEPHANIAH

But the reform was transitory. Subsequent return to irreligion brought martyrdom to the prophets, but not before they had foretold the inevitable political crash. In 586 B.C. Jerusalem fell to the new world power of Babylonia, and most of its citizens were exiled.

A CHURCH

In exile, Judah was transformed. Its religion could no longer be identified with Jerusalem, or the temple, or the land, or the king-

CAMEL TRAIL TO SINAI

dom, or the king, or the nation, for all these externals had been snatched away. If this religion was to survive, it had to be lived at a deeper level, where God was served for His own sake by a community which had become a church, and which saw the worship of God as the only reason for its existence.

It was again the prophets who helped Judah to reach this level — Jeremiah who wrote to the exiled nation that the only hope for the future lay with them; Ezekiel who taught them to see Yahweh's presence in their hearts; Habakkuk who raised the great problem of evil and attempted to solve it; and a group of Isaiah's disciples who spoke of the exiles as the Suffering Servant of Yahweh, willingly undergoing "death" in order to bring the knowledge of Yahweh to the whole world.

JEREMIAH
29–52
EZEKIEL

HABAKKUK

ISAIAH 40–55

All these looked forward to the return from exile as the beginning of a New Covenant.

With the monarchy ended, the leadership of the nation passed into the hands of priests. Their profound and distinctive spirituality was reflected in the priestly law which was to govern the lives of the returned exiles, and in their own retelling of Israel's past history.

LEVITICUS
Legislative parts of
EXODUS *and*
NUMBERS

These traditions, including the priestly account of creation, were later incorporated into the Pentateuch (the first five books of the Bible) as it now stands. An explanation of the Pentateuch will be given later in this essay.

GENESIS

Within fifty years of their deportation, the exiles found themselves free to return when Babylonia was defeated by Persia in 538 B.C. Their first uncertain efforts were encouraged by prophets whose preaching was crowned within twenty years by the rebuilding of the temple. But the following century saw the return of the old abuses, and prophetical reformers had again to be loud in their protests. The civil leaders, Ezra and Nehemiah, put their teaching into practice, and the reform was supported by a second "priestly" history of Israel as a church.

HAGGAI
ZECHARIAH 1–8
MALACHI
JOEL
Priestly history
(CHRONICLES-
EZRA-
NEHEMIAH)
OBADIAH

This reform, echoed in other writings too, encouraged a certain amount of narrowness and exclusiveness. This was countered by other elements in the new Israel, just as eager for religious renewal, but calling attention to the older prophetical ideal of an Israel no longer at daggers drawn with the pagan nations that surrounded them, but leading them to God. A final collection of all the old prophetic themes in the last pages of the book of Zechariah marks the end of the prophetical movement.

ISAIAH 56–66
RUTH
JONAH

ZECHARIAH 9–14

The last centuries before the coming of Christ were in many ways the most fruitful in Israel's history. The profound meditation which saw the whole of past history as God's love story is an eloquent witness of this, as also

SONG OF
SOLOMON

THE PROPHET AMOS EXHORTS THE PEOPLE, *a sixteenth-century woodcut*

PSALMS
PROVERBS
TOBIT

ECCLESIASTICUS
JOB
ECCLESIASTES

WISDOM

is the sustained worship which made the Psalter the "Prayer Book of the Second Temple." More significantly still, Israel's wise men concerned themselves with the problem of evil and retribution. An optimistic stream of thought continued to insist on the traditional teaching that this life sees the reward of virtue and the punishment of evil. A more critical and realistic school of thought insisted equally strongly that experience belied this, and demanded a more fitting solution. A final reassessment in the last century before Christ combined both views in a wider concept of life after death, and gave final precision to the whole movement's yearning for the divine Wisdom to come and bring Israel salvation.

The same confidence in a future life is reflected in two accounts of the fight for independence, forced on Israel by their Greek

FIRST *and*
SECOND
MACCABEES

DANIEL 1–6
JUDITH
ESTHER

DANIEL 7–12

overlords in 175 B.C. Politically the struggle was a success. Heartened by traditional stories which formed a parable of their own fight for independence, the Jews regained their freedom. But a more discerning minority saw that God's plans could not be achieved on the political level. The highest point of Old Testament thought is marked by an apocalyptic writing in which the whole of past history is presented in a series of apocalyptic visions, and which has abandoned all nationalistic ambition and yearns for a kingdom that can only come from heaven, ruled by the heavenly figure of the Son of Man. With all material hopes weaned out of them, a purified remnant is ready to receive God's final revelation of Himself.

THE TRUE ISRAEL

God gave this revelation in Christ. Having spoken His word in the heavens when He first created the world, and more explicitly

NEW
TESTAMENT

in the Law which He gave to Israel at Sinai, and more plainly still in the prophets who spoke in His name, He finally ordained that this Word should become flesh and dwell among us.

Here at last was the ideal to which God had been shaping His people all along, the true Israel into whom all men must be incorporated if they wish to share that title. Here at last the plan of God stood revealed in its fullness: to give Himself to men so that they may accept Him, and so be drawn up into His own life.

How Does the Bible Speak?

We said above that God did not *dictate* his thoughts to the men He inspired. If He used these men as His instruments, He took care that they should remain thoroughly human instruments, providing their own thoughts quite freely, and expressing them in their own quite individual ways. We must not imagine that the Bible dropped ready-made from heaven. It was painfully spelled out word by word by men of flesh and blood, whose inspiration was not something that took the place of their own culture and mentality, characteristics, style, and limitations. Their inspiration was embodied in these human terms. It became as it were "incarnate" in them, in somewhat the same way that the Son of God became the flesh of Jesus Christ, and did not merely substitute Himself for it.

A VARIETY OF HUMAN TEMPERAMENTS

There is no lack of variety in the human temperaments that may be found in the Bible. To turn the page from Ecclesiastes to Ecclesiasticus is to switch from a bleak pessimism to an almost smug self-satisfaction. The pedantic clumsiness of the book of Chronicles constrasts violently with the effortless poetry of some of the Psalms, and so does the fire and passion of St. Paul with the peaceful calm of St. John. Paul dictated his highly complicated thought at top speed, and the fact that the result is inspired does not stop it being highly complicated. The author of the second book of Maccabees, on the other hand, found writing a laborious and painful business, and his inspiration did not prevent him from concluding his work with "that is the best I could do." The human personalities stand out, as anyone who opens the Bible to read it

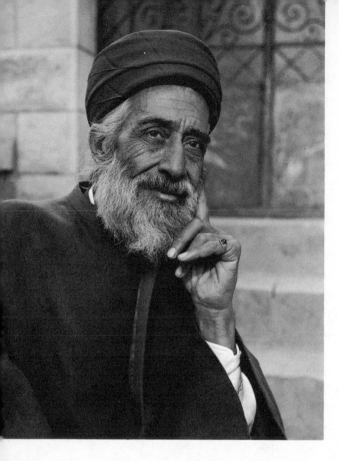

A Samaritan priest

can discover for himself. Nor is it only their style and personality which are thoroughly human. Their whole background, their whole mentality, their whole outlook has colored their writing through and through.

Authors are men of their time

These authors *thought* like men of their time. If all men of the time conceived of the earth as the center of the universe, a flat disc covered with a sort of colander through which the rain came down, then your biblical author is going to express himself in that way too. How else could he conceive of it? These authors *wrote* like men of their time. If it was the custom of the time to compose the history of your tribe or your people or your nation by simply stringing together all the various records and traditions you could lay your hands on (whether they agreed with each other or not), and leaving it to the reader to make his choice between the inconsistent details, then your biblical author is going to do the same; and to read his work as if it were history in our sense of the word would be to misunderstand him.

The *approach* of these authors was the approach of a particular civilization and mentality. When a westerner is presented with a story (Eden, the Tower of Babel, the Flood), his very first question is almost certain to be, "Did it really happen?" The Semite, when he is told a story, asks, "What does it mean?" The biblical authors are Semites (and that is true even of the New Testament writers). They are going to write with the firm conviction that the significance of a story is the most important (not to say the most interesting) thing about it. This does not mean, of course, that they are going to invent facts or deliberately falsify the facts at their disposal; but their eye is going to be on the theological meaning of the traditions they are dealing with, and not (as ours is) on their historical accuracy.

All this only amounts to saying that these people had, like anyone else, their own forms of expression and thought, for obvious reasons of time and culture.

LITERARY FORMS

We are constantly using our own forms of expression without even adverting to the fact. The speaker on a platform does not have to inquire into the genealogy and social status of every member of his audience before he allows himself to address them as "ladies and gentlemen." "Dear Sir" at the head of our letters does not necessarily imply either affection or respect. These expressions are merely the accepted literary forms for such occasions. To us, their meaning is clear from their context (the public speech, the business letter) and we might well complain if people digging up our letters in two thousand years' time misunderstood them by making no allowance for that context.

All this is very obvious when it is pointed out. But when we read the Bible, we treat it so uniformly as the word of God that we forget to allow for the fact that it has been "incarnated" into a whole library containing prose and verse, history and legend, legislation

E Z E C H I E L

THE PROPHET EZEKIEL
Michelangelo

FIRED CLAY CYLINDER *of Cyrus that tells of the peaceful occupation of Babylon and the return of the exiles to Judah and Jerusalem*

and prayer, national epics and private diaries, and a whole host of other literary forms for which no equivalent exists in our own literature. Each of these must be recognized for what it is, and judged according to the rules for that form. Otherwise we shall only understand the meaning of the words, not the meaning intended by the man who wrote them.

THE PEOPLE IN THE BIBLE

Anyone who has learned to see the Bible in this way will no longer be shocked by the men and women it portrays. We tend to think of Abraham, Isaac, and Jacob in the abstract, as a series of noble and edifying personages, walking across the stage of history with the dignity of stained-glass figures. We open the Bible to find that they were rather primitive Bedouins, with moral standards that were lamentably low, if not offensive to pious ears. Anyone who feels that, needs to do a lot more Bible-reading than he does. He needs to make the Bible his constant examination of conscience to see whether his ears are not perhaps too pious, to ask himself whether he has not become rather more fastidious than the God who came down to the level of men like this, the God who was not afraid to walk with them in order to draw them to Himself. When the Bible speaks of man, it speaks of him as he is, not as we would like to think him to be.

It speaks of people like Adam, whose first thought on being found out was to find an excuse and put the blame on someone else; people like Jacob, who decided that the ambition he had set his heart on was more important than the question of whether he told a few lies or not; people like Moses, who pleaded his lack of training in order to try and escape the responsibility put on him; people like Jephthah, who in the enthusiasm of the moment made a vow to God and then had to break his heart to be faithful to it; people like Ruth, who showed such unusual devotion to her mother-in-law that a book had to be written about it; people like Saul, who found it easy to fight God's battle but difficult to obey God's instructions; people like David, who one moment could dance like a child in the happiness of his intimacy with God, and the next fall from grace as miserably as anyone else; people like the Levite in the parable, who looked the other way after an accident on the Jericho road because he did not want to get mixed up in anything; people like Simon Peter, who had so much faith that he jumped into the sea and so little faith that he went under, who was willing to defend his Master with a sword and then broke down under the questions of a serving maid . . . people in fact like ourselves.

Because when all is said and done, this book is about us. The point is worth repeating because it is so regularly disregarded. This book is not just about the comings and goings of some Middle Eastern tribe. It is first of all about us, about our aspirations and falls, about our joys and our misery, about the beauty of our calling and our failure to be worthy of it. Because here is man as he is, as we know him to be, in all his weakness.

BRONZE AGE VESSELS *discovered at Gath*

And here is God as He is. Not an abstract first cause, but a God who is interested in men of flesh and blood, a father who bends down to appeal to His wayward children.

DIVINE TRUTH REVEALED IN A HUMAN WAY

The Bible, therefore, is the word of *God* which has come to live among *men*. Over-exaggerate either its divine or its human aspect, and you will be in danger of misunderstanding it. If considerable emphasis has been laid on its human aspect, it is because for centuries the prevailing tendency has been to neglect it, and because unless we make some attempt to reconstruct this as accurately as possible we are not in touch with God's word. We are only in touch with what we like to imagine God's word should be. Let us take an example.

The unscientific approach that ignores the human background takes the books of Joshua and Judges quite unquestioningly as history books pure and simple. This is what happened in the years 1250–1050 B.C., and it is recorded for that reason alone. This is the day to day account of how Joshua conquered the land of Canaan and of the opposition which the Israelites encountered. With books like that you do not ask questions about their theology. They are history and that is enough. It was the scientific method which first showed that such a view is rather naive. If the book of Joshua has given such a complete account of the conquest, why does the book of Judges start the whole story again from the beginning and contradict it so flatly?

Joshua is entirely in a heroic key. It gives the impression that all the twelve tribes, united closely under the leadership of Joshua, entered Palestine in one determined invasion, captured the first town of Jericho with magnificent ease, and then simply tore through the rest of the country, slaughtering all the inhabitants until the whole land was theirs.

The first chapter of Judges, recounting the same conquest, makes no mention of Joshua at all, but records the slow, very laborious efforts of individual tribes to carve out a portion of this land on their own account. Far from annihilating the natives, it has to leave the embarrassed record of Israel's failure to dislodge them, and of the constant thorn in the side that they remained ever afterwards. If the same author wrote both books (and this is undisputed) why was he so incredibly inconsistent? Why didn't he make it clear exactly what happened?

A THEOLOGIAN, NOT A HISTORIAN

Because he was not a historian but a theologian. Because he wanted to make it as obvious as possible that he is not interested in the events for their own sake but only in their meaning. He has taken up an optimistic tradition about the conquest in order to illustrate the fact that, from *God's* point of view, there is no difficulty at all in entering the kingdom that He has prepared for His people, that if God has promised His kingdom then He will give it, no matter what obstacles there are in the way. And the author has balanced that with a pessimistic account of the conquest to illustrate the fact that, from *man's* point of view, that kingdom is always eluding our grasp, because we are weak, because we are constantly falling, because we are constantly having to cry out for help to a God who is willing to forgive us seventy times seven.

It is not very good history, but it would be difficult to find better theology. And the truly Christian approach demands that we always finish on that note.

The Old Testament Analyzed

The Old Testament can be divided into three main sections, each seeking to introduce the reader to God in a different way, each, in other words, with its own purpose or slant. If we bear in mind as we read each section what its purpose is, we shall be meeting it on its own terms, treating it as the kind of writing its authors meant it to be.

1. THE PENTATEUCH

The first section of the Old Testament is the Pentateuch, the five Books of Moses: Genesis, Exodus, Leviticus, Numbers, and Deuteronomy. Until recently, the word "Moses" was taken quite uncritically, without much appreciation of the fact that the ancient world did not have our ideas of copyright. The text used to be taken quite simply as an accurate historical account of the origins of the human race and of Israel, without much appreciation of how fundamentally the ancient writing of history differs from our own. The legislation that these books contain (from the end of the book of Exodus through Leviticus and Numbers to the end of Deuteronomy) was taken quite unquestioningly as having been fixed once and for all by Moses at Sinai, without much appreciation of how law and legislation in any civilization must grow and be adapted to new circumstances.

Commentaries on the Pentateuch consisted, until quite recently, of an analysis of the text as a straightforward account of events from creation onwards, composed by Moses from notes left him by the patriarchs or from revelations whispered into his ear by the Holy Spirit. Even when the discoveries of science showed that the early chapters of Genesis can no longer be taken

as literally as they were, there was still no suspicion that these
chapters reflected any other age or mentality but that of Moses
in the year 1250 B.C. More recent scholarship has shown, however, that the process by which the Pentateuch was formed was
far more complicated than that. Again it was a question of the
inconsistencies acting as a warning light—the repetition, for
instance, of the same event in two or three utterly different styles
and mentalities, or the same legal case legislated for in two or
three different ways.

A MOSAIC OF FOUR GREAT TRADITIONS

Over the long years of analysis of these "doublets," it has
been established that the Pentateuch is a sort of mosaic of four
great traditions, each of which has its roots in the actual events
of which it speaks, but each of which had a long oral history
(with the inevitable modifications that such a history gives to
a popular tradition) before it was fixed in a written form centuries after Moses, and finally incorporated into the present form
of the Pentateuch only 350 years before Christ. The scholarly
approach is to distinguish these as accurately as possible, and
to detach them in order to appreciate the individual contribution
of each.

The "Yahwistic" tradition, as it is called, with its primitive
and childlike atmosphere of a God very close to man and its attempt to answer man's most fundamental problems, is a tradition which seems to reflect the enthusiasm of Israel's youth
in the early years of the monarchy. The "Elohistic" tradition
reflects the more developed and conscientious sense of the early
prophets about God's remoteness and supremacy, and the emphasis that this prophetic movement laid on Moses as the founder
of the Israelite constitution. The "Deuteronomic" tradition reflects the warmth and passion of the later prophets, with all
their experience of Israel's apostasy under its successive kings,
and their appeal to Israel's love as a response to the overwhelming
love of God. Here too all the emphasis is on a return to the principles of Moses, although this is expressed in a legislation adapted

to the events of the 7th century B.C. Lastly, the "Priestly" tradition reflects the final development of Israel's thought in the Babylonian exile, with all its concentration on cult and liturgy. Here the whole of history, from Adam down, is told as the story of a holy community bound to God by successive covenants, especially the Covenant of Sinai, to which is attached all the legislation which will ensure that Israel will in future be what it must be—a church devoted to the service of God.

Modern writers often refer to these four traditions—Yahwistic, Elohistic, Deuteronomic, and Priestly—by their initials: J, E, D, P. The Yahwistic goes under the initial J, since J can replace Y in the spelling of the word.

The four traditions are entirely parallel to one another. They deal with the same basic facts, but each from a new viewpoint. To distinguish them does not diminish the stature of Moses. It only emphasizes his importance as the supreme legislator to whom all future ages will look back. The stature of the Pentateuch is increased even more. It is no longer merely a record of the past, a sort of porridge in which everything is of the same grey consistency. It is a collection of all that is finest in Israel's tradition, from one end of their history to the other. This will forever afterwards be the Jewish Torah or Law, the expression of God's will which must be the yardstick by which the Jew measures his life.

2. THE PROPHETS

The second section of the Old Testament is called the Prophets. It begins not with Isaiah and Jeremiah, but with Joshua, Judges, Samuel, and Kings. This in itself is significant. It is we who called these books "historical," and took them as a straightforward account of events. The Hebrews called them the "Prophets," the work of the prophetical meditation on past events in order to draw a religious meaning out of them. The true approach to these books demands that we orientate ourselves to this angle in the sense of viewing life through a more Oriental perspective. Since the adoption of this approach is the main key to our under-

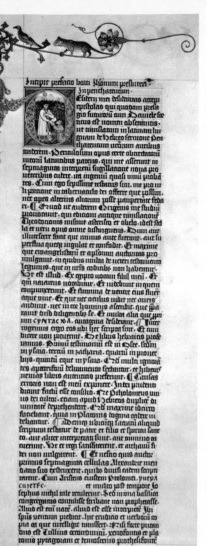

St. Jerome's preface to the Pentateuch,
from the Giant Bible of Mainz (1452 A.D.)

standing the Bible, especially of this kind of writing, it will be well for us to develop here some vital facts already touched on above.

AN APPEAL TO THE IMAGINATION

Westerners generally tend to think in the abstract, to present doctrine in an abstract form in a way which might appeal to a philosopher; the easterner never did this. He always presented his

doctrine in a way which would appeal to the imagination, and capture the interest and sympathy of the ordinary man. The rabbi
still embodies his teaching in a story, whether it be allegory or
parable or a seemingly historical narrative. The last thing he or
his disciples want to know is whether the persons or events or
circumstances in the story are real or fictitious.

The doctrine is everything: the mode of presentation has no
value independent of the doctrine. To make the story the first
consideration and the doctrine it conveys an afterthought, as we
do, is to reverse the eastern order of thinking, and to do injustice to all the narrative parts of the Bible, the New Testament included. To seize on the historical aspect of these books and to tie
oneself into knots in an attempt to reconcile their inconsistencies,
out of a sense of reverence to the author, is sheer stupidity if the
author never intended them to be taken as mere history.

They contain history but are not history books

Of course this must not be exaggerated. To draw the conclusion that these books contain no historical facts at all would be to
undermine Christianity. Christianity is a historical religion, and
if it does not rest upon historical facts into which God has entered
in order to reveal Himself, we have no knowledge at all of God.
That a conglomeration of Semitic tribes who later called themselves Israel occupied Palestine, that this small nation weathered
the vicissitudes of raids and invasions from other peoples who
were also intent on the same desirable property, that this group
finally set up a monarchy and had kings named David and Solomon and Rehoboam and so on ... all this is certain. We must not
question the historicity of anything unless we have grounds for
doing so. We must not come to the conclusion that history does
not matter so long as some religious theme is being taught. This
would be heresy. These books do contain history, as every page of
the Bible does.

But—and this is the point—they are not history books. They are
not books in which the main interest is the events themselves.
They are all theological interpretations of historical events. The

WILDERNESS OF JUDEA

same events are used by different theologians to express different theological truths. So that, in order to understand the purpose of these books (Joshua, Judges, Samuel, Kings and the rest), it is absolutely essential to have some notion at least of the theological viewpoint from which the author is writing: the Deuteronomic viewpoint, for instance, of the author of Joshua, Judges, Samuel, Kings, who wants to present a picture story of God's unmerited love and Israel's failure to respond to it; the priestly angle, for instance, of the author of Chronicles, Ezra, Nehemia, who wants to present a picture story of Israel as a church with only one vocation, the worship of God. If we fail to orientate ourselves to these angles, we shall miss the whole point of what we call the "historical" books of the Old Testament. They are not books written to inform their readers about the past, but to guide them into the future, and to give them a deeper understanding than their forebears had of what God's kingdom on earth must be.

WE MUST PLACE THEM ACCURATELY IN THE CONTEXT OF THEIR TIME

When we come to the prophets proper (Isaiah, Jeremiah, Ezekiel, Daniel, and the twelve minor prophets), the scholarly approach demands first of all that we place them accurately in the context of their time. And this, to begin with, will mean that some of our prejudices must go. Take a book like Isaiah, on which so much critical work has been done in the last 150 years. Is there really any point in refusing to budge from a conservative position about Isaiah, when all scholars of any standing have agreed that the second half of this book is not the work of the prophet Isaiah but of a school of disciples spreading over 300 years after Isaiah lived? It is not as if we were going to lose anything by accepting those conclusions. Who has a fuller understanding of the prophet Isaiah, the man who confines all sixty-six chapters to the eighth century B.C., or the man who insists that Isaiah's influence lasted over 300 years after he was dead? Who has a richer view of inspiration, the man who conceives of it as a rare gift bestowed here and there on a few individuals, or the man who sees it as something continually at work in the whole community, guiding it and enriching its meditation on the words of its prophets in the past?

A DEEPER UNDERSTANDING OF THE WHOLE
PROPHETIC MOVEMENT

But the greatest advantage in this insistence on the context in which the prophets belong lies in the deeper understanding it gives of the whole prophetic movement. In our neglect of this context, we have made the prophets a sort of Farmer's Almanac, a series of exact predictions of the New Testament — Malachi on the precursor of Christ, Micah on Bethlehem, Isaiah 7 on the Virgin Birth, Isaiah 61 on the miracles, Zechariah on Palm Sunday, Isaiah 53 on the Crucifixion and Resurrection . . . any school book will amplify the list. The rest of what the prophets had to say is not important at all. It is a mere envelope of pious exhortation, telling people to be patient. If this is all the prophetical books are, we might as well throw them away. The New Testament has made them redundant, except for those people who like to amuse themselves by looking back at all these "clues" which God gave hundreds of years beforehand, so that they can sit back and marvel at how clever He was.

The history of the Jews was not simply a waiting for Christ, as though God had nothing at all to say to them, except "Wait for it!" It was a history in which, constantly and continually, God revealed Himself and His nature and His will and His purpose here and now. And of that purpose the prophets were the spokesmen and the interpreters. They were not primarily concerned with foretelling the future, but with *forth*telling God's plans here and now, in the present. If they meditated on the past, if they looked forward to the future, it was always to focus the whole of it on the present, on the people of God who here and now needed His word.

They did not foretell the future so much as build it, shape it, make it happen; so that when their hopes were finally realized in Christ, He did not fit them like the second half of an equa-

OLDEST SURVIVING MANUSCRIPT OF THE BOOK OF ISAIAH, *found at Qumran among the Dead Sea Scrolls*

tion, but filled them to overflowing, to show that far from being exaggerations they were understatements. Their hopes were for the ruined temple to be rebuilt, so that God's presence could come and dwell in their midst again; instead God gave them His own presence in the flesh and blood of Christ, which all men could share for all time. Their hopes were for a future in which the kingship, the priesthood, and the prophetical office, so frequently at loggerheads, would be finally reconciled and at peace; instead God gave them one person in whom these three functions were fused into one, for all time the supreme spokesman for God to men, and for men to God. Their hopes were for the ideal king who would be the perfect representative of God's rule over His people; instead He came Himself to be with His people for all time.

If these prophetical books were simply a number of accurate predictions, we could throw them away when they were fulfilled. Their meaning would have been exhausted. But if instead they gave us something much wider—the constant proclamation of the nature of God's relationship to us—we shall never have done with reading them. When Christ comes as the final proclamation of this truth, we do not stop reading the prophets, we begin. We begin for the first time to understand what exactly they were getting at.

3. THE WRITINGS

The last section of the Hebrew Old Testament is called the Writings. It comprises the Psalms, the Wisdom books, and those miscellaneous writings like Ruth, Chronicles, Ezra, Nehemiah, Maccabees, Judith and Esther, which were composed too late to be included in the other two categories. About these miscellaneous books nothing more need be said here except to include them in the remarks made above about the "historical" books in general. About the Wisdom books and the Psalms, we may again assure ourselves that we have nothing to lose but everything to gain by being a little more scholarly, a little more critical, about the titles Solomon and David written at the top.

WISDOM BOOKS AND PSALMS

Considered as one consistent piece of literature, the Wisdom books become simply the pious maxims of a garrulous and rather self-contradictory king. In fact, they represent the most important development of Jewish thought in the last 500 years B.C. on the problem of evil, which traditionalists like Tobit, Proverbs, and Ecclesiasticus tried to by-pass, while pioneers like Job and Ecclesiastes put the tradition to the most severe criticism, in order to produce finally the serenity and calm of the book of Wisdom, only one hundred years before Christ.

As for the Psalms, when they were considered as a uniform collection of David's prayers, they were treated rather like the prophetical books, a dozen or so famous texts foretelling Christ,

ALTAR OF INCENSE, *an artist's conception, from a seventeenth-century map, of the altar of incense used in the Tabernacle*

surrounded by a lot of pious verbiage. It is by placing them as accurately as possible in their right context that more recent scholarship has shown the true value of the Psalter as a reflection of every age of Israel's history, from David down to the Maccabees, the meditation and the prayer of the whole of God's people on the march.

It is because the Christian knows that he belongs to the same caravan that he has recently become more and more conscious that he ought to put these prayers on his lips too. He does not have to be embarrassed by the words Jerusalem, Kingdom, Temple, Law, as if for him they had a completely different meaning, or did not fit in his mouth. They fit all the more readily once the Christian has seen all these key words fulfilled in Christ.

These prayers will forever be the words in which the Father has taught us by His Spirit to pray for the one thing that He wishes to give us, which is His Son.

Conclusions

This essay began with an outline of the reasons why reading the Bible is worthwhile — because it is the word that God speaks to His children. Then, after a glance at the historical framework in which the books of the Bible are set, the human background of their composition was emphasized because without some understanding of it God's word will be distorted. Finally, we analyzed briefly the general purpose and meaning of the three principal parts into which the Old Testament falls. The main facts that will enable us to understand and appreciate the Bible are now told. It only remains for us to think about their consequences. First, let us consider the question of the Bible's inerrancy.

1. Is the Bible true?

The church has always maintained that if God is the author of the Bible, then obviously it can teach no error. This was taken for granted by Christ Himself, who, like the apostles, appealed to Scripture as the infallible word of God. That this was always taken for granted by the church can also be seen from St. Augustine's wry complaint that St. Jerome apparently expects him to treat every one of Jerome's words as gospel:

> I must confess to your reverence that it is only to the canonical books of Scripture that I have learned to give this sort of respect and honor. It is of these alone that I firmly believe the authors were completely free from error. If I come across anything in these writings which seems to contradict the truth, I simply have to conclude that my text

INITIAL PAGE OF THE BOOK OF ES-
THER, *from the Giant Bible of Mainz*
(1452 A.D.*)*

is corrupt, or that it is a bad translation of the original, or that I have misunderstood it. But as for other books, however holy or learned their authors, I do not accept their teaching merely because they say so . . . And I presume, brother, that you feel the same way as I do on this. I presume you want to make a distinction between your books and those written by the prophets and apostles, whom it would be unthinkable to accuse of error [*Letter to Jerome*, 82, 1].

Now we must be careful to consider what we mean when we say that the Bible teaches no error. Our chief help here will be to reflect on what kind of writing we have found these books to be. But even before we come to this, common sense alone will throw considerable light on the question.

ERROR ONLY WHERE THERE IS A STATEMENT

Are there any parts of the Bible which cannot possibly be inerrant? Of course there are. From the very nature of things, by definition, there can be error (or lack of error) only where there is a statement. And there are many pages of the Bible that are not concerned with statements. If I say "It rained yesterday" or "It will rain tomorrow" I am making a statement, and it must be either true or false. Here there is room for inerrancy. But what if I say "I hope it keeps fine tomorrow," or "Prepare ye the way of the Lord," or "Let thine ears be attentive to the voice of my supplication"? Here there is no question of truth or falsehood and consequently no room for inerrancy or error.

Of its nature, inerrancy concerns a judgment about the truth of something, a statement that this is true or that is false. Do the sacred writers invariably make judgments and statements? On the contrary, more often than not they are concerned with consoling their readers, or threatening them, or warning them, or moving them, or attracting them. This was precisely the purpose, for instance, of the preaching of the prophets—and of course of their "historical" writing too, as was pointed out above. Insofar as they use any statement to bring about this effect, they have God's infallible truth to support them. But only to the extent that such a statement is deliberate. If the author is not even considering the truth of a statement, if he is only quoting it for example (as was also remarked above, the authors of the "historical" books might easily do this), then there is no question of inerrancy. Inerrancy needs a deliberate judgment. If this is absent then it has nothing to work on.

FURTHER LIMITATIONS ON INERRANCY

Now this already imposes considerable limitations on inerrancy. But they are not the only ones. Further limitations are involved by the kind of judgment the biblical author makes. Few judgments are universal. Most are made from one particular point of view. A botanist will consider a potato in a different light from one who has to peel it. A poet will see a star differently from an astronomer. Their judgment will be valid from their own point of view, not necessarily from any other. It is worth remembering that whatever matter the biblical author is dealing with—even if it is such an apparently "unreligious" matter as geography or chronology—he will be passing judgment on it from a religious point of

SAINT JEROME WITH
SAINT PAULA AND SAINT
EUSTOCHIUM
Francisco de Zurbaran

view. From any other viewpoint his judgment will not necessarily be valid. His inerrancy is inevitably limited.

Few judgments are categorical. Most are qualified with at least an implicit "probably" or "possibly." On a point of minor importance an author may pass no judgment at all. Here too it is worth remembering that God's truth can only support the degree of affirmation made by His writer. This does not mean that a biblical writer can put forward as only doubtful something which is in fact certain, or as certain something which is in fact only doubtful. That would be error. But if his investigation into a truth has not reached certainty—the classic example is St. Paul's explicit uncertainty about the number of people he baptized (cf. 1 Cor. 1:16), but there are many other implicit examples—then God does not guarantee his statement as certain. To that extent, his inerrancy is again limited.

Nor is every judgment of a writer meant to be passed on to the reader. Readers of a book may hold its author responsible only for those judgments of his which he wants to convey to them, not for those that they can read between the lines. Perhaps the author genuinely thinks that the sky is a solid dome with holes in it; he might even say so. But as long as he is not trying to pass that on to his readers, as long as he is using such a concept only to express something else, his readers cannot accuse him of error. Here too his inerrancy is necessarily limited.

THE CONTEXT OF THE WRITINGS IN THE BIBLE

The last paragraph will probably remind us of some of the difficulties brought up against the notion of biblical inerrancy. The 18th and 19th centuries saw the birth of many of our modern sciences—astronomy and geology, archeology and zoology, biology and anthropology, history and the rest. Day by day each of them began to produce facts which seemed to contradict the teaching of the Bible. An example may be found in almost every line of the Bible's first chapter, which apparently teaches that the universe was created in six days, that light is something distinct from the heavenly bodies, that there are three simple categories of flora and fauna, that the first man was made from clay, that all this took place in 4004 B.C., and so on. Many immediately concluded that the Bible was wrong, and lost their faith. Others doggedly maintained that science was wrong, and saw the various scientific discoveries as so many tests of their faith. Both solutions were obviously too extreme, but other attempts to solve the problem were not much happier.

Today we are in a better position to see that, if only allowance is made for the vastly different kinds of writing represented in the Bible, there is no problem at all. It is a false problem, one that rests on the false premise that the *context* of a piece of writing is unimportant and may be ignored. In fact anything can become a problem or even nonsense if it is ripped out of its context. Even the statement in Psalm 13 "There is no God" only needs putting back into its context to represent the author's meaning: "The

A village of Judea

fool has said in his heart, 'There is no God.' " And the first duty of
anyone who thinks he has found error in the Bible is to discover
something about the context in which its various books were
written.

Not that it is easy to discover the context of a literature which
extends across two thousand years or so. But unless we make the
effort, we condemn ourselves to the danger of constant misunderstanding. And in that effort we will find that what we once feared
as our enemy has become our ally. The discoveries of the last few
decades have raised all sorts of problems which never had to be
faced before. But they have also solved them by making it possible
to reconstruct the context in which the Bible was written: mental,
scientific, chronological, moral, and literary. Mention of these has
already been made; here no more need be done than to set them
out again briefly.

Mental context

It will only cause difficulties to read the Bible as if it was written
by a western mind, when it was in fact written (New Testament
as well as Old) by easterners. This subject of "mentality" is mentioned first because it is the most neglected, in spite of the fact
that it is the most far reaching in its consequences. Enough has
been said above about the difference between the abstract western mind and the concrete eastern one, which will always prefer
to convey its meaning through the medium of a story. The story
may be a parable, an allegory or even a piece of history. But its
only purpose and value, even if it *is* a piece of history, is the
teaching it intends to convey. The very first thing that the Bible
demands of us is that we untwist ourselves from our abstract
Greek mentality and adapt ourselves to the concrete Semitic mentality in which it was written. Perhaps as much as ninety per cent
of our difficulties over inerrancy are due to a failure to do this.

It is no good reading the Bible as if it was written by a twentieth-century scholar, when it was written by men who had neither training nor interest in the sciences. The views of the author
of Genesis on the make-up of the universe were as unscientific

MODEL *of the Hypostyle Hall in the temple dedicated to the God Amon at Karnak, near Thebes, the ancient capital of Egypt*

as those of any amateur at any time; and if he was not writing about the universe's composition at all but religion, then we have no more right to accuse him of error than we would the man who said: "The sun rises upon the good and the evil alike." In scientific matters (and this includes scientific history, scientific philology, scientific criticism, etc.) the Bible speaks as any non-specialist will speak. We may bewail the fact, but it would be stupid to neglect it.

CHRONOLOGICAL CONTEXT

We should also avoid regarding the Bible as if it dropped ready-made from heaven, when its composition was spread over thousands of years. Many of its supposed difficulties come from the fact that people have not allowed for this, and have read it as if there is no difference between 1000 B.C. and A.D. 100. God chose a people, and revealed Himself gradually — painfully, if you like —

in the checkered history of that people. To understand that revelation it is absolutely essential to place each element of it accurately in the period to which it belongs. There is no point in being scandalized, for instance, at a 550 B.C. statement that there is no life after death, when God did not clearly reveal His mind on the matter until 150 B.C.

MORAL CONTEXT

The same may be said about the moral context. If the faith of the Israelites could only be a progressive thing, it is no good expecting their morals to be otherwise. God did not choose a people who were already of great holiness; that was to be the end of the story, not the beginning. And if the beginning of the story shocks us, with all its insincerity and cruelty and sheer crudity, then we ought to be the more filled with wonder at the end to which God brought it. For if He was going to enter the story at all, He had to accept a people at the level at which He found them, with all their inadequate ideas of what was right and what was wrong. If He had not, He would have had no people to raise to higher things. St. John Chrysostom said: "When He forbade sacrifice to demons, He countenanced sacrifices that he did not really want in order to secure what He did want."

LITERARY CONTEXT

As we have seen, if we think we have found an error in the Bible it is usually because we have mistaken the form of expression the particular author is using. This form will be the "key" in which an author has deliberately composed his piece of literature, one that would have been well known to his original audience, but, naturally, less likely to be in habitual use among us. Many of the discords between Scripture and science have arisen out of an attempt to "play" Scripture in a key not intended by the writer. Each book—sometimes each chapter— has its own key, and this can be discovered only by a study of its background, its source, its purpose, and its point of view. Some of these keys are familiar to us (history, poetry, parable, metaphor, hyperbole, etc.), and as

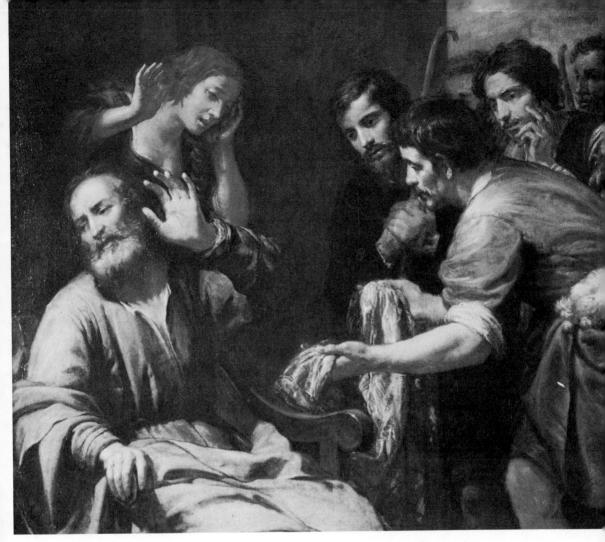

JOSEPH'S COAT BROUGHT TO JACOB
Giovanni Andrea de Ferrari

soon as they are pointed out to us we find no difficulty about playing them.

One of the many unfamiliar ones has already been mentioned: the placing of one or more divergent documents alongside each other (as with Joshua and Judges) and leaving it to the reader to make up his mind between them. We should not be surprised to find that there are other keys in which we moderns no longer play our music, such as pseudepigraphy (associating your thought with the name of someone more famous than yourself), pseudo-prophecy (seeming to foretell what is really past history), anachronism, approximation, inflated numbers, and so on. These may fall strangely on our ears, but it goes without saying that, if they were used, then we must recognize them for what they are.

OTHER, MORE IMPORTANT EFFECTS OF INSPIRATION

What has been said above may give the impression that the notion of inerrancy has simply been made more vague and tenuous so that it can include things which it was previously thought to exclude. In fact, it has been made more precise, pruned of false conclusions, and placed in the one position to which it belongs. If this position is more restricted than the one it previously occupied, making all the classical difficulties irrelevant, it is a matter for rejoicing. Our previous view made us think of inerrancy as the only effect of inspiration, and it loomed large in our minds. In fact, it is the least important of its effects, something merely negative that God could have achieved by giving His approval or *nihil obstat* to an exclusively human work. But inspiration is not to be identified with mere freedom from error. It has other more important and more positive effects, which still remain to be considered. Let us now, therefore, turn our attention to a more positive effect of inspiration: the unity of the Bible.

2. UNITY OF THE BIBLE

We believe the Bible to be a divine book, the word of God. It is God's revelation of Himself, the first expression of what He was later to reveal in its fullness in flesh and blood in the person of Christ. This means that the Bible has a relationship to Christ not only in the few texts which foretell Him, but in its entirety. It means that the whole of the Bible is directed to Christ, who does not appear on its last pages as something unexpected, or even as something merely expected, but precisely as the fullest expression of God's word. It is as if God said: "Look, this is what I have been trying to tell you all along. Now do you see?"

This unity of the Bible, this total relationship to Christ, is a

MADONNA AND CHILD WITH ANGELS
Hans Memling

direct consequence of the inspiration which makes it unlike any other book ever written. It means that we have not really understood the Bible until we have seen Christ on every page of it.

The authors refer to this Christ-directed meaning of the Bible as its "spiritual" sense as distinct from its "literal" sense. The terms are unfortunate ones; because they give the impression that there is nothing spiritual or doctrinal about the literal sense, the sense intended by the human writer. Whereas of course there is no page of the Bible that is purely historical or factual; every word of it is aimed, in the strict literal sense intended by its author, at fostering the spiritual life of its readers, at increasing their knowledge and love of God.

But there is a limit beyond which the writer cannot go, even under the control of inspiration. The end and perfection of God's revelation to men, the fullness of what He has to say to us, is Christ. This means that anything He revealed before the coming of Christ can only be a preparation for Christ, a first and partial expression of Christ. The man who has not seen Christ cannot possibly see this relationship to Christ. He is necessarily limited by his own time and place, and can only see a fraction of God's plan and revelation. But the man who *has* seen Christ can look back and see those fractions for what they actually were—an outline and a preparation for Christ, seeds which will eventually flower into Christ.

THE TRUE SPIRITUAL SENSE

To see this dynamic force which makes the realities of the Old Testament grow into Christ is to see their "spiritual" sense. Those who wrote of them could not see it, because they could not step outside themselves to see God's plan in all its fullness. But the Christian who has seen that plan in its entirety can look back upon those Old Testament realities and see them transfigured beyond the wildest dreams of those who first wrote of them. He does not change their original meaning, or add something different to them or read into them something that is not there. It was there all the time, as the flower is present in the seed.

The point can be illustrated by comparing the true spiritual sense with something that is a simple accommodation. The well known text of Isaiah 53:8 describes the servant of Yahweh as someone whose generation is unutterable: "Who shall declare his generation?" Verbally this would be a fitting description of the inexpressible mystery of Christ's eternal generation. Is this its spiritual sense? A study of the context indicates that in their literal sense the words describe the servant's childlessness; it is the climax of his suffering that he will have no son to perpetuate his name. Between this theme and the divine sonship of Christ there is no real connection. To apply the text to Christ's divinity is a mere play on words. On the other hand, the verbal similarity that exists between the names of Joshua and Jesus (in Hebrew both names are written in the same way: Jehoshua) is based upon something more solid, because there is a real connection between the two persons. Joshua's conquest of the promised land was not only *like* Christ's conquest of the kingdom but was in actual fact a *preparation* for it. The two events were links in the same chain. Joshua's work was the starting point of Israel's longing for the new Joshua who would perfect it. There was a divine purpose in the choice of the name Joshua-Jesus, which means savior. It is not being fanciful, but exactly in line with God's thought, to read the book of Joshua and see in it Christ's own conquest of the kingdom. That is its spiritual sense.

Another example may be taken from the story of Rahab (Josh. 2:1–21; 6:17–25), quoted frequently by early Christian writers as a figure of Christ's work of redemption. A Gentile woman is saved from God's judgment of Jericho by the scarlet cord: the Gentile church is saved from God's condemnation by the scarlet blood of Christ. But the similarity between the two is no more than coincidental. There is no real connection between them, no growth of one from the other, and to speak of one in reference to the other is merely a happy illustration. On the other hand, there is a real relationship between Christ's blood and the blood of the Passover lamb, or the blood of the sacrifice that sealed the Sinai covenant. Each was an expression in embryo of Christ's own pas-

sion, because it effectively prepared men's minds for it. The
Israelites celebrated the Passover and the covenant precisely in
expectation of a new and a better Passover and covenant. And
when Christ celebrated His passion He did not say "What a strange
coincidence!" He said: "This is the new Passover, for which the
old was a preparation; this is the new covenant in my blood."

A CHRIST-CENTERED HISTORY

This should make it clear that the spiritual sense demands
something more than a similarity in words or situation. It demands, between one event and the other, a real organic connection, in an unbroken line. It is not based on mere details which
happen to fit the realities of the New Testament in a rather unexpected way, as if God had deliberately chosen to express Himself in ambiguous words so that we could later admire His in-
genuity. The spiritual sense is not a sort of game which need not
be taken too seriously. It is the most serious thing about the whole
study of Scripture, because it reveals the overwhelming unity,
direction, and continuity of revelation. The Old Testament is not
simply a few promises that Christ would come, plus a number of
cryptic clues which nobody understood until later. The whole
of it is a Christ-centered history, in which every principal person,
institution, event and idea points to Christ.

The outline of a theme like that of God's kingdom will illustrate
this most clearly. It is one of the Bible's most fundamental themes,
expressed for the first time in the idea of a paradise in which God
holds undisputed dominion over the whole of His creation. This
dominion was disturbed by the sin in which man claimed the right
to run his own destiny, independently of God. It was restored at
least partially in Abraham, the man of faith, and his unreserved
giving of himself to God is already greeted in the book of Genesis
as the beginning of the return to God of all men: "In you all nations will be blessed." Abraham is a new Adam. But his union
with God was not reserved to himself; it was eventually extended
to the whole nation that claimed him as its forefather. At Sinai it
was the whole of Israel that received through Moses the title that

CHRIST CROWNED
WITH THORNS
Titian

consecrated it wholly to God, a "Kingdom of Priests." Moses was another Abraham, and in the community of which he was the head God's plan could be said to be achieved.

The theme gained in depth when the community conquered the land without which it could not exist. This land became the kingdom, the sphere over which the true God exercises His rule. Joshua was another Moses, and when he took Palestine the kingdom had truly come. Then the people demanded a human king to put them on an equality with the nations that surrounded them. At first this move aroused violent opposition, and it was regarded as an act of treason against the only true king of Israel, Yahweh. But by the diplomacy of Samuel this difficult step was also maneuvered, and the Israelite king was seen as Yahweh's representative on earth, ruling only insofar as he made visible the supreme mystery of God's invisible kingship. So Israel's kings became the "sons of God," the heirs who ruled in His stead over His universal and eternal kingdom. When David, another Joshua, was enthroned in Jerusalem, the kingdom of God was in all truth established on earth.

The decline of the kingdom followed. One by one David's successors proved unfaithful to the ideal laid down for them. The whole of Israel's subsequent history was a yearning for another David, who would bring to perfection all that Abraham and Moses and Joshua and David left unfulfilled. And in their constant disappointment, as bad king followed bad king and the royal line eventually died out altogether, they even reverted to the older hope that God Himself would come to establish His kingdom, which no mere human representative could do to perfection.

When Christ comes at the end of such a development of thought, He is no mere fulfillment of a promise; He is the explanation of the whole. When Christ comes God says: "*This* is what I have been trying to tell you and do for you all along." The full meaning, the "spiritual" meaning of all those events and persons from one end of the Old Testament to the other—Adam, Abraham, Moses, Joshua, David—is Christ. The Christian who reads these texts and understands them of Christ is not being frivolous; he is seeing the true meaning of the text for the first time.

THE ROAD BETWEEN BETHLE-
HEM AND JERUSALEM

3. THE LIVING WORD

Let us now consider another important effect of inspiration. If
the result of inspiration can truly be called the word of God, then,
it must be something which continues to act, for God's word cannot be inactive. God's inspiration cannot be conceived of as something merely static, once active but now frozen within the covers
of a book. It is something dynamic and still effective. The person
who reads the Bible is not in touch with a collection of archives
about events in the past, or even with a series of propositions about
God. He is in touch with God Himself, revealing Himself to men.
The purpose of the Bible is not only to inform us about God but to
give us God's presence dwelling with us. It is not something that
can be studied dispassionately with the mind alone; it is an encounter with God, who appeals to the heart as well as the mind,
and demands a commitment of the whole self.

We have to realize that there is some truth in saying that the
reader of the Bible is inspired when he takes it in his hands. The
Holy Spirit did not stop acting when the last page of Revelation
was written. He continues to act on the Christian who opens the
book He inspired in order to meet God there and listen to His
voice. We have to realize that the Bible is not simply a book for
specialists and scholars but that it belongs to every Christian. This

does not mean that scholarly study can be neglected; without it
the Bible will be misunderstood. But it does mean that all are invited to make this study, in order that here they may encounter
God.

In short, we have to realize that the Bible is a sort of sacrament:
that is, a tangible and material thing in which Christ is present
in an active manner. It is not merely a souvenir but a real presence of Christ. We should not find it fanciful to welcome the Scriptures with the same words in which we express our welcome to
the eucharist:

> O thou our reminder of Christ crucified,
> Living Bread, the life of us for whom He died,
> Lend this life to me then, feed and feast my mind,
> There be thou the sweetness man was meant to find.

In our concentration on one sacrament of Christ's presence, have
we neglected this other?

This essay began with the question, Why read the Bible? As
well ask a child why he should listen to the words of his father
when he tells him what he has planned for him, or a bride why
she should want to listen to the words of her husband when he
tells her how much he loves her. It has become a commonplace
to point out that it is a misnomer to talk about the four Gospels,
because the word means the Good News, and whether that good
news is told us by Matthew, Mark, Luke or John (or indeed by
Paul, Peter, Jude or James) it is the same. The Good News that is
told us by Moses, Samuel or David, by Isaiah, Jeremiah or Ezekiel,
is not different. They speak in a different accent and in a different
age, but their gospel is the same, the Good News of the love and
the mercy of a God who has made us for Himself, and who leaves
out hearts restless until they rest in Him.

St. John begins his first Epistle with the words:

> Something that has existed since the beginning,
> that we have heard,
> and we have seen with our own eyes;
> that we have watched
> and touched with our hands:
> the Word, who is life—

St. John the Evan-
gelist

this is our subject.
That life was made visible:
we saw it and we are giving our testimony,
telling you of the eternal life
which was with the Father and has been made visible to us.
What we have seen and heard
we are telling you
so that you too may be in union with us,
as we are in union
with the Father
and with his Son Jesus Christ.
We are writing this to you to make our own joy complete
        [1 John 1:1–4].

  Those words could be written at the top of every book of the
Bible. They are all of them the Word of Life, which people like
us, who cannot live on bread alone, need, and need desperately,
if we are not going to starve.

Books of Bible	History of God's People	Contemporary Events	Date
	A FAMILY		
Genesis 12–50	Abraham	Amorite invasion of Middle East	2000 B.C.
	Isaac and Jacob	Egyptian twelfth dynasty	
	Migration to Egypt	Hyksos kings in Egypt Egyptian eighteenth dynasty	
	Israelite slavery in Egypt	Egypt rules south, Hittites north	1500
	A PEOPLE		
Exodus	Exodus from Egypt under Moses Sinai Covenant	Wars between Egypt and Hittites	1300
	A LAND		
Joshua	Occupation of Palestine under Joshua	Hittite power ended	
Judges	Struggle for independence, especially against Philistines	Philistines invade Palestine	1200
1 Samuel	Saul anointed king	End of Egypt's power	1100
	A KINGDOM		
2 Samuel	King David	Assyrian Empire established	1000
Psalms	Israel's Golden Age		
Genesis 2–11	First writing of patriarchal traditions		
3 Kings	Solomon's Israelite Empire Schism of Kingdom into Israel (N) and Judah (S)		
4 Kings	Elijah and Elisha	Assyria extends Empire south	900
Amos			800
Hosea	Israel crushed by Assyria and exiled	Rome founded	
Isaiah 1–39	Judah in precarious position		700
Micah			
Jeremiah			
Deuteronomy	Religious reform in Judah	End of Assyrian Empire	600
Nahum	Writing of Joshua– Judges–Samuel–Kings		
Zephaniah	Judah exiled to Babylonia	Middle East ruled by Babylon	
	A CHURCH		
Ezekiel	Judah transformed in exile		
Isaiah 40–55			
Habakkuk	Judah tackles the problem of suffering		
Proverbs, Job			
Leviticus	Codification of Jewish Law		

THE EVENTS CONNECTED WITH THEM

Books of the Bible	History of God's People	Contemporary Events	Date
Genesis 1	Priests assume leadership		
Haggai and Zechariah	Return of exiles to Jerusalem	Persia takes over Babylonian Empire	
Psalms	Building of second temple		
	Schism with Samaria	Roman Republic established	500 B.C.
Ezra-Nehemiah Chronicles	Jerusalem rebuilt	Golden Age of Greece	
Malachi, Joel Obadiah Isaiah 56–66 Ruth, Jonah	Reform Movements		400
		Persia defeated by Alexander Greek Empire	
Zechariah 9–14	End of Prophetical Movement	Decline of Greek Empire Rise of Roman power Roman wars with Carthage	300
Tobit, Ecclesiasticus Ecclesiastes Song of Solomon Daniel	Greek influence		200
1 and 2 Maccabees Judith and Esther Wisdom	Maccabee revolt Jewish independence	End of Greek Empire	
		Rome rules the world Gallic Wars	100
	King Herod the Great	Pompey and Caesar Augustus, the first emperor	
Gospels	**THE TRUE ISRAEL** The Word is made flesh Ministry of John the Baptist		0
	Christ preaches the Good News of salvation	Tiberius	
Mark	Crucifixion, resurrection and ascension Gospel preached to Gentiles	Caligula	
Pauline Epistles Acts	Paul's journeys	Claudius	
Catholic Epistles Greek Matthew		Nero's persecution Jewish War of Independence Vespasian	
Luke Apocalypse	Fall of Jerusalem	Titus Domitian's persecution Nerva	
John	End of apostolic age	Trajan	A.D. 100

Language and Mentality of the Bible Writers

Luis Alonso Schökel, S.J.

The Bible is literature. When we realize this we have taken the first and most important step toward a proper understanding of God's word. It is Hebrew literature, a literature more vital, more immediate, more human, ever richer than our own Western, intellectual, abstract, technical language. Too often this vitality, immediacy, humanity, and richness is lost when we fail to realize that the language and mentality of the Bible writers were very different from our language and mentality.

GIANT BIBLE OF MAINZ (A.D. 1452), *first page of the book of Exodus*

The Old Testament Is Literature

THE AUTHORS who wrote or composed the books of the Old and New Testaments are not available to us as guest lecturers whom we can question about the meaning of their writings or their way of thinking. They have bequeathed us their books, and it is in and through these books that we discover a manner of expression which corresponds to a certain way of thinking.

And so, when we wish to introduce someone to the reading of Holy Scripture, it is not wise to begin with an examination of the author's mental processes in the hope of thus discovering a mechanism which will lead us to the understanding of his work. It is proper to begin at the other end: starting with the author's techniques of expression we reach back to the author's mind, and in so doing we shall learn how to live with his work.

IMPORTANCE OF OUR ATTITUDE TOWARD LITERATURE

When we open the sacred books of the Old Testament with the notion of finding there the doctrine of our faith, we may be disconcerted at the language (I do not mean the style, for many translations are stylistic masterpieces). We are surprised by what we find: instead of doctrinal statements we find poetry or narrative. While we generally distinguish the methods of writing used in science and literature, doctrine and poetry, the Old Testament portends to propound the doctrine of our faith, and offers us poetry and tells us stories to explain who God is.

Thus we come to a first and radical realization: the Old Testament is *literature*, is written in the language of literature. Let us accept this fact with humility and love. If we make the mistake of considering literary language as a mere relic of a barbaric culture which antedates the era of technology by some 2000 years, then we will lack the elementary respect and love to comprehend both the human and spiritual dimensions of Scripture. Nor is it enough that we consider literature as a part-time escape, a distraction in the daily routine. As long as literature means so little to us, we shall not be in a position to approach the Bible, because the Bible is written in the language of literature. As long as we take the position—at least in practice—that serious theology is to be found only in the manual, the learned monograph, in the works of the Barths and the Rahners, and that the Bible is "entertainment," our pose of intellectual superiority will make us read the Bible without seeing and will cause us to listen to it without hearing.

Thus a first principle emerges: The Old Testament frequently uses literary language. Those who know how to read literature properly—and this includes poetry—will easily begin and heartily continue to read the Bible.

GOD CHOSE THE LANGUAGE OF LITERATURE

A related aspect is devotion. If for doctrine we have the tract or the research paper, for devotion we have books of meditation, spiritual reading, and prayers. No one now thinks of writing a meditation in verse, but the author of Psalm 78 did exactly that. All the psalms are prayers, whether of praise, or petition, or thanksgiving. If, however, we think that verse cannot be serious, then we certainly shall not pray in verse. In short, we shall reject the psalms.

Thus we come to another conclusion: If God chose to speak in the language of literature, it is because He found it apt, even more suited to His purpose than the technical language of a particular culture.

LITERARY VARIETY

Our first general observation was that the Old Testament is literature. A further general observation is that the Old Testa-

WILDERNESS ON THE ROAD FROM JERICHO TO JERUSALEM

ment is a *collection* of literary works, that is to say, it contains
a variety of forms. The fact that it is a religious work certainly
puts it in a special category, but it does not reduce it to one literary genus. This is easier for us to understand inasmuch as our
own religious literature comes to us in a variety of literary dress.
In practice, what we need is an initial flexibility and an effort to
adapt ourselves to literary types which are different from those
to which we are accustomed.

FUNCTIONAL CHARACTER

One of the most important differences between this ancient
literature and our own is its *functional character*. It is literature
destined for worship, for the celebration of a victory or of a royal
wedding, a literature used to denounce sin or to announce a catastrophe, or to promise liberation. We also know and use this functional kind of literature, though generally it is not a major cate-

gory. It embraces publicity, journalism, teaching, etc., whereas great writers cultivate non-functional forms, not to mention poetry.

Now this functional character of Hebrew literature is something we must take as a positive value. For through these literary works the people maintained their unity, expressed their life, and developed their religious commitment. It is a literature which is at once extremely vital and rather popular in the best sense of the word. This might pose a problem for us, given our different way of life. But it can be an advantage for us too, since there are constants in the lives of all men, and these constants the biblical works express with great simplicity and force. Human life or the human condition is the terrain in which we encounter the biblical authors. Therefore, when we approach the reading of the Old Testament, it will be good to return to an attitude of simplicity: life and death, family and tribe, joy and sorrow, hope and courage, etc. It is not only a way of thinking, a biblical mentality, but rather a way of feeling or being.

FORMAL CHARACTER

Secondly, biblical literature is more *bound by form* than our literature is, not only because it is religious literature, but especially because biblical writers had not yet developed a personal style as have the moderns since the Romantic period. Biblical authors feel bound by the forms which the social function of the work and the tradition of their craft impose. It is true that within this more formalized literature there arise some great literary personalities like Isaiah, Jeremiah, Hosea; still, the Old Testament offers us a great deal of anonymous literature, of secondary elaboration and compilation. This formal quality of biblical literature can help us to understand the Old Testament, once we learn to classify each unity in its literary type.

If in reading the Old Testament books, we keep in mind these two points—the *functional* character and the *formal* character of biblical literature—the Bible will speak to us in a language more vital, more human, ever richer, than our intellectual, abstract, and technical language. To ensure a more attentive and penetrating reading of the Old Testament, it will help to examine this twofold character of biblical literature in some detail. In doing so we shall concentrate on some of the more characteristic techniques of *expression*, of *development*, and of *composition*.

Techniques of Expression

Among the techniques of expression used in the Bible it is useful to underline *antithesis and image*. Western intellectual style for the greater part consists in antithetical formulations. From dialectics we have inherited the habit of distinguishing and opposing in order to differentiate and make precise: "It is not a question of . . . but of . . . ; although . . . nevertheless . . . ; it is useful . . . but . . . ; on the one hand . . . on the other . . . ." We differentiate a concept, we qualify an affirmation, we nuance an idea; for this we use division and opposition. Antithesis is, for the West, a means of literary expression, because it is a way of thinking; the literary habit proceeds from the mentality and strengthens it. Authors who formulate with vigor but who do not use opposition, usually adopt an aphoristic style.

THE HEBREWS' USE OF ANTITHESIS

The Hebrew does not use this kind of antithesis. When we meet adversative formulae (the *wau*, the *ki'im*) in the Bible there is almost always question of a great passionate opposition; there is reference to the great contrasts and oppositions in religious life, sin and grace, crime and punishment, pride and humiliation, etc.: antitheses that are not elaborated to differentiate and nuance, but to confront the reader with definitive decisions, to denounce

CATTLE BOATS, *a wall-painting, dated* 2420 B.C.

his conduct before God, to introduce him into the drama of religious existence.

Thus, while for the Westerner antithesis is an instrument for precision, antithesis is for the Hebrew the act of conjuring up radical oppositions. The Hebrew thinks and contemplates generally in totalities: the totality is divided into its two exclusive halves, represented by its two extreme poles, conjured up in its dynamic tension. The Westerner restricts the field of vision, divides and subdivides rigorously, analyzes tirelessly, to know with precision, with exactitude.

We may speak of two styles, two mentalities, provided that we do not exaggerate. For our mentality and our literature of the West also know the Hebrew antithetical forms. Many Western literary types do not use the antithesis of precision, which belongs properly to an intellectual style; on the other hand, the writers of the New Testament, especially St. Paul, received along with the

Greek tongue the ability and the taste for fine distinctions, intellectual nuance.

ANALYTICAL AND SYNTHETIC: INEXACT LABELS

It is not exact to label Western style as "analytical" and Hebrew as "synthetic." For synthesis follows analysis – it does not precede it; and the Hebrew authors are at a stage prior to analysis, to differentiation. They are at the stage of simple intensity, unarticulated richness, and we must approach them with a mind open to the simple, the full, the intense. It is an understandable temptation and a dangerous one for many interpreters of the Bible to wish always to assign a precise meaning – precise in our sense – to the writings of the Old Testament, and even to St. Paul. Our differentiation will give us an authentic and partial viewpoint which must be completed by another partial aspect, and both must be directed to a further synthesis; and so the process of grasping will be as follows: from the full and undifferentiated to the differentiated and precise, to the final synthesis.

At this point we must correct the theory of T. Boman (*Hebrew Thought Compared with Greek*) – who labels the Hebrew mentality as analytical and the Western mentality as synthetic. J. Schildenberger's observation is more exact when he speaks of thinking in totalities: a concrete vision of the reality, the part as referred to the whole, the man in his integrated totality; truth is not purely intellectual, purely theoretical; the Hebrew sees or expresses in an individual the totality of the tribe, of the descendancy or lineage, of humanity; man is not the sum of soul and body perfectly separable, etc. (*Vom Geheimnis des Gotteswortes*, pp. 149–154).

IMAGES

Even more important than the procedure of antithesis is the *image*. Again we are confronted with a way of expression which shows a way of thinking and understanding. The language of the Old Testament, and somewhat less that of the New Testa-

AN ARAB DRINKING FROM AN
"IBREEK" IN JORDAN

ment, is substantially an *imaginative* language, which demands
an adequate viewpoint on the part of the reader. To secure this
we must first clear up blurred focuses due to our culture or
coming from false affirmations, accepted because repeated.

A special warning must be directed against the false characterization of the language of the East as imaginative, that of
the West as conceptual. The falsity of this is rooted in the elements taken to make the comparison. If we compare the Code of
the Alliance (Ex. 20:22–23:19) with the poems of Blake, we might
say that the Eastern is conceptual and the Western imaginative.
If we compare poetry with poetry, we see that the biblical images
are less refined, less daring, but no less vigorous. The exact distinction is, as we said earlier, that the Bible employs an imaginative
language for prayer, meditation, interpreting history, for preaching; while our culture reserves imaginative language for poetry
(except in some popular speech).

Another serious mistake which impedes a proper understanding of the Bible is to consider images as extrinsic decoration which can be stripped away without changing the content. And an even more dangerous mistake is to believe that the biblical author first thinks in concepts, and afterwards dresses these concepts in images for the sake of the uneducated reader. The interpreter who conceives the literary activity of the Bible writers in this way tries to force a reverse movement: retranslation of the image into the original concept so as to arrive in this way at the mind of the author, to arrive at what he "wanted to say."

Following this method we might translate the Bible into a more abstract and less expressive language, but we would not reach the original thought and meaning; for, generally speaking, before the image we do not have a concept but a pure experience not yet shaped; the image was the first shaping of the experience, the first vision or spiritual reflection, the first communicable formulation. With the image the author understood, in the image he expressed himself, and the image is what he wanted to say. A few examples will help to illustrate the dangers involved in conceptual translation.

Some examples

The tragic experience of the danger of death which is imminent, grows, is seen and shaped in the symbol:

For the waters threaten my life.
I am sunk in the abysmal swamp
    where there is no foothold [Ps. 69:2],

and therefore "danger of inevitable death" is a later conceptual translation, ours, but it is not the original formula of the author, preceding the symbol.

A man attacked by enemies and shaking feels

    as though he were a sagging fence,
    a battered wall [Ps. 62:3],

and he does not feel himself to be simply "a contingent being exposed to human hostility."

The complete longing for God is a biological thirst, an earthly thirst; the biblical author says:

> For you my flesh pines
>   and my soul thirsts like the earth,
> parched, lifeless and without water [Ps. 63:1].

It is we who translate the original as "complete longing for God."

Slander, calumny, false denunciation are precise concepts of our juridical or moral language; without reaching this cold intellectual precision, the biblical author feels intensely the attacks of the words of those

> who sharpen their tongues like swords,
>   who aim like arrows their bitter words,
> shooting from ambush at the innocent man
>   suddenly shooting at him without fear [Ps. 64:3–4].

Although this is less precise it is much more vivid, much more real and authentic.

THE MECHANISM AND LIMITS OF CONCEPTUAL TRANSLATION

Having discussed the dangers to look out for, we can now go on to say that conceptual translation is legitimate provided that we grasp the mechanism (the way in which we arrive at such a translation) and its limits. The mechanism can be sketched in this way: (1) experience, (2) conceptual formulation, (3) imaginative dress, (4) conceptual re-translation, so that (4) equals (2). This scheme is generally false. A second scheme may be constructed thus: (1) experience, (2) imaginative formulation, (3) conceptual transposition, so that (3) equals (2). This scheme is generally correct (taking into account that the symbolic configuration many times arises from or penetrates into the actual experience).

The first scheme is applicable to forms that are purely didactic, to some allegorical exercises of the apocalypses (Daniel); it is not applicable to the symbolic language of John or Paul, to the deeper parables, to the poetry of the Old Testament in general.

Whoever insists on applying the first mechanism will not really understand biblical language, but will substitute for it another language that is more conceptual, more precise, more propositional; and having reached this stage, the biblical text no longer interests him.

Secondly, it must be remembered that conceptual translation has its limits: what it gains in precision it loses in richness; what it gains in clarity it loses in magic; what is gained in manageability is lost in immediacy. The total of enuntiated conceptualizations does not equal a symbol, does not exhaust it, cannot replace it completely; biblical symbolic language continues to be needed.

Archetypal symbols

It was necessary to correct blurred focuses; now we are ready to offer some positive facts concerning biblical images. Some of these are great archetypal symbols; they are universal, and as such they can be grasped by any culture that has not been dehumanized. Thirst and drink, hunger and food, light and darkness, sea and sky, water and fire, fatherhood and motherhood, cycles of fecundity; the way of life, the sleep of death, the awakening of hope, the silence of the tomb, presence and absence, war and peace, storm, rain . . .

These elemental images can assume various forms, which do not veil but manifest the elemental depth. It is easy to capture them alive, repeating the deep experience in the symbol, provided that we do not try to take a purely intellectual attitude. Any man is "radically" human, that is to say, in the depths of his being, in his hidden roots; if he removes humbly the layer of culture that covers him, he will feel the touch of the symbol at his roots. The prayer of the psalms is intensely, profoundly human; less profound but no less universal is the wisdom of many proverbs; simply human are many situations of the narrative books. This imaginative world should not be an obstacle for the modern Western reader; if he still feels some difficulty, a

short training should suffice to teach him to discover the meaning
of these elemental symbols.

IMAGES FROM CULTURE

A second group consists of images tied to a specific culture.
At times they are the concrete realization of the archetypal
symbol, and then they can be reduced with little effort to the
former. The family institution is something radically human,
and it adopts the particular forms of matriarchate, patriarchate,
emancipation, etc.; the institution of law is something almost
universal, and it can adopt the forms of family vengeance, tribal
vengeance, the law of talion, tribunal of elders, arbitration,
Roman law . . .

Others belong to different types of culture diverse as the
imaginative world of hunter and fisher, of shepherd and farmer,
of nomad and city-dweller. The image of shepherd is a favorite
of the Old and New Testaments; it supposes a relationship of
man to nonhostile animals (not as in the hunt), even to peaceful animals (domesticated); it is typical of nomads, but can be
assimilated by an urban culture. For many members of our
modern industrial culture, however, the image of the shepherd
is not really alive, and at best is a fact, exotic and distant in
space or in time. Yet this image continues to be central in our
liturgy: the bishop is still the "pastor," and there is a science
and an activity that is "pastoral." If we lack direct experience,
even that of the tourist, of this human activity, we shall have
to make it up by reading, photography, with the help of movies,
television, or illustrated reviews. However, even if we do use
these helps the biblical image will not reach us with its original
immediacy.

IMAGES FROM HISTORY

Other images belong to the history of a people: above all,
a people tenaciously rooted in their geography, tenaciously mind-
ful of their history. Such a people will use a series of images
of their geography and history with a vital meaning; names alone

THE BIBLE WRITERS USED GREAT ARCHETYPAL IMAGES *such as hunger and food, light and darkness, sea and sky . . .*

are evocative and conjure up intimate realities. It is enough to recall Egypt, Sion, "If I forget you, Jerusalem," "the day of Madian," "they were as Sodom." These names are paradigmatic, symbolic names. What do they say to us? They must say something, since that history is our history, for we are the people of God. If we educate a child by making him study the history of his country, if we demand of the citizen of a country a knowledge of its geography and history, in the same way we should expect it of a member of the people of God.

A certain biblical culture, a degree of familiarity with our history as the people of God, is necessary in order that these images or names recover something of their splendor; what they lose in concreteness or individuality will not be a serious loss if they function for us with a symbolic meaning that is above the limitations of time and space. Thus Jerusalem will be for us an historical memory, a sign of the divine presence in the temple — in any temple — the name of the church on earth, the nostalgia for the heavenly city; and all this without passing through abstraction, through the cipher without content.

Irretrievable images

With regard to a series of images whose quality as image cannot be recovered, for example "horn," two observations, however brief, should be made: (a) These can be salvaged to some extent in an intellectual way, or by reducing them to images that are more or less equivalent to ours. (b) Against the opinion of those who classify the majority of biblical images in this category, we must affirm that this group is, as a matter of fact, rather small.

Anthropomorphisms

An anthropomorphism is a particular kind of image which attributes bodily members and human affections to God. If man is an image of God, it is logical to know and describe God in His human image; and as Christ is the supreme image of God, His incarnation founds and justifies the anthropomorphisms. On

ARAB PLOWING IN GALILEE, *using primitive methods of agriculture.*

the literary level we may distinguish the anthropomorphism of the patriarchal narrations from the anthropomorphism of the great lyric poets.

In the ingenuous, non-problematic anthropomorphism of the patriarchal narrations God walks, presents Himself, pays a visit. The modern reader can meet in these a poetic aura, remote and pleasing. Much more striking is the problematic anthropomorphism of the great lyric poets: when they see the inadequacy and yet proceed without shrinking. The author knows, of course, that God is not a man, that His ways are not ours; and yet he presents Him as "a warrior overcome by wine," as "awakening from sleep," "breaking the jaws of the enemy, whistling for the humming bees, taking upon His knees and caressing. . . ." The first impression of such anthropomorphisms is stupefaction, an encounter with the unbelievable. This reaction, however, drives us to a profound perception of an ineffable quality. Anthropomorphism secures the perception of God as a person, not as an impersonal force.

SYMBOLIC ACTIONS

There is another special type of non-literary images, that of action: these are changed into literary images when they are narrated—at times the prophets, before pronouncing an oracle, execute an action which presents the oracle as a pantomime. These, known technically as "symbolic actions," the scholars of fifty years ago found very hard to grasp. We, however, educated in the language of film images, easily understand and relish this oracular style. Jeremiah takes an earthen vessel, and in the presence of witnesses smashes it on the ground announcing, "Thus shall God destroy this people" (Jer. 19:1–20). Again, the prophet reads a curse against Babylonia, ties it to a stone and throws it into the Euphrates announcing, "Thus shall this city drown" (Jer. 51:59–64). Alongside these real actions there are some which remain in the realm of fantasy, whose only reality is literary. On the other hand, the rites of the liturgy, though symbolic actions, do not coincide exactly with oracular actions (see Schildenberger pp. 100–101).

IMAGES OF NATURE, ESCHATOLOGY, MESSIANIC BLESSINGS

Images of nature can have an overpowering and numinous character, such as the theophany in the storm. There are some which offer a vision that is ordered and serene, as in Psalm 104; there is the "domesticated" vision in which nature makes itself "at home," as in Psalm 147. Images of movement outnumber static views; in the Song of Songs the theme calls for many images of smell and taste.

Eschatology collects and accumulates images of nature when disturbed, the storm, earthquake, fire, combining them with military or historical images of the people.

The messianic blessings are concrete: benefits of fecundity,

OFFERING A CHURCH TO GOD, *an illumination used in the Book of Genesis in the Bible of Nekcsei-Lipócz (*A.D. *1335), showing donors offering to God their newly-built church*

of prosperity, of peace and just government. Pure materiality is surpassed and transcended by the character of "blessing" in which God acts and presents Himself, because the blessings overflow and inundate marvellously the cosmos (Hos. 3), or the animal world (Is.11); and also because in them a more interior and higher blessing begins to be realized: "You put gladness into my heart, more than when grain and wine abound" (Ps. 4:7).

FINAL COMMENTS ON IMAGES

Before ending our discussion of some of the more characteristic techniques of expression two final brief comments on images are in order: (a) More intense are the images which express the interior world of the affections: above all grief and anxiety, as in the psalms of lamentation, but also joy and serenity, as in the psalms of confidence. (b) It is evident that images take on the rapid-fire form of metaphor ("his anger burns"), or the more distant form of comparison ("as straw crackles in the flame" — Is. 5:24), or the form of juxtaposition ("you still the roaring of the seas, the roaring of their waves and the tumult of the peoples" — Ps. 65:7). These images create no problems for reading or interpretation.

Techniques of Literary Development

Some techniques of literary development found in biblical literature are very similar to ours, and they need no commentary. In narration we do not encounter such modern complexity as streams of consciousness, flashbacks, symbolic function of landscape. Biblical narration is simple, laconic, immediate, reduced to the essentials in action and dialogue; as such it is easy and accessible without special preparation. But it is very important to remember that it is a "theological" narration, as we shall see later.

DEVELOPMENT BY WAY OF REPETITION

On the other hand, lyrical or thematic development has special forms. We are accustomed to develop a theme by analytical division, differentiating the theme into its branches; we like to move ahead without repetition, handling objections, drawing conclusions. The Hebrews often use a kind of musical development, by repetitions and variations of a theme or motif: parallelism is a case in point. A totality, a situation unfolds in two movements; it unfolds again in two more movements, then another two: it seems that we are not moving ahead, but rather

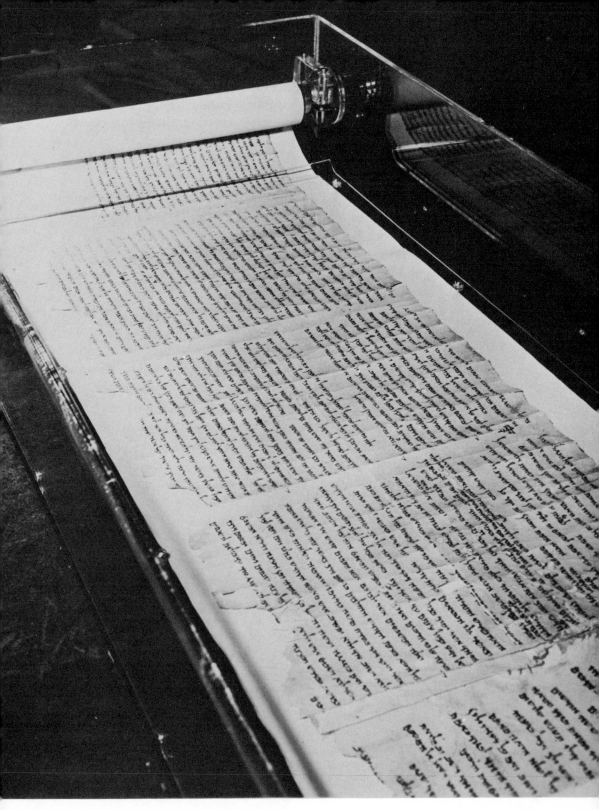

THE ISAIAH SCROLL, *one of the Dead Sea Scrolls (about 100* B.C.–A.D. *100)*

circling around the object examined, without losing sight of its totality. When it seems that we have finished, the author starts over from the beginning.

DEVELOPMENT BY WAY OF ORGANIC SITUATION

Another modality of the literary development used by the Hebrews is by way of *leitmotif* or catchword: the key word recurs with organic changes of meaning, conjuring up in this way a complex and powerful reality. We search for logic in cause and effect, in consequences, the dialectic of objections and distinctions. Consequently, the biblical world disconcerts us. Where is the logic in the divine discourses of Second Isaiah? What is the logic of the monologues or dialogues of St. John? It is not exactly our discursive logic but what we may call "the logic of organic coherency." Having supposed an organic situation, one member implies the other, one member explains the other; organic coherency dominates: the step from one member to the other is justified by the objective unity. For example, the love of God and the love of neighbor are, according to St. John, an organic situation: it is legitimate to pass from one to the other, proving, explaining, arguing—this, however, is not done according to the laws of our logic. Again, Amos, having supposed the organic situation of the intimacy between God and the prophet, proceeds to launch a series of seemingly disconcerting questions, which in reality hammer in the theme by implication (Amos 3:3–8).

FURTHER FORMS OF LITERARY DEVELOPMENT

Some further forms of literary development used by the Hebrews should be mentioned. Very simple and evident is the development by violent change of situation. The scheme: "since you have done ... for this the Lord will do ... and there will happen ...", with its particles *'al kenlaken-wehaya*—all this is not different from normal Western techniques of development: cause, effect, consequence. Nor is there a distinction between Hebrew and Western development by contrast or by enumeration.

In one of the last writers of the Old Testament we meet a refined technique of development: he divides a reality into two parallel aspects, and goes ahead applying a verse to each side, as if passing between two lines, greeting alternately. Such are the two fragments of chapter 42 of Ecclesiasticus.

As far as the degree and extension of development is concerned, we may distinguish the conciseness of Isaiah, the unrestrained rush of Jeremiah, the baroque amplification of Ezekiel, the smooth monologue of Qoheleth (Ecclesiastes), the controlled enumeration of Ben Sirach (Ecclesiasticus), the Alexandrine amplification of the book of Wisdom. An image can be hinted at, concentrated into one verse, pushed to its extreme as in Ezekiel, and it may offer a unifying theme in a poem.

Dialogue can assume the overruling function for the literary development of a work, as in Job. And, finally, there are pieces which are not the result of a development but of a secondary grouping, as the series of proverbs, the anthologies of oracles.

Techniques of Composition

In a literature which collects and uses again, adapting and interpreting anew, in a literature strongly conditioned by traditional forms, composition plays a capital role. The repeated effort of analyzing and assigning to sources may cause scholars to lose sight of this element; for this reason it has to be emphasized. Composition has a function which is not purely formal, but which frequently is also meaningful: it reveals organic connections, gives each element its place in the hierarchic structure, shows the unifying principles. Consequently this all too frequently overlooked aspect requires special treatment.

The German biblical scholar, H. Gunkel, made a decisive step in this direction. He established a series of patterns of composi-

SHEPHERD AND HIS FLOCK *in the mountains of Judea*

tion typical of different literary genera. He succeeded in determining the generic in the Psalms, and the specific in the narratives of Genesis. His attempt in prophetic literature went astray because of prejudice. After Gunkel this branch of biblical research has made solid progress, rediscovering the unity, original or secondary, of many passages: credal formulas (von Rad), covenant (Mendenhall and Baltzer), prophetic oracles (Westermann), etc.

NUMERIC COMPOSITION

Among the Hebrews numbers frequently have a symbolic meaning: the three, the seven, the ten, the twelve, the fourteen, the forty, besides being quantitative designations, may have a qualitative meaning. Certain passages may, therefore, use such numbers as a skeleton for a meaningful structure: for example, in Psalms 78 and 105 there are seven plagues; there are ten in the Exodus narrative (7:14–12:29). In Exodus the first two plagues are ambiguous because the magicians were able to imitate them; the third revealed the finger of God; the fourth begins with a new introduction; in the sixth the magicians have to withdraw leaving the scene empty for the seventh, which opens very solemnly with a theophany and closes with Pharaoh's confession; after the seventh there is a new introduction, and in the eight and ninth there are concessions leading to the tenth, which is the definitive plague. So we see that the number ten unifies, and is not simply an enumeration, because the third, seventh, and tenth order the whole series qualitatively and dynamically.

More refined is Genesis 1, combining a structure of ten words of God with a structure of seven days—the first divided into two halves of five each for heaven and earth, and the second stressing the first, fourth, and seventh day. Psalm 106 recounts seven sins of the people in the desert, not chronologically, but placing the adoration of the golden calf in the center. The great dialogue of Joshua with his people at the renewal of the covenant at Shechem is ordered by fourteen occurrences of the verb *bd*, meaning to serve or to worship; at the seventh, Joshua professes his fidelity to Yahweh, at the fourteenth the people do likewise.

Sometimes seven or ten means simply plenitude, totality of enumeration, without a specific structural intention: Psalm 105 enumerates seven plagues beginning with the darkness and ending with the death of the first-born; Psalm 78 also enumerates seven plagues, but begins with the changing of water into blood; Psalm 115 expresses the emptiness of the idols by enumerating seven forms of incapacity; Psalm 18 opens by invoking the Lord under ten titles; Psalm 148 is a hymn with seven imperatives and one jussive of praise addressed to the heavens, and one imperative and one jussive addressed to the earth, i.e., ten altogether, with strong emphasis on heaven; the last psalm (150) of the Psalter invites the orchestra to praise in ten imperatives; the genealogy of Christ, according to Matthew, counts 14 generations to David,

THE ISRAELITES WORSHIPPING THE GOLDEN CALF
Nicolas Poussin

14 to the Exile, 14 to Christ; while Luke counts 77 names between
Jesus and God.

Schildenberger (pp. 136–149) mentions the numerical proverbs – "three things and a fourth," the seven thunder-claps of
Psalm 29, the seven functions of the anointed in Isaiah 61:1,
the 21 adornments of women in Isaiah 3:18–23, the 21 properties
of Wisdom in Wisdom 7:22, groups of 7 throughout Revelation, etc.

ALPHABETIC COMPOSITION

When the scribes developed a consciousness of the letters,
the authors began to take the alphabet as a constructive element,
sometimes writing 22 verses, or else using each letter of the alphabet to begin each verse, or half verse, or every second verse,

or three verses in a row, or eight verses in a row (*see* Psalms 111, 119, 145; Lamentations).

CONCENTRIC STRUCTURE

A frequent form of composition in the Bible is the so-called concentric structure (Galbiati). Also known as "chiasm," this structure consists in disposing the elements in the pattern: a b c n c' b' a', with thematic and verbal correspondences, the central element being stressed. We can find such an artificial disposition in legal series, narratives, exhortatory passages, and poems of various styles. The following verses from chapter 34 of Isaiah will serve as an illustration:

10 It will lie waste *from age to age*
11a   the jackdaw and the hedgehog *will take possession of it*
11b   the Lord will suspend over it the *plummet line*
12b   her nobles will be no more
16   none of these will be missing
17a   He distributes to them with *a cord*
17b   they *will take possession of it* for ever
17 *from age to age* they will inhabit

The psalm *Miserere* is an interesting case of structure. It is divided into two parts, the first the realm of sin, and the second the realm of grace. In the first part, after the opening invocation, the name of God does not appear again. This part is dominated by the theme of sin, the root *ht'* appearing six times, and synonyms being used six times. It is constructed with a concentric inclusion: *wipe* . . . wash . . . cleanse . . . . . . cleanse . . . wash . . . *wipe*." In the second part the name of God reappears to create anew. There is a triple reference to *spirit* and the root *ht'* appears the seventh time, a synonym for sin. The last verse of the original composition repeats many key words of the psalm: "sacrifice . . . spirit . . . crushed . . . heart."

Such techniques of composition puzzle us when first we hear of them, and if we do not hear of them we do not observe them; but their occurrence is so frequent that they cannot be over-

RUINS OF ANCIENT
JERICHO

looked. They may be used to organize pre-existing materials, or in an original composition. It has been shown (by Vanhoye) that the whole Epistle to the Hebrews is composed with such devices of concentric inclusion.

OTHER TECHNIQUES OF COMPOSITION

There are other techniques of composition which are less artificial, used to organize previous materials, e.g., prophetic oracles, or for original compositions. The pattern of salvation history may dominate a narrative: grace – sin – punishment – penance – grace; this pattern may become almost cyclic, as in the book of Judges. It is very frequent in the Bible. Sometimes the editor will add an oracle of salvation after an oracle of doom. We may also find a technique of composition that uses the juxtaposition of blocks thematically related. And often it will not be possible to determine whether we are dealing with a real composition, or with a simple compilation of oracles or proverbs.

Recent research, mainly on the Gospels, has shown that the last editor is a real author, very conscious of his intentions, and master of the techniques required to carry them out. It is no longer permissible to despise the anonymous last editor, who may have said the most important things. Nor can we forget that the canonical text of the Bible is the present text, not the original text, or any intermediate stage.

STRUCTURES OF LITERARY GENERA

Literary genera are types of literature distinguished from each other by distinct form and structure adapted to content. The structure or disposition of its elements, therefore, is a characteristic factor of a literary genus. The basic structure admits of variants. Two examples will serve to illustrate this technique of composition.

Structures of psalms according to Gunkel:
  Hymn. Introduction: imperatives – Body: divine attributes – Conclusion.
  Supplication. Introduction: invocation – Body: lamentation, petition, motives – Conclusion: certitude, promise of thanksgiving.
  Thanksgiving. Introduction – Recalling of past suffering – Account of the prayer and liberation – Hymnic conclusion.

Structures of the prophecies according to Westermann:
  Prophesy of doom for the individual. The sending – Denunciation of the sin – "Therefore thus says Yahweh" – The sentence.
  Prophecy of doom for the people. Introduction – Denunciation of the sin, generic and specific – "Therefore thus says Yahweh" – The sentence: God's intervention, and the results of this intervention.

There are genera of reduced extension where composition does not count, e.g., the proverbs. Other literary works have a strong and individual structure not reducible to a pattern, e.g., the book of Jonah—in such a case a special introduction to the reading will be necessary.

Theological Reading of Scripture

Everything said thus far has been subordinated to the religious reading of Scripture, for Scripture is before all else a religious book: the expression and nourishment of the religious life of a people. If "theology" is to speak of God, all Scripture is theology, since it speaks of God and of man in the light of God; yet it is not speculative or systematic theology in our style. And it is here that we find the root of one of the difficulties for the modern reader: to one accustomed to a technical theology, to a systematic treatise, conceptually differentiated, the Old Testament (and even the New) with its narratives and poetic symbols is a puzzle.

A NARRATIVE THEOLOGY

The theology of the Old Testament, and somewhat less that of the New, is for the most part a narrative theology; and we must know how to read these narratives, listening for their theological meaning, their authentic sense. If we fail to do this and read the Old Testament as an edifying story from which to draw moral lessons, we read in a way diametrically opposed to revelation.

REVELATION IN HISTORY

The biblical author knows that God reveals Himself in action, he knows that divine revelation is the deep meaning of the deed:

THE PROPHET ISAIAH
Michelangelo

for this reason he tries to tell the deed declaring its meaning. He knows that salvation has God for protagonist and that history is its realization; and for this reason he tries to present history showing God as protagonist. Although man seems to work independently, in reality he acts before and under God; although man seems to assume the main role, there is a higher horizon, the divine, which goes far beyond.

To be saved is to live in history with God; to speak of God is to tell this history. For this reason the Old Testament is full of history: in narration, in meditation, in preaching, in history, recent, remote, and future.

GOD AS PROTAGONIST

The narrator shows us God present, the protagonist, with His action and with His word. A particular action can be a miracle, which is a sign; it can be a theophany, which is an apparition in power. A series of actions are assumed in the initial plan, developed in their course against human opposition, brought to their goal; thus we have achieved a higher unity of the divine manifestation. The oracle is the divine word which penetrates history to direct and explain it; sometimes we have a real oracle, at other times the later narrator employs the oracle as a literary procedure, to explain a step in history. The real oracle we find with Elijah or Isaiah; the oracle as literary technique would be the introductions to the narration of the plagues. In such cases the protagonism of God appears within the narration, informing it. At other times the author explains the meaning outside of strict narration by putting speeches of recapitulation into the mouth of his characters (as does the Deuteronomist), or by taking himself the role of speaker, interrupting the story on the spot or at its conclusion, or by framing the narration in a theological explanation, as in the book of Judges.

When in a biblical narration we lose sight of the protagonism of God, we must remember the law of context. For the people are "the people of God." Whoever attacks them attacks God. Man

THE BIBLE USES SYMBOLS *to express religious experience—the experience of mystery*

responds to God, nature serves God, and the whole multiplicity is unified in the plan of God.

A SYMBOLIC THEOLOGY

Joined to narrative theology we encounter a symbolic theology. We have already said that symbols are not an extrinsic embellishment but a means of perception and of expression. As such they are a highly important theological instrument, and we must learn to read them. We shall, therefore, discuss the Bible's use of symbols in conveying a sense of mystery, transcendence, and religious experience; we shall also mention briefly the symbols known as "types."

MYSTERY

Salvation is a mystery, veiled and yet unveiled in the historical event; a global reality, inexhaustible. It resists conceptual articulation or any precision which limits it; it can, however, make itself present in the symbol which by nature is global, unarticulated—above all in the great poetic symbols which appear in myths. Thus the crossing of the Reed Sea can be explained as a phenomenon, an arid wind which dries up and makes passable a strip of water; it can be narrated by introducing God as protagonist who sends his oracle to Moses; but the mystery of the sovereign action of God, who controls nature and directs history, can be expressed in a symbol of mythical ascendancy, the primordial dragon or the rebellious ocean which God crushes and quarters.

TRANSCENDENCE

Salvation is a transcendent mystery which is made present by way of signs in history and also in nature; such signs have a symbolic structure, insofar as they overflow, surpass, manifest something more than their own being; for this reason the literary symbol is the great instrument for expressing the symbolic structure we mentioned. The transcendence of God who punishes takes as sign the invasion of the king of Assyria, although he himself is not aware of his symbolic function; the Assyrian king does not go beyond the immanent vision "I have done . . . I will do . . ."; the prophet Isaiah declares the transcendent meaning in the symbol "rod of my wrath" (cf. Is. 10).

RELIGIOUS EXPERIENCE

The mystery of salvation, or its contrary, is lived by man in the depths of his person, in a psychological unity that is anterior to differentiation, and with total impact. This interiority is articulated in concepts with difficulty; they break the unity and limit the totality. But the non-notional experience can be expressed in symbolic formula. The Psalmist thirsts for God, seeks the face of God, contemplates God and becomes radiant, feels the companionship of darkness, God is his light, his rock, his refuge, his advocate, God sounds his depths, penetrates him, surrounds him, covers him, reaches him, God is far away or near at hand. All these symbols and many others express religious experience, which is the experience of mystery; but the conceptual formulation will have less richness and intensity and could even threaten the mystery.

Joel saw a swarm of locusts which darkened the skies and laid waste the earth. He sees them as an invading army: it is the army of the Lord executing vengeance, and the darkness is the dark cloud of theophany. This symbolic vision penetrates to the deeper meaning of an agricultural catastrophe. Hosea had one of the most sublime revelations of God's love in the Old Testament when he gazed into the symbolic depths of his marriage experience: in a remarkable poem he formulates his religious experience in literary symbols.

The symbolic formulation, besides achieving richness and depth, can transform an individual event into a meaningful image, so that the event transcends its individual limitations and the symbol remains applicable to similar events: e.g., the "rod of my wrath" in chapter 10 of Isaiah.

TYPES

Archetypal and mythic symbols have already been mentioned. A slightly different theological operation consists in explaining one historical fact according to the model of another previous and particularly important historical event. The latter in this way becomes a prototype. For example, the Exodus is a model for the return from the Exile, and of the eschatological reunion from the diaspora. Sodom and Gomorrah are prototypes of the eschatological punishment. David's election is the model for further elections of kings and anointed ones, and the Messiah.

REASONING THEOLOGY

Narrative theology and symbolic theology are probably the basic form of theologizing used by the inspired authors. A third form is closer to our reasoning method in theology, namely asking

A CLOUD OF LOCUSTS

"why?": the Deuteronomist applies this questioning method for pastoral purposes. He wants to understand the past so as to illustrate the present. Chapter 8 of Deuteronomy starts from a present situation of prosperity in which God is forgotten, analyzes its psychological process and, to find a remedy, searches the reasons of God's acting in the past. Deuteronomy contains theology in exhortatory form. Later theologians analyze and explain passages of "Scripture" in the technical sense: Ben Sirach, whose teaching reaches up to the New Testament, is a typical example.

SAPIENTIAL LITERATURE

The sapiential (wisdom) literature of Proverbs is not theology in the same way. However, it cannot be reduced to a purely human ethic. First, religious references are frequent. And, above all, there is the law of context: sapiential activity and sapiential literature are incorporated into religion, and they are, as it were, converted into a type of humanism with God. This is evident in Ecclesiasticus. We may say that prior to the incarnation "His humanity has appeared" in those sapiential sayings.

THE NEED FOR CAUTION

It is well known that in order to understand ancient texts or those far distant from us, it is not enough to know the language only; one must also know the kind of language in the text studied. In the case of the Bible, one must know the meaning of the religious concepts of the Old and New Testaments. We have an advantage inasmuch as our religious life is a development and continuation of that expressed in the Bible, and this guarantees a fundamental empathy. But at the same time it creates the danger of forgetting semantic development in the concepts, even within the Bible itself, and still more in later Christian tradition; this mistake in perspective can be serious when theology, preaching, and ascetical principles have lost living contact with Scripture. For example, what do we understand when we read in the psalms: "those who fear the Lord," "the Lord reveals his justice"? Many times it will be good to move carefully, to consult dictionaries of biblical theology, and theological notes.

FORMULAS

It is not enough to know words, be they concepts or symbols. No less important are the "formulae" with theological value. For example, "You are my people and I am your God" is a technical formula which sums up the covenant of God with His people; it is not enough to understand the terms if we are unaware of the global, technical meaning of the formula. When we read "who brought us out of Egypt," we are presented with an attribute of God, condensed into an article of the Israelite creed, professing the initial salvation of the people. "Thus says the Lord" is the prophetic formula for introducing oracles; "Is there anyone who wishes . . . ?" is a wisdom formula whose purpose is didactic. We need much attentive reading to become familiar with the many

THE SEA OF GALILEE *with the Mount of Transfiguration in the background*

biblical formulas characteristic of the different genera, situations, or religious practices. Here, too, the principle holds: the phrase counts more than the word.

Especially interesting is the case in which the biblical authors, above all the prophets, take a classical formula and with slight change adapt it, twist it, fill it with new meaning or expressive force. Always God says "I brought you out of Egypt and led you to the promised land"; but in chapter 19 of Exodus we read: "I brought you out of Egypt and led you to myself." The author of the book of Jonah employs this technique to present ironically the "anti-prophet" in contrast with the exemplary attitude of "the wicked."

Complementary to the formulas, with more action, are the motifs characteristic of themes or situations: thunder, fire, earthquake; or motifs of theophanies. According to Matthew we meet, in the death of Christ, a heaping up of motifs of theophany. The invocation of sky and earth as witnesses is a motif of the litigation of God with His people; the assault of beasts is a motif of personal lamentation. These motifs can migrate and be transformed by adopting different formulations.

Summary

This discussion of the language and mentality of the Bible writers has been aimed at helping us toward a better understanding of the Bible. The first step toward this understanding is the realization that the Bible is literature. To understand this literature we must have a knowledge of the Bible writers' techniques; for example, their techniques of expression, techniques of literary development, techniques of literary composition: starting with these we can arrive at the authors' mentality.

Beyond this we must realize, in our approach to reading the Bible, that though the Bible is "theology," since it speaks of God and of man in the light of God, it is not speculative or systematic theology in our style. We must not, therefore, expect this kind of theology in our reading of the Bible. Rather, we must understand how the Bible theologizes—for instance, by way of narratives and symbols—if we are to grasp the authentic sense as we listen to God speaking to us in His Scripture.

The Influence of Israel's Neighbors

John McHugh

Israel did not live in a cultural vacuum. It took the raw materials of its life and culture from the world around it—there was no other source. We should not, then, be surprised to find that Israel borrowed liberally from its neighbors' myths, legends, legal forms, and social customs. In borrowing from these, however, Israel took care to alter or reinterpret them in the light of its own unique religious faith. The half-truths and obscurities of pagan culture were rejected, and all that was good and worthwhile was caught up and fused into a new vision of life.

THE GREAT SPHINX OF GIZEH, EGYPT

Problems in Understanding
the Old Testament

MOST READERS of this volume have probably decided at some time or other to "read the Bible regularly." How many, I wonder, have begun with Genesis and given up the struggle sooner rather than later? The fairy-tale atmosphere of those first pages of the Old Testament seem to create difficulties against faith, not to nourish it.

FACT OR FICTION?

What is the reader to make of the magic trees in the Garden of Eden, of the creation of woman from man's rib, and of the talking serpent? Is the Christian expected to believe that there was once a flood which covered the whole earth and drowned the entire human race and all the animals in the world, and that only Noah and his family along with certain animals survived in a very unseaworthy boat? Did Methuselah really live to be 969 years old (Gen. 5:27)?

The book of Exodus is equally puzzling to the twentieth-century reader. In one account of the vocation of Moses, God seems to be using His omnipotence to play conjuring tricks: He changes a stick into a serpent, and then changes it back again (Ex. 4:1-4). This is not very edifying to the Christian reader, and it is not very credible either, when we read that certain Egyptian sorcerers did the same (Ex. 7:8-13). Again, was the river Nile really turned into blood (Ex. 4:9; 7:20-24), and did the people of Israel really walk "on dry ground through the sea, the waters being a wall to them on their right hand and on their left"? (Ex. 14:29). The Christian who perseveres through the first hundred pages of the Old Testament finds the story growing ever more puzzling instead of clearer, and when he comes to the tediously repetitive laws of Leviticus, his resolution to "read the Bible" will probably have taken a severe knock.

THE GOD OF LOVE: ADVOCATE OF CARNAGE?

But worse is to come: the books of Joshua and Judges are a tale of carnage. When the Israelites captured Jericho, "they utterly destroyed all in the city, both men and women, oxen, sheep, and asses, with the edge of the sword" (Josh. 6:21). A little later, we read that "the Lord said to Joshua . . . you shall do to Ai and its king as you did to Jericho and its king" (Josh. 8:1-2), and the command is duly carried out: 12,000 men and women are put to death (Josh. 8:25). As each of the towns of Canaan is captured, the same merciless slaughter is repeated (Josh. 10:28-39).

All this is said to have been done at the express command of the Lord (Josh. 11:15), who had said to Moses: "when the Lord your God gives them [i.e., the inhabitants of Canaan] over to you, and you defeat them, then you must utterly destroy them; you shall make no covenant with them, and show no mercy to them" (Deut. 7:2).

The Christian who takes up his Bible for spiritual edification may well wonder whether this is the same Lord who said to the people of Galilee: "Come to me, all who labor and are heavy-laden, and I will give you rest. Take my yoke upon you, and learn from me; for I am gentle and lowly in heart, and you will find rest for your souls" (Matt. 11:28-29). What is the Christian to make of the Old Testament, when so much of it (e.g., the Flood, the Exodus) seems historically improbable, and so much else (e.g., the story of the conquest of Canaan) is not merely un-Christian but positively inhuman?

SCIENTIFIC RESEARCH INCREASES UNDERSTANDING

One hundred and fifty years ago, it would have been impossible to answer this question honestly and satisfactorily. But since the beginning of the nineteenth century immense progress has been made in research into the history and culture of the Near East.

ARCHEOLOGISTS WITH ARTIFACTS *discovered in the Negev near the Dead Sea*

Doors which had been locked for two and three thousand years have been thrown open, and it is no exaggeration to say that our own generation is better informed about the life and background of ancient Israel than any other generation of the last two thousand years.

The writing of the ancient Egyptians, Assyrians, and Babylonians has been deciphered, and by comparing the literature of Israel (i.e., the Old Testament) with that of those neighboring lands, much in the Old Testament that has for centuries been obscure or incomprehensible is seen in a new light.

Archeology, too, has progressed from what it used to be in the eighteenth century, when Pompeii was first excavated; then, it meant systematic hunting for ancient statuary and coins to fill museums, whereas today it is an honored science whose aim is to discover how people lived in the past. The modern archeologist is just as interested in a broken jar from a peasant's kitchen as in a granite statue from an Egyptian palace.

Ethnology, too, has taught us much about certain passages in the Bible. In short, the historical background of the Old Testament has suddenly sprung to life, and this has totally transformed our attitude to those books. The discussion of a few examples that now follows will serve to illustrate this point.

Myths, Genealogies, and Legends

Long before any page of the Old Testament was written, there circulated in Mesopotamia a myth about a great flood. The most complete and best-known version of it relates how the gods decided to destroy mankind by causing a flood in the region of the river Euphrates. One of the gods, however, warned a certain Utnapishtim of the impending disaster, and advised him to build himself a boat, and to take on board every kind of animal and ample stores (compare this tale with the indicated parallel texts from the Genesis story of Noah: Gen. 6:13-21). When the storm came, the hero, Utnapishtim, survived.

After seven days of storm, he opened the hatch of the boat, and discovered that it had lodged on a mountain-top (Gen. 8:4). Seven days later, he sent out a dove (Gen. 8:8) which could find nowhere to rest, and therefore returned; the same happened with a swallow, but finally he sent out a raven (Gen. 8:7) which did not return (Gen. 8:12). Thereupon Utnapishtim opened the doors of the boat to let the animals out (Gen. 8:13-17). He offered a sacrifice, and "the gods smelled its sweet savor" (Gen. 8:21), so that one of them exclaimed, "I shall not forget, I shall remember these days" (Gen. 8:21-22; 9:12-17).

As the cross-references to the book of Genesis show, this

ancient Mesopotamian myth tells basically the same story as the Bible tells about Noah. The divergences between the two narratives are insignificant, except for one. At the end of the Mesopotamian myth, Utnapishtim becomes one of the gods, whereas at the end of the biblical narrative, Noah dies. This detail provides the key to the interpretation of the whole story of the flood and of Noah's ark.

ADOPTION AND ADAPTATION OF PAGAN MYTHS

Someone (we do not know who; perhaps we never shall) took a myth current in ancient Mesopotamia and adapted it for his own religious purposes: he gave a new moral to the story by stressing that man is sinful and that God is both just and merciful. We do not know who first retold the story in this form; the myth may have been adapted and reinterpreted nearly two thousand years before Christ and then handed down by word of mouth for several generations before it was first set down in writing about 1000 B.C.

But the point of interest here is that Israel did adopt and adapt a myth of pagan Mesopotamia; some modern scholars stress that Israel adopted such stories, and conclude that the religion of Israel is just one form of Near Eastern religion, not essentially different from any other. We should emphasize rather that whenever Israel adopted anything from a neighboring culture, it always reinterpreted the material in the light of its own religious faith.

The story of Utnapishtim is not the only Mesopotamian myth whose influence can be discerned in the Bible, but it provides the closest parallels. There are, however, several other myths of ancient Babylonia which have some bearing on the interpretation of the book of Genesis—myths about creation, about the innocence of man in the first days of his existence, about his quest of immortality, and even about quarrels like that between Cain and Abel. There is no space here to recount them in detail, nor any need to do so.

FOLKLORE USED TO TEACH RELIGIOUS TRUTHS

What the modern reader needs to remember is that some of the material in the Bible has been taken over from a very old pagan

THE EUPHRATES RIVER, *an aerial view showing its circuitous course*

culture, and adapted to point a religious lesson for Israel and ourselves. God can, if He chooses, teach us about Himself through folklore as well as through straightforward history, and if the first eleven chapters of Genesis are read with this in mind, then we shall no longer trouble ourselves with irrelevant questions (such as wondering why Cain should have been afraid of being murdered when, after the death of Abel, he was the only person apart from Adam and Eve who was alive). Rather, we should look for the religious message which the Bible contains.

GENEALOGIES

Ancient Babylonia supplied some of the ideas used in the Bible; the deserts of Arabia contributed also. Many of the puzzling genealogies in Genesis and elsewhere make perfect sense when

they are seen as genealogies not of individual persons, but of
tribes.

All the members of an Arab tribe are held to be descended from
one ancestor, and are known as "the sons of. . . ." When a man
joins the tribe, he is "adopted," and acknowledges the tribe's
ancestor as his own. Sometimes a small tribe will amalgamate
with a large one to secure protection, and in that case a genealogi-
cal relationship will be thought up to link the ancestors of the two
tribes as brothers, or cousins, or as father and son. Something
similar takes place whenever several small tribes join together,
and this is what happened in the early years of Israel's settlement
in Canaan.

The implications of this last statement must be drawn out explicitly. The twelve tribes of Israel are commonly regarded as the
physical descendants of one man, Jacob, and anyone who reads
the Old Testament without a knowledge of the nomadic background will conclude that the Bible means to say this. But the
tribes were in reality a confederation, allied together for common
action, and bound together in the end by their common rejection
of all gods except Yahweh, the God of Jacob.

It is interesting to note, for example, that in the story of Joseph
(Gen. 37-50) the only sons of Jacob who are actively involved are
the sons of Leah (Reuben, Simeon, and Judah) and of Rachel
(Joseph and Benjamin). Now these are the names of the tribes
that occupied the southern part of Palestine after the conquest:
Reuben occupied the region east of the Dead Sea; Simeon and
Judah settled south of Jerusalem; Benjamin near Jerusalem; and
the two tribes of Joseph (Ephraim and Manasseh) further to the
north. Moses and Aaron belonged to the tribe of Levi (Ex. 2:1,10;
4:14), another son of Leah (Gen. 29:34).

Is it mere coincidence that the six sons of Jacob who play a part
in the story of Israel in Egypt (Reuben, Simeon, Levi, Judah,
Benjamin, and Joseph) are also held to be the ancestors of the
tribes which occupied the southern part of the land? Is it mere
accident that the tribes which lived in the north of Canaan (Asher,
Naphtali, Zebulun, Issachar) are never mentioned in the story of

BEDOUIN DWELLING IN THE VALLEY OF SINAI

Joseph or of the Exodus, except where we come upon a list of all Israel? In the light of what we know about the customs of Arab tribes, the reader may well think that the Hebrew tribes which escaped from Egypt first conquered the southern half of Palestine, and were then joined (after their initial success) by a group of tribes from the north (Asher, etc.) who sought alliance with them.

Perhaps the scene described in chapter twenty-four of the book of Joshua is an account of the formal ratification of this union by a religious ceremony at Shechem. After that, it would have been normal for the ancestors of the northern tribes to have been "genealogized," i.e., to have been counted as sons of Jacob, and

The Holy Land

God's revelation, though addressed to all mankind, had its setting in the history and geography of a chosen people. Since this is so, the Holy Land must always be of particular interest to all who believe that it was here that God's revelation was given, and here reached its fullness in Jesus Christ

SUNSET OVER JERUSALEM, *the city that outranks all other cities of the Bible in importance because of its prominence, throughout its long history, in the story of mankind's salvation*

THE GREAT PYRAMIDS *of Egypt were built 2700–2200* B.C. *Most modern schol-ars believe Abraham lived between 1900 and 1700* B.C.

RUINS *of the Temple of Jupiter at Baalbek in modern Lebanon*

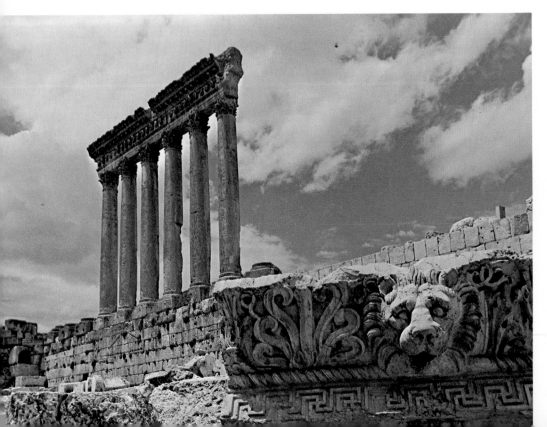

VIEW *from the traditional site of the Garden of Gethsemane looking toward the Golden Gate in the wall of Jerusalem*

CHAPEL *on the summit of the Mount of Olives. The Old Testament mentions the Mount of Olives only twice: 2 Samuel 15:30 and Zechariah 14:4*

BETHLEHEM, *about six miles from Jerusalem, though best known as the birthplace of Jesus, was also the home of King David*

ST. STEPHEN'S GATE, *Jerusalem, so called because traditionally it is said to be the place where St. Stephen was martyred. It is also known as the Sheep Gate because every Friday morning sheep are bought and sold near here, a custom that has continued for many centuries*

THE SEA OF GALILEE, *also known as the Lake of Gennesaret and the Lake of Tiberias, is about 13 miles long north to south, and some 8 miles broad at its greatest width*

RUINS AT JERASH *(Gerasa) date from the Roman period when the city was taken by Pompey (63 B.C.). Earlier it had been occupied by Alexander Janneus, King of Judea (ca. 103–76 B.C.)*

VIEW OF THE MOUNT OF OLIVES — *in the distance — as seen from near the Dome of the Rock in Jerusalem*

ASKAR, *an Arab village that until recently was identified with Sychar. It is probable, however, that Sychar was the Old Testament Shechem near which was the field Jacob bought (Gen. 33:19)*

RUINS *of the ancient sea front at Caesarea, a city on the coast of Palestine, about twenty-three miles from Mount Carmel*

to have been named as if they too had taken part in the great migration across the Sinai peninsula.

The various plagues which enliven the story of the Exodus (Ex. 7:20-12:32) point to yet another influence, that of Egypt. All of them except the tenth (the death of the first-born) are natural disasters which can and do happen in Egypt: for example, ancient Egyptian texts speak of the Nile's being turned into blood (cf. Ex. 7:14–24) when red sandstone is carried downstream instead of silting up in the river, and a fierce sandstorm can all too quickly produce "darkness" (cf. Ex. 10:21–23), as all who have experienced one will confirm.

According to the Bible, Moses was empowered by God to produce these natural disasters by a mere gesture or a word of command; if we read these events as history, this sounds incredible, or at least most improbable. Is there any way of making this story acceptable to a rational, twentieth-century mind?

At the risk of mildly shocking the American reader, may an English writer suggest that the key to this problem lies close at hand for him, in the stories of "Buffalo Bill" and Jesse James? There is what we may call "the true history of the Wild West" and also what we may call "the legend of the West." It is not always easy to discern where history ends and legend begins, even though we live at a distance of only one hundred years from the events. But it is certain that the legends of Buffalo Bill and Jesse James are based ultimately on a hard rock of fact; and it is equally certain that if we wish to know what kind of men these two outlaws were, legend can paint as true a picture as factual history.

This illustration is not meant as a joke; it helps perhaps more than any other to throw light on the obscurity of Old Testament history, for if legends can flourish in a civilization as sophisticated as that of the United States, is it not more likely that they would have thriven in ancient Israel? St. Francis of Assisi provides yet another example: the legends collected in *The Little Flowers of St. Francis* teach us everything about him – he must have been an extraordinarily gentle and Christ-like person for such stories to have been made up. The legends about St. Patrick prove the same point, but let us return to Moses.

If the narrative of the ten plagues of Egypt is read as history, it does seem incredible; but if it is read as legend, i.e., as a story handed down by tradition and popularly regarded as historical, then it makes excellent sense. Here we have Moses, the great liberator of the slaves, calling down upon Egypt every kind of natural disaster until the Pharaoh lets the people go free. Moses leads the Hebrew slaves out of Egypt, and a great sirocco suddenly creates a dry passage through the marshes north of Suez, which were known as "the Reed Sea" (not the "Red Sea," which is a mistranslation). Little wonder that later ages embellished the tale, with typical Oriental hyperbole, by speaking of the waters standing up like a wall to the right and left! The Exodus is an epic, and can only be properly understood as such.

Ancient Egyptian literature has many legends of a similar kind, and it is highly likely that several of the biblical stories about Joseph and Moses are based on themes familiar in Egypt. There is, for example, a story about a young man who was maliciously accused of proposing adultery to his brother's wife, after he had in fact rejected her advances; it is broadly similar to the tale of Joseph and Potiphar's wife in the thirty-ninth chapter of the book of Genesis.

So far, no such precise parallels have come to light to illustrate the life of Moses, but the very frequency of legends about great figures of the past show that this was not an uncommon form of storytelling in Egypt. And why should Israel not have made up its own legends about Moses, telling how God redeemed His people "with a mighty hand and an outstretched arm"?

The account of the conquest of Canaan

But perhaps the greatest stumbling block to the Christian reader of the Old Testament lies in the bloodcurdling account of the conquest of Canaan: did God really order Moses and Joshua (Deut. 7:1-3; Josh. 8:2) to kill every man, woman, and child in the cities they captured? If He really did, then the Christian will think there is an unanswerable case for rejecting the divine inspiration of these parts of the Old Testament. Can it be said that God did

RELICS OF A CANAANITE TEMPLE

not order these massacres, when the Bible expressly states that
He did?

In order to interpret the story of the conquest of Canaan cor-
rectly, two points must be kept in mind: (1) in tribal warfare at the
time (around 1200 B.C.) it was not uncommon for the victors to
exterminate the other tribe—as, indeed, has often happened
within living memory on the northwest frontier of Pakistan,
among the Pathans; (2) the biblical account of these massacres
was set down in writing centuries after the event. With these two
principles in mind, a solution of the theological problem is possible.

There can be no doubt that in the course of the conquest of
Canaan the Israelites waged war as mercilessly as their opponents, whom they were trying to dislodge; and there is no reason
whatever to doubt that they did slaughter men, women, and

children indiscriminately. Like the Canaanites, they saw life in black and white, in bleak alternatives: either you made peace with a tribe, settled down beside them, intermarried, and accepted their gods, or you made war to exterminate them. The middle path was centuries away! Some of the indigenous tribes, like Asher, Naphtali, etc., settled for peace, intermarriage, and Israel's religion; others did not, and met their fate. Such are the historical facts of the conquest of Canaan.

BIBLE WRITERS' ATTITUDE TO CONQUEST OF CANAAN

Scholars still debate about the date when the book of Deuteronomy was composed, or the book of Joshua put into its present form; but all are agreed that neither was put into its present form until at least five centuries after the death of Moses and Joshua — let us say, at the earliest around 700 B.C. By then, the Israelites were firmly established in the land, but they were always in close contact with their pagan neighbors like the Philistines and the Phoenicians; and the books of Kings and the prophets show how difficult it was to keep Israel's religion uncontaminated by foreign elements.

The religious rites practiced by the Canaanites and the Phoenicians embraced a fair share of what we today would call devil-worship; obscene fertility rites were commonly practiced in the shrines of their gods, prostitutes of both sexes lived there and by their trade helped toward the upkeep of the temples, and in certain circumstances new-born children would be burnt to death as a sacrifice to Moloch, the god of war. Against this type of religion, Elijah and all the prophets after him fought unceasingly, and in the books of Kings, in Deuteronomy, and in the final edition of Joshua we read today the judgment of condemnation passed by Israel on all these evil customs.

The Israelite historians of the conquest of Canaan knew that their ancestors had exterminated many of the Canaanites without pity; looking back on the events five centuries later, and seeing around them the unspeakable atrocities of their pagan neighbors, they concluded that it was the will of God that the Canaanites

THE LAND OF CANAAN

BEFORE THE ISRAELITE CONQUEST

Copyright, The Westminster Press
International Copyright Secured. All Rights Reserved

SCALE OF MILES

0 5 10 15 20 25 30

BOUNDARIES
UNCERTAIN
BOUNDARIES
CITIES AND TOWNS   o
ROADS

THE GREAT SEA

Sidon
Zarephath
Ahlab,
Meheleb
Tyre
Kanah
Hammon?
Achzib   Abdon
Accho
Rehob?   Neiel
Achshaph?   Cabul
Salmonah?
Helkath? Hannathon?
Harosheth?   Adami?
Japhia   Gath-hepher
Jokneam   Sarid   MT. TABOR
Dor   Anaharath
Megiddo   Shunem Hapharaim
Aron
Yaham   Taanach   Beth-shan
Ibleam   Rehob
Aruboth?   Dothan
Gath-carmel   Hammath
Sochoh   Bezek
MT. EBAL   Tirzah?
MT. GERIZIM   Shechem
Gilgal
Aphek   Tappuah
Joppa   Bene-berak   Adamah
Ono
Lod   Hadid
Beth-horon   Luz
Lower   Bethel
Beeroth?   Ai
Gezer   Chephirah Gibeon   Jericho
Aijalon
Ekron?   Kirjath-baal,
Zorah   Kirjath-jearim
Ashdod   Beth-shemesh   Jerusalem
Libnah   Jarmuth   Jebus
Azekah   Bethlehem
Ashkelon   Keilah
Gath   Mareshah
Eglon   Lachish   Salt
Gaza   Kirjath-arba   Sea
Beth-eglaim   Hebron
Kirjath-sepher   River Arnon
Gerar   Debir
Raphia   Sharuhen   Arad
Beer-sheba
Aroer

Ijon?
MT. LEBANON
MT. HERMON
Abel
Laish   River Abana
Dan   Damascus
Yano'am
Kedesh
Hazor   Aduru
Merom
Beth-anath?
Chinnereth?   Sea
Rakkoth?   of
Madon   Chinnereth
Hammath
Ayyanu
Enu-anabi
Ashtaroth   Karnaim
Beth-arbel
Ham   Ramoth-gilead
Pella
Jabesh-gilead
Zaretan
Zaphon?
Succoth   Panuel
River Jabbok
Rabbath-ammon

KINGDOM OF GARU
KINGDOM OF OG
Raphono
Kenath,
Nobah,
Qanu
Edrei
Tob?   Bozrah

KINGDOM OF SIHON
(founded during the 13th century)

KINGDOM OF AMMON
(founded in the 13th or 12th century)

KINGDOM
OF
MOAB
(founded during the 13th century)

Brook Zered

KINGDOM OF EDOM
(founded during the 13th century)

Kadesh-barnea?

Jordan River

HOLY CAPE

should have been destroyed, or else Israel itself might have been seduced into their ways.

The prophets and the writers of Deuteronomy and Kings saw individual Israelites going astray "after other gods"; knowing clearly what this apostasy entailed, they used the strongest language at their command to condemn it. They recalled the history of the conquest of Canaan and told their own generation very bluntly that God had wanted the Canaanites exterminated for these very crimes. So they placed on the lips of Moses these words:

> When the Lord your God brings you into the land which you are enter- ing to take possession of it, and clears away many nations before you . . . , and when the Lord your God gives them over to you, and you defeat them; then you must utterly destroy them; you shall make no covenant with them, and show no mercy to them. You shall not make marriages with them, giving your daughters to their sons or taking their daughters for your sons. For they would turn away your sons from following me, to serve other gods; then the anger of the Lord would be kindled against you, and he would destroy you quickly [Deut. 7:1–4; *compare also* Ex. 34:11–16ff.].

PERVASIVE INFLUENCE

Thus as we read through the Old Testament, we are confronted at every turn with the influence of Israel's neighbors. The biblical writers took over Mesopotamian myths, and adapted them to their own religious themes; they wrote up genealogies to justify tribal federations, as the Arabs of the deserts have so often done; they told legends about their great national heroes, as all nations do. Sometimes they reacted violently against the influence of their neighbors, as when they rejected the religious influence of Ca- naan and Phoenicia.

Israel's Unique Religious Genius

During the last fifty years, many writers have published books which stress the close affinities between Israel and its neighbors. Unfortunately, some of these writers go too far, and claim that the religion of Israel is only a natural development, an inevitable happening in that part of the world; if Israel had not seized on the elemental religious truths contained in the faiths of Egypt and Mesopotamia, etc., some other nation would have done so—the Greeks, perhaps, or the Persians. The "ifs" of history are always fascinating, but as history, they are generally irrelevant, and particularly so in the present instance. The plain fact is that no other people did grasp the elemental truths in each of the Near Eastern religions, and certainly no other nation discerned truth from half-truth with such unerring insight.

We see this especially whenever we compare a non-Israelite version of a myth with the version given in the Bible (e.g., when we compare the story of Utnapishtim with that of Noah). It is safe to say that Israel adopted no myth, no legend, no custom from any other land without altering or reinterpreting that myth, legend, or custom in the light of its own unique religious faith. It took the raw materials of its life and culture from the world around it—there was no other source, and Israel did not live in a cultural vacuum (as, for example, China may be said to do today). But the great leaders of Israel then refined these raw materials, purged away all that was incompatible with their religion, and stamped them with a distinctive seal. The process may be illustrated by looking briefly at an Israelite law.

A STEP FORWARD IN MORALITY

Of all the laws in the Old Testament, undoubtedly the most familiar to Christians is that found in the twenty-first chapter of the

THE MOUNT OF MOSES IN
SINAI

book of Exodus, verse twenty-four: "eye for eye, tooth for tooth."
Christians, remembering the words of Jesus in the Sermon on the
Mount (Matt. 5:38) tend to regard this Mosaic statute of "an eye
for an eye" as a harsh and terrible precept, and are puzzled to
know how it ever could have been laid down in the Old Testament as part of God's Law. But to understand it rightly, one must
see it in its historical context, partly as a law *restricting* the extent of punishment for injury ("*only* an eye for an eye"), and
partly as a sanction which was necessary to preserve order in a
society which had no police force.

Where vengeance was the only sanction on crime, blood feuds
between families could rapidly increase and multiply; and therefore many precepts of the Mosaic Law were designed to set limits
to vengeance and to curb blood feuds. Against this background,
the Mosaic law about "an eye for an eye" becomes intelligible, and

can be seen as a step *toward* the morality of the Sermon on the Mount (Matt. 5:17), not as a contradiction of it.

ISRAEL'S DISTINCTIVE INTERPRETATION

Many similar laws are found in other countries of the Near East, of which the most famous collection is the Code of Hammurabi, written about 1700 B.C. All these collections (Babylonian, Assyrian, Hittite, and Mosaic) have several points in common, and from this it may be deduced that the resemblances are to be explained not by direct borrowing but by the influence of a single widespread customary law. In other words, the laws of Moses are Israel's codification of the common law of Near Eastern lands.

As might be expected, Israel did not adopt this common law without interpreting it in the light of its own religion. The Law itself was said to have been given by God to Moses on Mount Sinai: this meant that the God of justice had underwritten all its statutes and all its sanctions. If the people kept the Law, God would protect them; if they broke it, He would punish them. Thus the whole weight of Israel's religion was cast on the side of good order and civilization.

At the same time, the faith of Israel stressed that God was all-merciful and compassionate, and thus we find in the laws of Israel generous provision for those who have injured their neighbor unintentionally: there is a splendid example in the book of Deuteronomy (19:4–7). The laws of Deuteronomy in particular are full of solicitude for "the stranger, the orphan and the widow"; we find, for instance, the following:

> When you reap your harvest in your field, and have forgotten a sheaf in your field, you shall not go back to get it; it shall be for the sojourner, the fatherless and the widow; that the Lord your God may bless you in all the work of your hands.... You shall remember that you were a slave in the land of Egypt; therefore I command you to do this [Deut. 24:19–22].

There is nothing so exalted in the legal codes of other countries, and it was this which led the psalmists to describe "the Law of the Lord" as "perfect, right, enlightening, enduring for ever" (Ps.

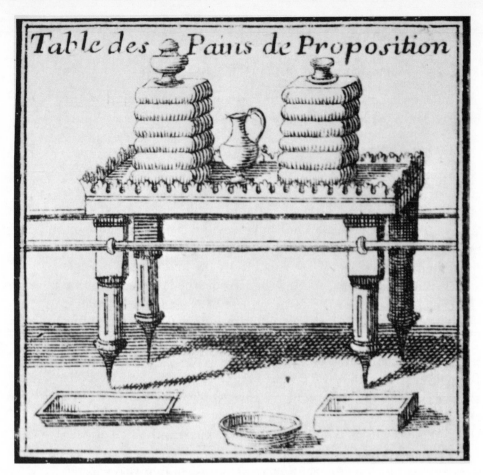

TABLE OF SHOWBREAD, *an artist's conception of the table of showbread used in the Tabernacle*

19:7-9). One wonders how many Christians would be prepared to live up to these standards.

NEIGHBORS' INFLUENCE ON ISRAEL'S LITURGY

Even in the liturgy the influence of Israel's neighbors was felt—in the externals of worship. The architecture of Solomon's temple followed the pattern customary in Syria and Phoenicia, and this is not surprising, since so much of the work was done by Tyrian craftsmen. Obviously, Solomon wanted to build a temple richer than any in Phoenicia to express the superiority of the God of Israel over any pagan deities. In this, he was no different from any other monarch of the time: all wished to present their own god as more important than others.

But in the beautiful prayer which the Bible attributes to Solomon at the dedication of the temple we read how Israel rejected the idea that God dwelt in any earthly city:

> Behold, heaven and the highest heaven cannot contain thee; how much less this house which I have built! . . . And hearken thou to the supplication of thy servant and of thy people Israel, when they pray toward this place; yea, *hear thou in heaven thy dwelling place*; and when thou hearest, forgive [1 Kings 8:27,30].

Here we see that though Israel may have copied the plan of the temple buildings from Syria, it stood firmly by its own theology.

LITURGY COMMEMORATES HISTORICAL EVENTS

One last word must be said about the liturgy of Israel. In the surrounding countries, and particularly in Mesopotamia, certain rites were practiced at fixed times of the year (e.g., at the new year) to commemorate and to re-enact by mime and word episodes of mythology. In Babylon, for example, the epic of creation, of the struggle between Marduk (the patron-god of Babylon) and the forces of chaos, was recited on the first day of every new year, and the god himself was acclaimed in the words "Marduk is king!" Elsewhere, myths about fertility gods and goddesses were recited, and mythological dramas performed. Several scholars have therefore suggested that in Israel too there may have been liturgical ceremonies, at great feasts, based on mythology.

Against this theory, it must be unequivocally stated that there is not a single reference to such rites in the Old Testament, and that the texts adduced to prove the existence of such rites are certainly capable of bearing a quite different meaning. Israel did have its liturgy, but the events commemorated were always historical, not mythological: Israel observed annually the Passover, the Feast of Tents, and in later times, various other feasts as well. The one feature common to them all is that they all became linked with particular events in the history of Israel's salvation.

It is quite true that these feasts may originally have been fixed at certain times because of pagan influence: e.g., the Passover may have been originally a springtime sacrifice of a lamb in order to secure fecundity for the flock—the Arabs celebrated such a feast in the first month of the spring. But Israel adapted these customs to its own ends, just as the church, in later days, fixed the feast of the Nativity of our Lord on December twenty-fifth in order to displace the old Roman pagan feast of *Sol Invictus* – the Unconquered Sun-God. No one concludes that Christians are therefore worshipping the sun.

A NEW VISION OF LIFE

Wherever we turn in our investigation of the Old Testament, we find that Israel had the Midas touch: whatever it handled, it turned into pure gold. The dross and the alloys were purged away; the half-truths and obscurities of pagan culture were rejected; and all that was good and worthwhile in those Eastern civilizations was caught up and fused into a new vision of life. For this was the genius of the Hebrew people: to see steadily and clearly that man's life on earth is to be lived in the presence of God. All Christians, and more especially students of the Old Testament, must echo the words of the final verse in Psalm 147: "He has not dealt thus with any other nation; they do not know his ordinances."

The Development of Doctrine in the Old Testament

Robert W. Fisher

Israel's faith was a historical faith. The very idea of history implies change, so it should not surprise us that Israel's understanding of God's revelation was a developing one. Revelation was involved in the change and growth of the Hebrew people. In speaking of the development of doctrine in the Old Testament, however, we must be careful about what we mean by "doctrine" and "development." For the Hebrews there was no such thing as doctrine in our sense of the word. Nor was there development in the sense that the Hebrews always progressed from an inferior to a superior understanding of revelation.

Vɪᴇᴡ ꜰʀᴏᴍ ɪɴsɪᴅᴇ ᴀ ᴄᴀᴠᴇ ᴀᴛ Qᴜᴍʀᴀɴ, *one of the caves in which the Dead Sea Scrolls were found*

Man's Developing Understanding of God

WHY IS IT that there are some places in the Old Testament where God seems to be a vengeful tribal deity of war while elsewhere He is shown to be a loving father of infinite compassion? Why is it that in the book of Joshua we read of an entire family being punished for the misdeed of only one of its members while in the book of Ezekiel we are told that each person is to be held responsible only for his own actions, and no one is to suffer for the wrongs of another? Many people have often been puzzled by such apparent contradictions as these and others like them which are to be found throughout the Old Testament. It is the purpose of this essay to try to shed some light upon these questions by a consideration of the development of certain ideas within the Old Testament.

ADVANCE IN BIBLICAL SCHOLARSHIP

Happily, there is a wealth of knowledge available to help us in this task. Today we are able to understand the meaning of the Old Testament in a way which was not possible a century or two ago. In the last one hundred years or so, scholars have succeeded in learning much about the Israelite people, their history, their thought, and their literature. We have come to a much better understanding of the way in which the Old Testament grew from its very early beginnings to its present form: we know much more about the various books of the Bible—who wrote them, why, to whom, and when—than we have ever known before. Of course, there are still many baffling problems and frustrating questions which we have not been able to answer, at least not yet, and these must not be minimized. But the fact remains that our knowledge of all facets of biblical literature has vastly increased over past decades.

AERIAL VIEW OF EXCAVATIONS A
TYRE, *showing columns of th
market, remains of Roman an
Byzantine houses, and the Rc
man baths*

One result of this increased knowledge is that we have some idea of the order in which most of the biblical documents were written. This order is by no means infallible since we are still quite uncertain as to the date of origin of some biblical materials, even at our advanced stage of biblical studies; nevertheless its general outline is fairly secure. This is a very important achievement in the study of Scripture because it allows us to trace the changes which took place in the Hebrew understanding of God as well as in Hebrew religious life as a whole. And change there was indeed!

This fact of a changing understanding of religious concepts within the Old Testament should not surprise us; on the contrary we would be surprised not to find it. Israel's faith was a historical faith. It was her conviction that God revealed Himself through His mighty acts in history, and of course the very idea of history itself implies change. History never stands still, and if it is the stage for the self-revelation of God, then at least man's comprehension of this self-revelation will be a developing one. Indeed, throughout the Old Testament, God is the God who acts; He is always "on the move," and Hebrew conceptions of God were always very dynamic and alive.

It should be made clear, however, that we are dealing here with man's understanding of God and not God in Himself. Inasmuch as the Hebrew Scriptures came into being over a period of some one thousand years, it is only natural that there should have taken place during this time what has been called "the development of doctrine in the Old Testament." It is this phenomenon which we shall study and attempt to clarify in the following pages.

Dangers Involved in this Study

Before we begin we should be very careful to recognize that there are three real dangers involved in this attempt and we should be on our guard against them at all times. We would do well to discuss these at some length at this point and thus be forewarned.

THE DANGER OF THE TERM "DOCTRINE"

First, we must be cautious about the use of the term "doctrine" in this essay, because, as a matter of fact, there is no such thing in the Old Testament, at least not in our sense of the word, i.e., authoritative and systematic teaching. In the first place, the ancient Hebrew simply did not think systematically. We are dealing here, for the most part, with an ancient, "pre-logical," poetic mind that expresses itself in rich and varied imagery, a mind whose thought processes are much more dynamic and integrative than static and analytical, and whose faith is pounded out on the anvil of active and concrete relationships rather than in the solitude of religious contemplation. Note, for example, the prophet Jeremiah and his struggles, not only with men, but with God.

Such a mind could hardly be expected to produce "systematic theology"; indeed, this would be false to its own nature and genius.

However, these men did think thoughts about God, man, the world, and so forth; they were forced to deal with problems that were basically "theological" and in this way it is possible to speak of what has been called an "implied theology" in the Bible. However, we must never forget the vital and dynamic nature of this "theology" which in the final analysis simply cannot be reduced to an abstract system.

A WORSHIP SETTING

This fact becomes particularly clear when we stop to consider a second point. One of the crucial gains of modern biblical scholarship is the recognition that a large part of the Old Testament arose and/or was preserved in a *worship* setting. This includes such unlikely materials as historical narratives and law codes. Thus we realize that the primary activity in which the biblical writers were engaging was not theological speculation, but the praise and worship of God, and they set forth their religious ideas only incidentally, only by the way as they took part in this more fundamental process. They did not reflect upon their "theology" so much as they participated in its meaning; they did not contemplate the essence of God so much as they celebrated His mighty acts in history and His presence with them in the cult.

Now this is hardly the way we approach the subject today. We are not attuned to this kind of thinking. We are accustomed to concepts being deliberately thought out in a cool, detached, intellectual atmosphere according to rigid standards of logic. The Old Testament simply did not come into being that way; it is the product of a very different process. Which process is superior is another, and perhaps irrelevant, question. At this point we need only be aware of the difference, for it is very important.

A final caution with regard to the use of the term "doctrine" in this essay stems from the fact that we cannot speak of "the" doctrine of the Old Testament. There are places where we find a variety of differing and sometimes conflicting positions on the same question. We discover that there is no set, standard view on many issues. For instance, during the period following the Babylonian exile, most of the Jewish community adopted a rather exclusivistic attitude, represented by Ezra and Nehemiah, but at the same time a strong protest was raised against these tendencies by a small minority with a very universal and inclusive point of view, represented by the books of Jonah and Ruth.

We must at least speak of "doctrines" in the plural and realize that the Old Testament represents, not a monolithic system of dogmatics, but the religious deposit of a highly variegated community recorded over a period of more than a thousand years. It can be seen, from the preceding considerations, that the use of the term "doctrine" represents a certain hazard to the purposes of this essay.

THE DANGER OF THE TERM "DEVELOPMENT"

The term "development" is even more misleading than "doctrine," and stands in greater need of clarification. If the term "development" implies automatic and inexorable progression from an inferior to a superior religious understanding and conviction, then we must confess that, like "doctrine," there is no such thing in the Old Testament. In fact, some of the most profound elements in the Old Testament, those which form the very foundation of the Hebrew faith, such as the idea of the covenant and of election, are to be found in the very earliest biblical material.

To be sure, there is change over the centuries, there is movement from a more primitive to a more sophisticated understanding and mode of expression. But whether or not this movement always represents "progress" from a "lower" to a "higher" level is altogether a different question. We may well ask if the faith represented by Abraham is inferior to the nationalistic pride and vengeance of the book of Esther, which was written perhaps five hundred years after the stories relating to the patriarch were first recorded, or if the ethical zeal of the Mosaic covenant is inferior to the priestly casuistry of the post-exilic period, seven or eight hundred years later. Of course, there were sound historical reasons for the negative feelings of the later eras, but still we cannot ignore the fact that they are among the most recent parts of the Old Testament.

No SIMPLE, CHRONOLOGICAL PROGRESSION OF THOUGHT

The point to remember is simply this: the fact that an idea or an attitude is later does not necessarily make it more advanced or true, religiously speaking. It is quite possible for the crude images of an early period, e.g., the anthropomorphisms (the use of human imagery in referring to God) of the first part of Genesis, to convey some very profound thoughts. On the other hand, the great age of a passage is in no way a guarantee of its depth of religious insight; there is hardly a less noble thought in the whole Old Testament than that expressed in the haughty and hateful Song of Lamech (Gen. 4:23–24), one of the oldest poems of the Bible.

What we find within the Old Testament itself is not so much a "development" from a "primitive" to an "advanced" stage of religious thought, but rather a situation in which both less advanced and more advanced ideas are present in all periods of biblical literature with a continuum of thought existing between the two poles of tension, between what we would call "lower" and "higher" religious concepts. During certain periods, one or the other of these poles would appear to predominate somewhat over its opposite; however, this was never a case of "either-or" but rather "both-and." If we extend our perspective to the New Testament, then it cannot be denied that ultimately, but not necessarily immediately, all paths lead upward. However, it is interesting to note that even in the New Testament a number of the "lower" concepts still persist.

SUBJECTIVE CHARACTER OF THE TERM "DEVELOPMENT"

One of the difficulties in dealing with the idea of "development" when it is equated with progress is the pronounced subjectivity involved. "Development" in this sense often becomes simply

EZRA READING THE LAW, *a wall-painting, dated first or second century* A.D., *from a synagogue in Dura-Europos, a city of ancient Syria*

what is pleasing to the individual in question. However, what is pleasing to one person is almost inevitably displeasing to someone else. For example, was it "development" when the Israelites passed from the prophetic era of the pre-exilic period to the priestly era of the post-exilic period? Obviously the answer to this question would depend upon whether one were inclined toward the prophetic or the priestly enterprise. In any case the term "development" must not be understood in the sense of simplistic progression. Its basic meaning, here at least, is change, the movement from one stage of thought to another, without any implication as to the quality of those stages.

CHRONOLOGICAL ORDER OF BIBLICAL TEXTS: SOME PROBLEMS

Even when development is properly understood as change we are still faced with the difficulty mentioned earlier: we are not altogether certain as to the date of origin of some of the biblical material, e.g., many of the psalms. It is important here to remember that great progress has been made in this field. In fact, it is precisely at this point that biblical scholarship has advanced sufficiently to allow us to undertake the task proposed in this essay. But there are still some puzzles which have not been completely solved.

One reason for part of the confusion is the fact that some of the biblical material probably existed in oral form of one kind or another long before it was written down. Which period does it represent? For example, there is very strong evidence that some of the ritual laws in the Old Testament were not collected, edited, and written down until the Exile or later, and yet many of these give every indication of being highly archaic and of great age. How does one evaluate such material with regard to the "development of doctrine"? At what point is it to be "fitted into" the sequence?

In this connection, we must beware of the fallacy of judging a passage to be late or early because we think that the ideas it expresses are late or early. This is a very tempting procedure and exceedingly difficult to avoid. Indeed, many have succumbed to it, and it may not be possible to escape it entirely, but as a regular method it is much too subjective and circular to be followed.

There is one thing that we definitely do know, however, concerning the order in which the biblical documents were composed and it is this: they were not composed in the order in which we now find them in the Old Testament. How and why they came to be arranged as they are is not completely clear in every case, but there are some places where we have gained some very helpful light on this question. This is particularly true of the first five books of the Bible, sometimes called the Pentateuch (from the Greek, meaning "five rolls").

ADVANCES IN THE STUDY OF THE PENTATEUCH

Tradition has held that these books were written by Moses, although the Old Testament itself nowhere makes this claim. If this assumption were true, then these five books would indeed

SAMARITANS ON MOUNT GERIZIM *celebrating Passover*

be the oldest documents in the Bible and would rightly stand as the very first of the Scriptures. However, over a long period of careful and reverent research, biblical scholars concluded that the Pentateuch could not have been written by one man, and certainly not by Moses; rather it was composed of various strands of tradition from different periods which had been brought together at certain points in Israel's history and edited by different men. This process was not completed until after the Exile and thus stretched over more than seven hundred years.

FOUR PRIMARY STRANDS OF TRADITION

There is no unanimity among Old Testament experts with regard to the details of this process, and indeed scholars are still working on and developing important aspects of it. However, the basic tenets of what was originally called the Graf-Wellhausen or "documentary" hypothesis are now accepted by most biblical researchers as established fact.

In broad outline they are as follows: there are four primary strands of tradition in the Pentateuch; the oldest of these, designated by the letter "J," is of southern or Judean origin and is now dated as early as 950 B.C.; the second strand, known as "E", is from the north and is usually dated around 750 B.C.; sometime after the fall of the northern kingdom of Israel in 721 B.C., the two strands were merged into a single unit, known as JE; at some period prior to its discovery in the Jerusalem temple in 621 B.C., the third strand, called "D" because it consists of material found in Deuteronomy, was committed to writing; later, either shortly before or a little after the fall of Jerusalem in 587 B.C., "D" was inserted into JE, thus producing "JED"; finally, during and after the Exile (587–ca. 400 B.C.), the priestly writers ("P") collected their material and both inserted it in and used it as a framework for "JED"; thus they gave the Pentateuch approximately the form it has today.

The development of this theory of the composition of the Pentateuch was of the greatest significance for the study of the Old Testament, for it provided an explanation, consistent with the

BAS RELIEF OF THE ARK OF THE COVENANT, *sculptured in rock at the ancient synagogue of Capernaum*

nature of the biblical material, of the numerous purposeless and even scandalous contradictions, doublets, and anachronisms which have hounded the steps of many serious readers of the Bible since the very beginning. Why is Moses' father-in-law called Jethro in one place and Reuel or Hobab in another? Why are certain incidents, such as the promising of a son to Abraham (Gen. 15, 17, and 18) or the revelation of the name of Yahweh (Ex. 3 and 6), repeated in very awkward and pointless ways? Why are camels mentioned in a story relating to Abraham when these animals were apparently not domesticated until several centuries later?

It is clear from the pitifully short sketch of the composition of the Pentateuch given above that such a process, with its several variant sources plus the interweaving and editing which took place at numerous stages, would inevitably produce precisely the kinds of inconsistencies which have been found in these books.

Shedding light on the chronological order

Moreover, the "documentary" hypothesis provided a great deal of knowledge regarding the age of the various passages of the first five books of the Bible, and it was discovered that they were not at all in their chronological order. A classical example of this disarray is found in the first two chapters of Genesis, at the very threshold to the whole Bible. In its present form, the first chapter of Genesis is from the "P" source, the latest one of the four Pentateuchal traditions; whereas the second chapter of Genesis is from the "J" source, the oldest of the four. A quick reading of these two chapters will readily reveal some of the repetitions and inconsistencies referred to above and will also demonstrate the way in which the preceding theory accounts for them.

Thus, to summarize, there are some points at which we are still faced with a degree of uncertainty concerning the age of particular biblical materials. This fact should cause us to proceed with caution at these points. However, biblical scholarship has made great advances in this field as the development of the multiple source theory of the composition of the Pentateuch makes quite plain, and in general, we are fairly certain as to the dates of most of the biblical documents. We simply must be careful not to become naively overconfident in this regard.

The danger of modernization

The last danger of which we need to be aware in this essay is the peril of modernization. It is simply not possible to apply modern terms and concepts to Old Testament thought straight across the board. The men of the Old Testament are separated from us by a gulf of over two and sometimes three thousand years, and also by an immense gap of culture and custom. Their ways and their thoughts are not our ways and our thoughts, at least not for the most part. They were ancient Semites, we are modern westerners. If we want to understand the meaning of the Old Testament, then, we must try to understand how these Hebrews of long ago thought and what was the meaning which these words had for them when they were first addressed to their particular historical situation.

It is very easy to slip into the rather comfortable habit of conceiving of ancient concepts in twentieth-century terms, but this is a temptation we must resist. The categories are not the same, they do not fit, and we shall never come to grips with the real meaning of the biblical message in this way.

A related temptation to be noted here is that of trying to force our own attitudes and opinions upon the biblical material. We must not attempt to make it say what we want it to say, even if we think that is what it ought to say, even if we think that is the pious and religious thing for it to say, because sometimes the Bible can be very impious and unreligious—that is, to our limited unimaginative modern Western minds.

In this regard we must be particularly careful about "reading back" into the Old Testament later ecclesiastical doctrine. Of course there are many later ideas and institutions which grew out of Old Testament ideas and institutions, but we are obliged to look at these from the Old Testament perspective and not from our own modern point of view.

OLD TESTAMENT IS NOT TO BE JUDGED BY THE NEW TESTAMENT

The Christian finds himself in a somewhat paradoxical position at this point. For him, the final standard against which all things must be measured is the spirit of Christ in the New Testament. But according to what has just been said, this is precisely what we must not do with regard to the Old Testament. We must not judge it by the New Testament, but rather on its own terms. Indeed, since the Old Testament came first and had no knowledge of the

SCHOLAR CAREFULLY UNFOLDS PIECES OF PARCHMENT OF ONE OF THE DEAD SEA SCROLLS

New Testament, it would be manifestly unfair to criticize it on the basis of the latter's standards.

To avoid these various forms of modernization will require what has been called "a difficult thrust of historic imagination," but it is a thrust we must make if we are to deal meaningfully with the Old Testament.

METHOD OF TREATMENT

These, then, are some of the dangers of which we should beware in this essay. They are not insurmountable and they should not deter us as we seek to come to a better understanding of the Old Testament by observing the changes ("development") which took place with regard to the ideas expressed in it ("doctrine") during the course of its formation. For the sake of this study, these ideas will be rather arbitrarily grouped under the following headings, which will undoubtedly overlap to some extent: God, Man, Ethics, and Worship. Incidentally, this is a fragmentation of thought of which no ancient Semite would ever be guilty; however, perhaps we can learn something just by noting the contrast between this example of our way of thinking and what we have learned and shall learn about theirs.

The Development of the Idea of God

The crucial starting place for the Old Testament idea of God is the Exodus from Egypt and the covenant at Mount Sinai, not the stories in Genesis. It was not until their deliverance from Egypt that the Hebrews actually became a people and Yahweh became their God. It was here that they learned who He really was (i.e., His name, "Yahweh") and it was in these events that His nature and characteristics which would be determinative for all later thought and religious formulations were revealed to them. His love, shown in His election of Israel; His power and sovereignty in history shown in His bringing the people out of Egypt; His glory and holiness, which were manifested at Mount Sinai; His faithfulness and righteousness which were manifested in the covenant.

There was no distinctly Hebrew view of God until the Exodus; after the Exodus almost all Old Testament thought was conditioned by the understanding which derived from it. Thus the Exodus was *the* constitutive, creative event in Israelite religion. Of course, this does not mean that all of these implications were immediately realized by the people. This process took a long time, in some cases centuries, but the basic constituents had been given. The spectacles through which the people viewed these basics varied down through the centuries, and sometimes these spectacles were strongly influenced by the immediate historical situation, but the basics themselves never changed.

This is not to say that the wandering forefathers of the Hebrews who have come down to us in the figures of Abraham, Isaac, and Jacob had no religion, but it centered around tribal deities who were associated with the individual who founded their cult, i.e., the Shield of Abraham (Gen. 15:1), the Fear (or Kinsman) of Isaac (Gen. 31:42, 53), the Mighty One of Jacob (Gen. 49:24). These family or clan gods stood in intimate relation both to the group and to the individual and in many ways served as a fitting preparation for the later Yahwistic faith which began with the Exodus.

In any case, these earlier tribal deities were clearly identified with and coalesced into the covenant God Yahweh at Mount Sinai. In one of the accounts of Moses' encounter with God at Sinai (Ex. 6:2–3) we read: "And God said to Moses, 'I am Yahweh. I appeared to Abraham, to Isaac, and to Jacob as God Almighty (Hebrew, *El Shaddai*), but by my name Yahweh I did not make myself known to them.'" In this connection it should be remembered that according to our best knowledge of the composition of the Old Testament today, the Genesis accounts of the patriarchs were not written down until long after the Exodus and therefore these narratives were viewed and recorded from the perspective of the Yahwistic faith. Indeed, one of the writers, the great author of the "J" source, did not hesitate to read back the knowledge and worship of Yahweh all the way to the time of Adam's grandson, Enosh (Gen. 4:26). Even the faith of the fathers was seen in the light of the Exodus event.

INFLUENCE OF THE EXODUS IN FORMATION OF ISRAEL'S RELIGION

This centrality of the Exodus in the formation of Israel's religion—and thus her concept of God—is clear throughout the Old Testament. For Hosea, God identifies Himself as "Yahweh your God from the land of Egypt" (Hos. 12:9); to Jeremiah He is "Yahweh who brought us up from the land of Egypt" (Jer. 2:6); and according to Ezekiel Yahweh chose Israel in Egypt and led her out of that land in spite of the fact she was already rebelling against Him (Ezek. 20:1–13). Likewise, the fact that prior to the

A VIEW OF MOUNT SINAI, *in mist.*

Exodus the Hebrews had not worshipped Yahweh is unashamedly admitted in such a passage as Joshua 24:2, 14. [Joshua said to all the people] "Thus says Yahweh, the God of Israel, 'Your fathers lived of old beyond the Euphrates, Terah, the father of Abraham and of Nahor, and they served other gods...' Now therefore... put away the gods which your fathers served beyond the River, and in Egypt, and serve Yahweh." These statements should leave no doubt but that the religion of Israel proper had its origin at the Reed Sea and Mount Sinai.

It has already been noted how during this formative period of her existence Israel came to know the basic characteristics of her God: love, sovereign power, glory, holiness, faithfulness, and righteousness. These fundamentals were to remain the central facts of Israel's faith as long as she existed, but, as mentioned above, many of their implications were not immediately recognized and had to be worked out over a long period of time. Moreover, Israel's understanding of these fundamentals was always

colored in one degree or another by her current historical setting. Therefore we shall not be surprised to find elements in the
history of her religion which do not correspond to these basic
principles, at least not from our modern Western point of view.

SOME EARLY IDEAS OF GOD

Thus, at various times but particularly in the early period, the
Hebrew people thought of Yahweh: (1) as a storm God, associated
with a certain mountain; (2) as a God of war; (3) as a tribal deity;
and (4) as a rather anthropomorphic God (i.e., one conceived of
and represented in human terms).

A STORM GOD

It is possible that the first of these images, the storm God of a
mountain, grew out of Israel's initial and crucial encounter with
Yahweh at Mount Sinai. The external circumstances surrounding
this formative event in her history surely tended to give such an
impression of the deity. There are a number of passages in the
book of Exodus in which the presence of Yahweh is represented
in terms of violent exhibitions of natural power. For instance, in
Exodus (19:16), as Moses is about to ascend Mount Sinai, we read:
"On the morning of the third day there were thunders and light-
nings, and a thick cloud upon the mountain, and a very loud trumpet blast, so that all the people who were in the camp trembled."

The fact that these early Israelites first experienced their covenant God as a mighty storm deity as well as a righteous and sovereign Lord had a lasting effect. Of course the latter aspect was
always primary, but even centuries later we find storm imagery
being used with reference to Yahweh. In Judges (5:4), when
Yahweh comes from Sinai to help Deborah, He is pictured as
riding the storm. The psalmists in particular were inclined to
describe the presence of Yahweh in these terms: "He bowed the
heavens, and came down; thick darkness was under his feet. He
rode on a cherub, and flew; he came swiftly upon the wings of the
wind" (Ps. 18:9–10).

A VIEW OF THE EUPHRATES RIVER, *showing fisherman drying his nets*

STORM GODS NOT UNCOMMON

It should be noted that the characterization of an important deity as a storm god was not at all uncommon in the ancient Near East. For example, the young and powerful deity Baal of the Ugaritic texts, about whom we have learned so much since the discovery of these tablets in 1929, is precisely a god of the storm and of fertility. He is customarily pictured as a helmeted warrior in a short kilt, striding into battle with a thunderbolt as a spear and a mace in his uplifted arm. He also thunders from heaven, rides upon the clouds (exactly the same phrase appears in Ps. 68:4), and in various other ways is described in terms which are often very close and even identical to those used of Yahweh.

These similarities are neither surprising nor disturbing. Such terminology was the common medium in which to "speak of God" in those times; indeed, perhaps this kind of language provided the only meaningful forms with which these unsophisticated Hebrews could conceptualize, identify and represent deity, especially deity as dynamic as they knew Yahweh to be. Perhaps these concepts were the highest at their disposal. In any case, as we shall frequently see, the terms themselves are not the important thing, but rather the content, the meaning with which they are filled.

THE FUNDAMENTAL DIFFERENCE

However, there was one crucial and fundamental difference between Yahweh and all the other gods which set him completely apart in a unique category. In spite of these outer trappings which remind one of a storm god, Yahweh was not primarily a nature god like Baal and numerous other such deities. From the very beginning Yahweh was first and foremost a God of history, who revealed Himself in His mighty acts in history, not nature. His relationship with Israel is understood and described throughout the Old Testament in terms of history. This is an important principle which must be kept in mind.

A GOD OF WAR

Another way in which the Hebrews thought of Yahweh, again particularly in the early period, was as a God of war, doing battle for His people and leading them to triumph. In one of the early Israelite victory songs, the so-called Song of Moses in Exodus, we find the exultant cry, "Yahweh is a man of war, Yahweh is his name" (Ex. 15:3). In the account of Joshua's victory over the kings of the Amorites, when "the sun stood still at Gibeon," we are told that "Yahweh fought for Israel" (Josh. 10:14) and David told Goliath, "I come to you in the name of Yahweh of hosts, the God of the armies of Israel" (I Sam. 17:45). Indeed, the title of one of the Old Testament's early source books, now lost, was "The Book of the Wars of Yahweh" (Num. 21:14).

A Hittite stele, *dated 1530 B.C., which was found in the ruins of the royal castle of Babylon*

However, it is important that we see this concept of Yahweh as a God of war against the background of Israel's historical situation, in order that we do not misinterpret it. It is clear that Israel's very survival frequently depended upon her victory over those people with whom her mere presence brought her unavoidable military conflict, especially in the formative period of her existence. Defeat at this point would have spelled annihilation. The idea of Yahweh as a God of war meant that Yahweh was with Israel as her covenant God in this enterprise, so important at that moment, as He was with her in all her other undertakings.

Under these circumstances it was necessary for Yahweh to be a God of war, even from a theological point of view. It had always been a basic tenet of Israel's faith that Yahweh had promised her a land of her own, and this promise, which was traced all the way back to the patriarchs, could hardly be realized without military conflict. Thus Yahweh as a God of war is a necessary though ultimately a secondary element in Israel's life and thought.

A TRIBAL DEITY

The idea of Yahweh as a tribal deity is likewise understandable against the background of Israel's origins. Indeed, it was her firm belief that Yahweh had chosen her to be His people and had said that He would be her God. The whole concept of the covenant relationship was based upon a special and unique bond between Yahweh and Israel. The election of Israel may have been for service, even for suffering; indeed it may have been totally necessary, but it was election nonetheless, and it gave rise to a tension between exclusivism and universalism which remained basically unresolved throughout the Old Testament. In truth, we may well ask whether Christianity itself has resolved this tension vis-à-vis the other religions of the world today.

AN ANTHROPOMORPHIC GOD

Frequently the Old Testament makes use of human imagery in referring to God. For example, God speaks, walks in a garden which He has planted (Gen. 3:8), hears (Ex. 16:12), sees (Gen.

6:12), smells (Gen. 8:21), laughs (Ps. 59:8), shuts the door of the ark Himself (Gen. 7:16), and so forth. These are called anthropomorphisms. The Old Testament anthropomorphisms are a problem, because it is usually not clear when these human terms are applied to God in a purely figurative manner and when they are used in a more literal sense. But there is a basic difficulty involved here with which even modern theologians still struggle: how is a human being to speak of the divine, or anything else for that matter, without using human language? Added to this is the peculiar fact that Old Testament man always expressed himself in very concrete and realistic terms drawn from immediate experience, regardless of how abstract his subject matter might be.

Having said this, one must realize that there is a tendency for these expressions to be understood less figuratively in some of the earlier strata of the Old Testament. Certainly in the later writings of the Old Testament they decrease in number, and in the Targum, the Aramaic translation of the Old Testament, they are usually avoided altogether. In any case, such language is by no means a necessarily "primitive" way of speaking of God; it can be and is used in the service of very "advanced" and "sophisticated" theologies, e.g., Isaiah 40–55.

THE EFFECT OF THE ENTRY INTO CANAAN

When the Israelites settled in the land of Canaan, some very significant changes took place in their idea of God. For one thing, He could no longer be thought of as residing exclusively at His far-off sanctuary, Mount Sinai, and thus He became the Lord of the land in which His people now dwelt. Although it was very modest, this revision marked the beginning of a movement toward wider horizons.

In the shift from Sinai to Canaan, Yahweh took over the functions of the agricultural deities. While the Israelites wandered in the arid steppeland, there was obviously no necessity for such a deity, but as they gradually turned from their seminomadic way of life to farming, they needed a god who was able to vouchsafe to them the necessary conditions for plentiful crops and herds—

ILLUMINATED PAGE *of the book of Genesis, from the Bible of Nekcsei-Lipócz (1335 A.D.).*

rain, fertility, and so forth. Of course, this had been precisely the role of the Canaanite baals (fertility gods), and many Israelites naturally began to worship them often while still maintaining the worship of Yahweh as well. However, the loyal Yahwists simply added these functions, powers, and prerogatives to the concept of their covenant God. Indeed, the very fact that they did not surrender Yahweh for the baals of Canaan is a remarkable witness to the strength of His hold upon their allegiance and devotion.

OPPOSITION OF CONSERVATIVE GROUPS

There were certain conservative groups among the Israelites who resisted this transition to a settled, agricultural existence, preferring instead to cling to the old nomadic ideals. Their reasons were as cultural and ethnic as they were theological. To such circles we are indebted for the preservation of the story of Cain and Abel (Gen. 4:1–16), in which the offering of the herdsman, Abel, finds favor with God while that of the farmer, Cain, does not.

Actually this story reflects an age-old cultural conflict between what has been called "the desert and the sown" which goes back thousands of years, even to prehistoric times. This rustic reaction lasted long after Israel's settlement in Canaan. Even as late as the time of Jeremiah we hear of the Rechabites, for example, who would not even dwell in houses or touch wine (Jer. 35:1–10). However, such is not representative of the large majority of Hebrews, who were content, even eager, to settle in the land.

Thus there took place a further enlargement and diversification of the Israelite idea of God. Yahweh was no longer the source of life and well-being for a nomadic people only, but He was now the source of agricultural plenty as well. More and more, His people understood Him to be Lord over nature (this is not the same as a nature god) as well as Lord over history.

THE MIXING OF ELEMENTS FROM DIFFERENT RELIGIONS

This development inevitably resulted in a certain degree of syncretism, i.e., the mixing together of elements from different religions. It was noted above that after settling in Canaan many Israelites worshipped both Yahweh and the baals. Under these circumstances numerous Canaanite practices were bound to creep into the worship of Yahweh, and so they did, especially the sexual ones associated with the fertility cult. (We might also note, in passing, that the worship of Yahweh influenced Canaanite practices, but that aspect of the question does not concern us here.) To be sure, the Israelite concept and cult of Yahweh was greatly enriched by contact with Canaanite religion, but there were times when the latter threatened to swallow up the former completely, when it seemed as if it were actually the baals who were being worshipped under the cover of the name of Yahweh.

This syncretism continued throughout the entire period of the Old Testament, even until the latest phase, and the prophets had to struggle against it constantly, lest the unique heritage of Israel should be so altered that it lose its original identity altogether. It is important to remember that, in this struggle, the prophets and other loyal Yahwists were always in the minority. The majority of the Israelites preferred to follow a mixed religion of the popular type which contained many Canaanite elements.

GOD OF THE SKY AND THE HEAVENS

In the course of time Yahweh also became a God of the sky and the heavens. The fact that He had already been thought of as a storm God, controlling thunder and lightning, would have associated Him with the sky and made this development natural and simple. However, an even more significant preparation is to be found in the pre-Mosaic worship of the god El by the Hebrew patriarchs and by the Canaanites as well.

The word "El" (plural, "Elohim," sometimes used with singular meaning) served a number of purposes in the Semitic languages of the ancient Near East. (1) It was the generic term for "god." (2) It designated the senior, high deity of various ancient Near Eastern pantheons; and of special interest to this study, (3) it was used to refer to the particular deity of the wandering ancestors of the Israelites. Both biblical and extrabiblical sources show clearly that El was a god who was closely associated with the heavens. In Genesis (14:19) we find Melchizedek, king of Salem, blessing Abram in the name of "El Elyon ('God Most High'), maker (or possessor) of heaven and earth," and at ancient Ugarit, El was worshipped as the father of the gods and the lord of heaven.

THE IDENTIFICATION OF YAHWEH WITH EL

As we have seen, the Israelites quickly identified Yahweh with El, or perhaps better, the various Els, who had been worshipped under one form or another by their forefathers. In this process Yahweh assumed the attributes of the latter, and this development definitely contributed to His becoming a god of the sky and of the heavens. Such a development could not avoid having a broadening effect upon the Hebrew concept of deity. A god of heaven is no longer bound to a specific locality in the old way, although he may have a special relationship to certain places as, indeed, Yahweh did. In any case, Yahweh's power and sovereignty

A Bedouin's home

were thus extended beyond the bounds of territorial or tribal limitations and this extension could not help but tend toward universalism.

Yahweh as a God of Righteousness

Another central concept which assumed ever greater importance in the Israelite idea of God was the righteousness of Yahweh. As we have already noted, this concept had been present from the very beginning, since Israel's entire relationship with Yahweh was based on the covenant, and the conditions upon which the covenant rested were the stipulations of the Law, which at least in part was an ethical code. However, from the very beginning this aspect of Israel's faith faced a continuous crisis and it was in the context of this crisis that the prophets labored to make the implications of Yahweh's righteousness clear to all the people. Let us look at this problem more closely.

The settlement of the Israelites in Palestine resulted not only in a confrontation between Yahweh and the baals, but also between the culture, the mores, the whole way of life represented by their respective peoples. The Israelites came from a seminomadic background where there was little private property and thus where no one was very rich or very poor. The Spartan conditions of life in the wilderness fostered a sense of solidarity, equality, and justice which never left them.

On the other hand, the Canaanite culture was a complex, relatively sophisticated, commercial one with a stratified society and all of the inequities attendant upon such a civilization. Private property, trade, credit and the like made possible a situation in which there were a few rich and many poor, and the worship of the baals tended to preserve this status quo rather than call it into question. Inevitably the Israelites were affected by this kind of environment and soon began to follow the lead of their new neighbors.

Thus the conflict between Yahweh and the baals involved not only the question of which one was really God and to be worshipped by the people, but it was also a matter of which way of life, which system of ethics was to prevail in Israel. These two elements are quite inseparable.

Elijah

Relatively early in this conflict, it seemed as if perhaps the battle might go to the baals. Jezebel, the Phoenician queen of King Ahab, mounted a determined effort to establish the worship of her god, Baal-Melkart of Tyre, in the land. So forceful and thorough was this attempt that it almost succeeded. However, at this moment of grave danger in the history of Israel's religion, as in all such moments, a prophet arose to stand in Yahweh's name against all that would subvert the sovereignty of the God of the covenant.

The well-known story of Elijah's triumph at Mount Carmel over "the four hundred and fifty prophets of Baal and the four hundred prophets of Asherah, who eat at Jezebel's table" (I Kings 18),

RUINS ON TOP OF MOUNT NEBO

whatever it may represent in actuality, shows that he was successful in thwarting this particular threat to Yahwism. Never again was there an attempt to make the worship of a baal the official religion of Israel. At the same time, the story of Elijah's condemnation of Ahab for having Naboth murdered in order to gain possession of his vineyard (1 Kings 21) shows the revulsion of the loyal Yahwist to the odious and oppressive Canaanite ways which the king and many of the people had accepted.

THE CONTRIBUTION OF THE PROPHETS

Thus it was down through the history of Israel. As the people fell away from Yahweh and worshipped the baals, or at least mixed Canaanite elements with the worship of Yahweh, and as they turned to follow various unjust Canaanite practices, prophets would arise to proclaim anew not only Yahweh's sovereignty, but His righteousness as well. Israel was to be a righteous people precisely because Yahweh was a righteous God, who demanded justice and not meaningless sacrifice. With the work of Amos and Hosea, the implications of Yahweh's righteousness became clearer and clearer, and with Isaiah of Jerusalem this thought received its climactic statement: "But Yahweh of hosts is exalted in justice, and the Holy God shows himself holy in righteousness" (Is. 5:16).

Thus these prophets stood for a God who was very different from the Canaanite baals in His relation to human social structures. He was not the sanctifier of the status quo like the local deities of Palestine, but He was the standard of creative change and reformation.

ISRAEL SUBJECT TO JUDGMENT

This concept of Yahweh as a righteous God, who demanded of His people not only their loyal devotion but righteousness and justice toward their neighbor as well, had very far-reaching implications. For one thing, it contributed to the idea that Israel was subject to judgment and punishment for her misdeeds. If Yahweh was indeed "of purer eyes than to behold evil" (Hab. 1:13), then He surely could not tolerate the wrongdoing of His own people and would be forced to punish them for their wickedness.

Such an understanding is a far cry from the usual relationship between a god and his people found elsewhere in the ancient Near East. There the deity was intimately dependent upon his people and could not punish them severely without endangering his own welfare; thus he was ordinarily obliged to protect them regardless of their devotion or behavior.

THE SOVEREIGNTY OF YAHWEH

On the contrary, in Israel the covenant relation between Yahweh and His people was precisely contingent upon the fulfillment of certain mutual obligations: Yahweh was to be Israel's God and Israel was to be loyal to Him and obey Him, which obviously included dealing righteously with others since Yahweh Himself was righteous. If Israel did not fulfill these requirements, Yahweh was no longer beholden to her in any way; indeed He had to punish her for her evil because it contradicted His righteousness. Yahweh was not dependent on Israel, but Israel could not live without Yahweh. Thus, in proclaiming the righteousness of Yahweh, the prophets from Elijah to the Second Isaiah not only made unmistakably clear the central place which ethics and morality had in the Yahwistic faith, but they also contributed to a more exalted and profound conception of Yahweh's own greatness, which exceeded all human considerations. Yahweh, judge of Israel and judge of the nations, was indeed "exalted in justice."

INDIVIDUAL EMPHASES OF VARIOUS PROPHETS

All of the prophets shared in this common task of working out the implications of Yahweh's righteousness, of which Israel had known since the very beginning at Mount Sinai. But at the same time each individual prophet made his own special contribution to Israel's faith by working out the implications of some other important characteristic of Yahweh which had also been there all along. For example, while Elijah and Amos dwelt on Yahweh's righteousness, Hosea stressed His love and grace; Isaiah emphasized His holiness and majesty which make Him worthy of man's unqualified faith; Jeremiah showed forth a God to whom man can turn in repentance and intimate communion; for Ezekiel, Yahweh was a God of glory and honor before whom man knows himself to be totally profane; and for Second Isaiah, He was a God of universal power who was over all the earth and beside whom there was no other. Thus one by one the prophets refined and clarified Israel's understanding of God until by the time of the Exile it was almost complete.

THE IMPACT OF THE EXILE

The Exile marked a crucial watershed in the faith of Israel, an important turning point in the history of her religion. The fall and destruction of Jerusalem in 587 B.C. deprived Israel of the material focal points of her faith; the temple, the king, the holy city, even the land itself were all gone, and most of the people were carried off into exile in a strange, yet rich and attractive country. This event caused some rather fundamental changes and reformulations in Israelite religion; at the same time it finally established some traits which had been developing for a long time.

THE NECESSITY FOR NEW SYMBOLS OF THE FAITH

For one thing, the people were forced to adopt less external symbols for their faith and more non-material means for the exercise and expression of it. Thus the Torah, the Law, which was now a written book and no longer oral guidance, began to assume a dominant position, and certain of its requirements, such as circumcision and keeping the Sabbath—which could be observed anywhere—became the chief signs of belonging to the covenant people.

YAHWEH NO LONGER A LOCAL DEITY

Moreover, the Exile permanently laid to rest any lingering ideas, left over from an earlier time, that somehow Yahweh was necessarily bound to a specific locality. As we have seen, the people now found themselves in a distant land, far beyond the borders of their own country, and yet, for some of them at least, Yahweh had not become any less real. This is one of the meanings of Ezekiel's chariot throne vision in the first chapter of his book. God's throne was now movable, it was no longer fixed in Jerusalem as it was for Isaiah; indeed, God had come to His prophet in far-off Babylon.

THE RISE OF UNIVERSALISM

But what is perhaps even more important, the Exile created a definitive crisis with regard to Yahweh's power and control over all the world. The fall of Jerusalem had to mean one of two things: either Yahweh had been overcome by a more powerful deity, in this case Marduk of Babylon, and thus was no longer worthy to be

ELIJAH AND THE RAVEN
Girolamo Savoldo

worshipped, or else it was precisely He who had done all this, He who had brought the Chaldeans to accomplish His holy will, He who was using this foreign nation to execute judgment and punishment upon His people for their sin in hopes that this chastisement would purify them of their evil and restore them to their right relationship to God. Either Yahweh was nothing, or He was Lord of all.

Many undoubtedly came to the first conclusion and fell away from their ancestral religion forever, but some did not, and for those who remained faithful, the Exile erased for all time any doubt as to Yahweh's universal sovereignty. He indeed was the ruler of all the kingdoms of the earth.

Second Isaiah, the great unknown prophet of the Exile who composed the matchless oracles in Isaiah (40–55), gave this concept its most sublime expression and represents in the eyes of many biblical theologians the very pinnacle of Old Testament "doctrine."

THE END OF THE OLD TESTAMENT PERIOD

In general, the end of the Old Testament period witnessed a retreat from the magnificent and profound view of God taught by Second Isaiah. The historical conditions of the times make this fact wholly understandable. After the Babylonian Exile, the small group of Jews who returned to their devastated homeland faced a very perilous situation. On the one hand, their economic condition was so wretched that their very existence was endangered. But an even greater threat to the life of the community lay in the possibility of their simply being swallowed up by the much more numerous pagans and semipagan Jews who inhabited Palestine and in whose midst they now dwelt. Confronted by these dangers, they banded together into a closed and exclusivistic community and sought to separate themselves from the outside world, from everything that was in any way impure.

Ezra and Nehemiah were leaders in this movement. Such a particularistic attitude was bound to result in a narrow view of God, and so it did. Gone was the lofty universalism of Second

Assyrian boundary stone,
dated twelfth century B.C.

Isaiah and in its place there grew up a strong nationalism, a fanatical devotion to religious peculiarities, and a rather negative attitude toward other peoples and races, all of which they felt God condoned. It is important to remember that the very survival of Israel depended on this vehement exclusiveness, but we can only view as a great irony the fact that the same Exile which released Israel's faith from old dependences and helped to universalize it was also responsible for the narrowness and particularism of its latest representatives.

The protests of the books of Jonah and Ruth

This prevailing attitude of the post-exilic period did not escape significant protest, however. There was a small minority who held to a broader view of God's concern for man and who earnestly appealed for a more tolerant frame of mind toward non-Jews. To them we are indebted for those charming and completely disarming stories known as the books of Jonah and Ruth, which so eloquently preach the message of brotherhood and which are un-excelled in the Old Testament for their breadth of vision and largeness of heart. But although this little group has infinitely enriched our biblical heritage by their witness to God's love for all men, their point of view remained that of a tiny minority.

THE INCREASING TRANSCENDENCE OF GOD

As the historical situation continued in its miserable state and did not improve significantly, many of the people of the Jewish community began to lose confidence in this world as the proper sphere of God's activity. One result was the exalting of God into such a transcendent deity that He had little to do with man at all. For some, God became completely supra-mundane, hidden and inaccessible, beyond all worlds. Since the relationship between God and man was no longer a direct one, it had to be mediated by intermediate beings of some kind, and it is in this period that we find the growth of a system of angelology. Note, for example, the book of Daniel. Even the prophetic experience of revelation came to need the help of the mediating office of these angels (*see* the book of Zechariah). Indeed, a God of such transcendence hardly needed a prophet anymore, but rather a priest who acted for Him on earth. Thus it is not surprising that this view is reflected in some of the late priestly writings of the Old Testament, such as parts of the "P" tradition of the Pentateuch.

THE RISE OF APOCALYPTICISM

Another result of this depreciation of the current historical situation was the rise of apocalypticism — a type of thought and style of expression portraying in symbolic terms the end of history and the transformation of this world into another. For the apocalypticist, earthly conditions had become so deplorable that there was no longer any hope that God would manifest His salvation within the existing frame of history. However, God would soon intervene from beyond history with great supernatural power, abolish the present economy of existence, destroy the impious evildoers, and establish a trans-historical kingdom of

THE ARCHANGEL GABRIEL
Gérard David

blessedness for the loyal saints. In this situation, the devout Jew was exhorted to stand fast in the faith, for the end would soon come. Such was the message of hope and encouragement which the apocalypticist proclaimed in veiled and coded language to his suffering people in their hour of extremity. "How long, O Lord, how long?" asked the pious in despair. "Soon," answered the apocalypticist, "be faithful."

The most prominent example of apocalyptic literature in the Old Testament is the book of Daniel, which became a model for later apocalypses; but parts of Isaiah (chapters 24–27), Ezekiel, Zechariah (chapters 9–14), and Joel can also be considered as belonging to this category. Although it may be lacking in other respects, the apocalyptic view of God is impressive in its emphasis on the divine power and transcendence. In spite of the difficulties we may have with its imagery and its ever impending "end of the world," apocalypticism's confident assurance that God is in control of history and is directing it according to His good pleasure conveys a message of timeless meaning to men of all ages.

The Growth of Individualism

Although the development of the idea of God was of central importance in the growth of Old Testament thought, there were other concepts involved in this process of formulation which deserve our attention as well. In some instances, these tend to parallel the development of the idea of God and much of what has already been said can be applied to them. Thus, in many cases, we shall be able to consider them in much briefer scope.

THE OLD TESTAMENT VIEW OF MAN

"Ein Mensch ist kein Mensch," "One man is no man" (i.e., not really a man at all). This little maxim, coined by a German biblical theologian, states the basic core of the Hebrew understanding of man. According to this view, *the group* was of primary importance; the individual had very little significance in himself. Indeed, he was not thought of as existing at all apart from the group, he had no independent status. His rights, his worth, his importance were all submerged in those of the group; whatever meaning or worth he might have derived from his membership in a larger whole. This fact was one reason why the tribe and tribalism was so important in Old Testament thought and why it continued to exert its limiting influence for so long. However, the centrality of the group presented no great difficulty for ancient man because even he was unable to conceive of himself as an entity existing separately from it. Life for him was a very corporate affair.

VIEW OF THE DEAD SEA AND THE MOUNTAINS OF MOAB, *showing Mount Nebo on extreme left horizon*

CONCEPT OF "CORPORATE PERSONALITY"

This idea has been expressed and developed in the concept of "corporate personality" whereby the group is seen as a single personality in its solidarity and cohesion. This solidarity extended not only to the present members of the group but also reached forward and backward in time to those already dead and those yet unborn. Thus the devout Hebrew could celebrate the great events of his people's history, such as the Exodus, in a very real way, actually participating in them himself in an exceedingly concrete manner, as he said, for example, "A wandering Aramean was my father; and *he* went down into Egypt . . . And the Egyptians treated *us* harshly, and afflicted *us* . . . Then *we* cried to Yahweh the God of our fathers, and Yahweh heard *our* voice . . . and brought *us* out of Egypt with a mighty hand . . ." (Deut. 26:5–8).

This concept also allowed a single person to represent the whole group quite literally, as for example the king was understood to do. Moreover, it is possible that this idea has important implications for the development of the concept of vicarious suffering and sacrifice, where one suffers in the place of others and clears them by bearing the penalty that they deserve. The well-known "Servant of the Lord" in Second Isaiah is a case in point.

EXTENSIVENESS OF CORPORATE VIEW

It should be noted in passing that the Hebrews were not the only ones to hold this corporate view of man; they shared it with all of the peoples of the ancient Near East, not to mention other ancient cultures. It is not hard to understand why this view was so widespread when one realizes that primitive man had little chance of survival apart from a group of some kind. The depth to which this concept was rooted in Hebrew thought is shown by the fact that it continued to be an important part of their understanding of man down through the centuries, and even today exercises a very wholesome influence on Jewish family and community solidarity and on the keen Jewish sense of social justice. Certain Christian concepts, such as the church as the body of Christ, may have been informed by it also.

GROUP RESPONSIBILITY

In the Old Testament, this corporate view of man accounts for many situations and events that appear quite strange to modern Western man. For example, one man could inculpate a whole group by his wrongdoing and often the group would have to bear the punishment. Thus, in the instance mentioned at the very beginning of this essay, when Achan violated the taboo of the holy war by appropriating some of the sacrosanct spoils of Jericho for his own purposes, he brought defeat upon all the people of Israel. Likewise, when he was discovered, not only he, but his whole family and all of his possessions were destroyed (Josh. 7). As members of the same corporate body, they shared the same fate. We would consider such a procedure wanton and cruel, but it was based, not on cruelty, but on the fundamental, consistent, and universally accepted principle of group solidarity, without which ancient Hebrew society would have collapsed.

ANATHOTH, *birthplace of Jeremiah*

By the same token, vengeance was a group or tribal matter. For example, in the days of David, the Israelites were stricken by a severe famine. When it was determined that the famine was caused by an earlier slaughter of the Gibeonites by Saul, David did not hesitate to hand over to the surviving men of Gibeon two of Saul's sons and five of his grandsons, completely innocent men from our point of view, to be put to death as expiation for the blood guilt of their father and grandfather. Examples such as this are numerous in the Old Testament. Against this kind of background, the biblical injunction, "eye for eye, tooth for tooth" (Ex. 21:24 Lev. 24:20; Deut. 19:21), can be seen, not as a heartless legalism but rather as a merciful and prudent check upon the excesses of nomadic vengeance.

CENTRALITY OF THE GROUP IN RELIGION

The corporate view of man also influenced the Hebrew understanding of the way in which Yahweh dealt with His people. He was primarily the God of the nation and He approached His people primarily as a group. He punished the whole group for the wrong-doing of some, and it was said that He visited the iniquity of the fathers upon the children to the third and the fourth generation (Ex. 20:5). However, He was also willing to forego punishment because of the goodness of a few (Gen. 18), and it was likewise said that He showed steadfast love to thousands of generations of those who loved Him (Ex. 20:6).

Religion as a whole was considered a corporate affair; in ancient Israel there was no such thing as "personal" or "private" religion in the modern sense. The traffic between man and God went by way of the group. God was related to the group and man was a part of the group; this was usually the extent of their relationship. It may have been possible for the individual to have what we would call "personal" experiences of the divine (note some of the psalms), but this was always within the context of his member-ship in the group, and the God he encountered was always the God of Israel and not some private deity.

So also there were always exceptional individuals who arose to mediate the relationship between God and the people, men like Moses, Samuel, and the prophets, but these men were themselves members of the group and were able to approach Yahweh precisely because of, for the sake of, and within the framework of the group. They were "individuals-in-community," the only kind of indi-vidual that the Old Testament knows.

THE RISE OF INDIVIDUALISM

Such was the basic view of man in the Old Testament and what development or change there was in this concept centered around the way in which, while still retaining its corporate understanding of man, the Old Testament made more and more room for the individual. However, this process must not be seen as a simple one according to which in the early period there was only the corporate understanding of man and in the late period only the individual understanding with a neat line drawn between them. There were significant instances of individualism in the early period and the corporate view never lost its hold upon the people. Nevertheless, it cannot be denied that the individual did gain a certain status in the later period that he had not had before. Let us look at a few of the major reasons for this change.

ENTRY INTO CANAAN

First, the same transition from the nomadic life of the desert to the commercialized town life of agricultural Canaan which had an important effect on the Hebrew view of God also affected their view of man. In this new setting, with its private property, different economic classes, and generally complex civilization, the old tribal cohesions grew weaker and weaker, and as they did, the individual slowly began to emerge.

CONTRIBUTION OF THE PROPHETS

The great prophets of the Old Testament also contributed to the growth of individualism. First, by their own example, they showed the necessity for moral and religious nonconformity. It had become painfully clear that the group, in this case the Israelite nation, was not always right and when it went wrong the situation demanded that someone step aside and call it to task. This act in itself, even though it was done by a member of the group, was an act of individualism.

Perhaps more important was the prophet's own individual experience of the divine, his own direct encounter with Yahweh. Jeremiah is a classic example in this regard. Separated from his people because of his prophetic vocation, despised by those whom he loved, condemned to a life of loneliness, Jeremiah was forced to hammer some meaning and purpose out of his own solitariness. He had nowhere to turn but directly to Yahweh, even if at times he felt abandoned by Him as well. Thus Jeremiah came to know God in a very real and immediate sense, and so movingly did he tell of the heights and depths of this direct relationship that it was impossible for those who heard or read his words to remain unaffected by them. Although he was a prophet and thus in a special category, Jeremiah's experience was of such a nature that it was difficult not to look upon it as a possibility for others also.

The same holds true for the rest of the prophets as well. Their encounters with Yahweh may not have been so explicitly and eloquently described, but they were no less direct and each of them made his contribution in one way or another to this nascent individualism.

EXILE

One of the most significant forces which helped to make room for the individual in Hebrew thought was the experience of the Exile itself. With the destruction of the external symbols of the old national group, the Israelite was forced to approach life and religion on a more individual basis. To be sure, the old sense of community solidarity still existed, but many of the traditional ideas had to be radically revised in view of the present situation. Thus the same event which lifted Israel's eyes to international horizons also allowed them to turn inward in the direction of a greater recognition of the individual.

The Exile also raised the problem of divine justice with regard to the individual in a new and pressing manner. It was understood that the people were suffering for the apostate sins of the nation, but before long there were few left who were actually responsible for their sad plight. Under these new conditions of mass suffering and together with some of the recently released forces mentioned above, the thought that innocent people should suffer for the guilt of others began to be intolerable.

It was against this background and out of a deep sense of pastoral concern for his people that the prophet Ezekiel was led flatly to deny the old orthodox doctrine of corporate responsibility. "What do you mean by repeating this proverb concerning the land of Israel, 'The fathers have eaten sour grapes, and the children's teeth are set on edge'? As I live, says the Lord Yahweh, this proverb shall no more be used by you in Israel . . . The soul that sins shall die. The son shall not suffer for the iniquity of the father, nor the father suffer for the iniquity of the son . . ." (Ezek. 18:2–3,20). Once pronounced, such statements as these became in themselves powerful influences for individualism.

THE PLAIN OF THE LAW, *adjoining Mount Sinai*

Thus, bit by bit, the old tribal solidarity, while not abdicating its place altogether, made way for the "individual-in-community." We shall now investigate the effect which this development had upon human relationships.

Ethics

The development of ethics in the Old Testament was closely related to the development of the two concepts already discussed, God and man. The influences of the idea of God can be seen in the very formation of Old Testament ideas about right and wrong. From the outset, the Hebrews were a highly ethical people. The strict morality of their semi-nomadic desert origins had a formative influence upon them. But more importantly, it was their understanding of Yahweh as a righteous God who demanded that His people likewise be righteous which placed them under a categorical imperative, an inescapable obligation to act justly themselves.

THE LIMITATION OF ETHICAL OBLIGATION

However, this obligation was limited, and here the Hebrew concept of man becomes relevant. We have just seen that throughout much of the Old Testament man is seen primarily as a member of the group, usually the tribe or the nation. As a result, the various codes of ethical behavior were customarily understood as applicable only to members of the group; they did not ordinarily extend to those outside of this category. Thus the sense of moral obligation was limited to a relatively small number.

In most cases, this limitation had little significance because practically all day-to-day contacts were confined to the group. Within these bounds, moral behavior and ethical practices were understood to be rigorously required. Of course these requirements were frequently not met, but such dereliction was always recognized as wrong and was thoroughly condemned, at least by the representatives of authentic Yahwism. This moral censure, together with the rebuke of religious apostasy, constituted the major burden of the great prophets of the Old Testament.

However, beyond these bounds, this sense of moral obligation was largely absent. It must be said that Israel's historical situation, which involved frequent hostilities with outsiders, was not particularly congenial to the growth of international brotherhood. Nevertheless, as her view of man – and God – became slightly less tribal, so did her sense of moral obligation. The record of this period witnessed one of the most restricted views of ethical responsibility to be found in the whole Bible. Indeed, this was a problem which the Old Testament was never able to solve satisfactorily – nor have we today!

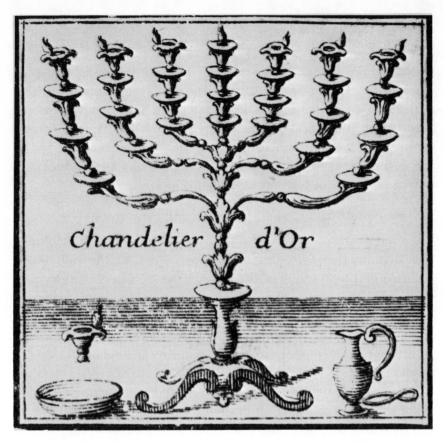

GOLDEN MENORAH, *an artist's conception of the seven-branched lampstand used in the Tabernacle and the Temple*

THE EXPANSION OF ETHICAL RESPONSIBILITY

Yet there were places where Israel's moral perspective widened and, even if there was not a breakthrough of clear-cut universalism, crucial seeds were sown which are still bearing fruit in our own time. As early as the eighth century B.C., the prophet Amos saw Yahweh as a God who was not only Lord of Israel, but who held the nations responsible for their cruelty to one another as well (Amos 1-2). However, it was the books of Ruth and Jonah, written after the tragic but broadening experience of the Exile, that represent the high point of the thrust for brotherhood and tolerance beyond national bounds in the Old Testament. Undoubtedly the magnificent vision of the universality of God proclaimed by Second Isaiah during the Exile had influenced the authors of these matchless little tracts on interracial harmony (Ruth) and Yahweh's love for all men (Jonah). As we have seen, these books were intended to rebuke the narrow exclusivism of the post-exilic community, but they stand today as a condemnation of our own modern provincialisms as well.

THE INCREASING APPRECIATION OF THE INDIVIDUAL

We have already observed in our consideration of the Hebrew idea of man that the increasing appreciation of the individual resulted in a weakening of the old concept of collective responsibility and retribution. Thus we find the growing conviction that each person should be responsible for his own guilt, but not for the guilt of others. This change in itself marks one of the most significant developments that took place in the field of Old Testament ethics.

However, in the last analysis it must be remembered that, despite its changes and limitations, Old Testament ethics has left us with a prophetic and uncompromising demand for justice, especially social justice, which continues to inform our moral thinking, even today.

Worship

This essay can perhaps best be concluded with a short consideration of the changes which took place in the way man worshipped God in the Old Testament.

WORSHIP AMONG THE PATRIARCHS

Among the patriarchs, the wandering ancestors of the Hebrews in the second millennium B.C., worship was largely a clan or

CEDARS OF LEBANON—*Solomon ordered straight cedars such as these for the building of the Temple*

family affair, informal in nature and conducted by the regular leader of the group. By the time of the Exodus and the experience at Mount Sinai, certain ritual acts were being observed, as is evident from the ceremonies connected with the making of the covenant (Ex. 18–19,24). In turn, this event itself became the source of new rites and practices.

WORSHIP IN THE PERIOD OF THE SETTLEMENT

The entry of the Hebrews into the land of Canaan was the occasion for an extensive enlargement of their worship. The Canaanites were the possessors of a rich cultic tradition and the Hebrews naturally adopted many of their forms of worship. In most cases they filled these forms with a new content so that they lost their old pagan coloration and became quite "Yahweh-ized." For example, they took over the Canaanite sanctuaries, such as Dan, Gilgal, Shechem, Shiloh, perhaps Bethel, together with much of their ritual and even hymnody (*see* Ps. 29, which appears to have originally been a hymn to Baal). They appropriated their agricultural festivals and transformed them into celebrations of the great events of Israel's history. Thus a spring festival related to the beginning of the grain harvest was associated with the Exodus from Egypt and became the Feast of Unleavened Bread or the Passover. An early autumn harvest festival was associated with the wandering in the wilderness and became the Feast of Booths, later expanded to include the whole complex of observances surrounding the New Year. This process was typical of the way in which the historical always took precedence over the natural in Israel's faith.

ADOPTION OF CANAANITE FORMS OF WORSHIP

The Hebrews' adoption of many Canaanite forms of worship had both positive and negative aspects. Positively, it greatly increased the scope and richness of Israel's worship. Negatively, there was always the danger that the old content would creep back into the old forms, and indeed, for many Israelites, it did. For them, Yahweh simply became Baal by another name. This was the risk which had to be taken, however, if the people were to develop meaningful forms of worship in their new situation.

THE TEMPLE

The construction of the Jerusalem temple by Solomon was one of the high points in this process. This building provided both a shrine for and a symbol of the religious synthesis which David had brought together out of traditional Yahwism on the one hand, and various other sources on the other, especially the ancient cult of El Elyon, "God Most High," of Jerusalem. The temple itself, built by the workmen and artisans of Hiram of Tyre, seems to have been an interesting combination of Canaanite, Phoenician, and Egyptian influence. By this time, the period of the monarchy, the worship of Israel had become a rather extensive affair, with its various ceremonies, sacrifices, festivals, and priests. The king sometimes took an important part in the cult, but this role was obviously eliminated by the fall of the kingdom.

RUINS OF AN ANCIENT SYNAGOGUE AT CAPERNAUM

THE REFORM OF JOSIAH

The reform of King Josiah (640–609 B.C.) served to give the temple a place of undisputed centrality in the religion of the people by abolishing local shrines and concentrating all worship in Jerusalem. This action did have the effect of reducing, at least temporarily, the rampant syncretism (the mixing together of elements from different religions) which had been flourishing up until then, but it also tended to foster a false sense of security among the people, as if this change in itself was all that was necessary to please Yahweh. Consequently the blow which came with the destruction of the temple in 587 B.C. was all the more terrible.

As we have had occasion to note several times already, the Exile had a crucial effect upon every aspect of Israel's life and thought, and not least of all upon her worship. The destruction of the temple, the cessation of the cult and its sacrifices, and the removal of the people to a strange land inevitably gave rise to new modes of worship—meetings for prayer, praise, preaching, and teaching. From such beginnings as these the synagogue eventually arose.

THE RISE OF THE PRIESTHOOD

It was during the exilic and post-exilic period, also, that the priesthood reached the peak of its power, although it had begun to rise in importance considerably earlier than this. Even in the pre-exilic period, as Israel's worship became more complex, the priests, who were versed in these matters, had begun to assume greater significance and more prerogatives. However, with the fall of the nation, and especially the disappearance of the king, the priest became an increasingly important figure of authority.

As we have seen, the material symbols of the faith were replaced at this time by symbols of a more non-material nature, especially the Law, and it was precisely the priest who was in charge of the Law. Moreover, as the people came more and more to conceive of God in terms of an ever greater transcendence, it was the priest, not the prophet, who was the more appropriate agent to act for Him on earth. Thus as the Old Testament period comes to an end, we find a man such as Ezra, "the priest, the scribe, learned in the matters of the commandments of Yahweh and his statutes for Israel" (Ezra 7:11), standing as the post-exilic ideal more than any other figure.

So it was that worship in the Old Testament moved from the relatively simple family worship of the patriarchs to the highly developed ritual of Judaism.

The Great Theologians of the Old Testament

David J. Bourke
and John McHugh

There are various ways of gaining an under-standing of the "theology," or religious teach-ing, of the Old Testament. The approach here is through a discussion of the great "theo-logians" whose religious teaching is contained in the Pentateuch (first five books of the Bible), in Second Isaiah (chapters 40–55 of the book of Isaiah), and in the Wisdom books (chiefly Job, Proverbs, Ecclesiastes, Wisdom, and Eccle-siasticus). The Pentateuch is the work of "theo-logians" who today are named: "the Yahwist," the "Elohist," the "Deuteronomists," and "the Priests." The "theologian" who authored the final chapters of the book of Isaiah is called "Second Isaiah." The Wisdom books are the work of "theologians" who are, for the most part, interested in the religious and moral principles which lead to a virtuous (and there-fore a happy) life for the individual.

MOSES WITH THE TABLES OF THE LAW
Rembrandt

The Basic Ideas of Old Testament Theology

To MOST Christians today, the Old Testament is as flat and monotonous and uninformative as a map on which only the rivers, cities, and political frontiers are marked. If you look at a cheap school atlas, the first things you notice are the political frontiers, because they are generally distinguished by colors; and yet we know that in many respects they are the least important boundaries (life is very much the same in Denmark and in Sweden, in Toronto and in Niagara Falls). So, in the Old Testament, the first thing you notice is that there are a lot of different books, marked off into "The Historical Books," "The Prophets," and "The Wisdom Books" as into three great continents. Yet in many respects these divisions are the least important: the prophets relate a great deal of history, and the historical books contain a good proportion of prophecy. The division should be noticed, like the political boundaries between states; but geography is not primarily concerned with political boundaries, and the theology of the Old Testament cannot be sensibly discussed by following the divisions between biblical books, because the divisions do not follow "natural boundaries."

LESSER-KNOWN FIGURES ALSO IMPORTANT

A school atlas can familiarize us with the names of the great cities, but what about the small towns and villages, which are just as real a part of a country's life? So the lesser-known figures of the Bible have their importance alongside the great names like Abraham, David, and Isaiah. One cannot understand India if the only fact known about it is that it has four big cities called Bombay,

Delhi, Madras and Calcutta; and it is folly to expect to comprehend the problems of the Old Testament merely by having some
general ideas about its leading personalities.

Rivers, too, are important: we can trace the connections between cities by following the line of a river. So we can trace the
connection between the great figures of the Old Testament by
recalling that Moses was descended from Levi, and thereby from
Abraham, whose faith he inherited and passed on to his people.

And yet the time comes when we must put away the things of a
child, and begin to study more detailed maps. So we pass on to
maps of ethnic distribution, of crops and minerals, of rainfall and
temperature, in summer and in winter. These many different
maps are essential in order to grasp the full complexity of the
factors affecting the life of a country, and each of them must be
studied with care by anyone who wishes to take geography seriously. The same procedure must be followed by anyone who
wishes to advance beyond a child's understanding of the Old
Testament. He needs to look at the various books from a variety
of angles to appreciate the different factors which have gone to
their making. But (as in geography) it is useful to start with a
bird's eye view of the terrain as a whole. For convenience, then,
we shall sketch out first a "school map" of the teaching of the Old
Testament, to give the over-all picture.

An elementary map

The central tenets of Israel's faith might be stated as follows.
There is but one God, who made both heaven and earth, and controls the destiny of the world. He chose one man, Abraham, and
from his descendants one nation, Israel, to be His favored people
so that through them He might bring all other nations to acknowledge His supremacy and to worship Him. He therefore revealed
to Israel certain basic truths about Himself and about man's nature and destiny, and gave them certain rules of conduct, which
they in turn were to spread to the whole world. He also promised
to supply Israel with the strength needed to achieve this historic
vocation.

God also made a covenant with Israel by which He promised them certain blessings, and they solemnly undertook to remain obedient to His laws. By the terms of this covenant He undertook to be *their* God, to lead them into a fertile land and to bless them with every happiness on earth, provided only that they on their side remained loyal and obedient to Him. They in turn promised to be *His* people, acknowledging no other god but Him, and reproducing in their lives (both as individuals and as a nation) His attributes of holiness, purity, justice, mercy, and truth.

God then provided Israel with leaders whom He endowed with His spirit. There were leaders who preached His word to the people, like the law-givers and the prophets; there were leaders in worship, like the priests and Levites; He gave the nation leaders in war and leaders in peace. Above all, God gave to Israel the Davidic house of kings, and promised that from this house there would arise a Messiah (an "Anointed One"), so called because He, more than all others, would be anointed with the Spirit of the Lord. He would rule over all the nations of the world forever, with justice and wisdom, and His reign would be an age of immeasurable prosperity and peace.

A righteous remnant

This was God's purpose and plan. But the Old Testament also tells us that one section after another of the people lost their right to share in the promised blessings because they proved unfaithful to the covenant. Some went astray by pursuing wealth at the cost of justice and mercy; others followed the less exacting moral codes of Canaanite gods. And so the Old Testament repeatedly proclaims that only a "righteous remnant" would be found still faithful when God sent His people the promised Messiah, "the consolation of Israel," and that this remnant would consist for the most part of the poorest and most afflicted members of the community. Many of the rest, by their apostasy, were to turn the blessing of light and life with God into the curse of darkness and death in separation from Him. Yet for one and all there was always hope of regaining God's favor by heartfelt repentance and a sincere

SACRIFICE OF ISAAC
Rembrandt

"conversion" (i.e., "turning") from evil ways to good. The theology of sin and repentance is therefore an essential and major element in the total message of the Old Testament.

OLD TESTAMENT THEOLOGY MORE COMPLICATED

This brief, and perilously over-simplified outline is an attempt to convey the essential unity and coherence of what is basic to Old Testament theology as a whole. It seems necessary to commence with this precisely because of the great diversity of outlook and interpretation which is found in the particular Old Testament "theologians" whose thought will be expounded in the following pages. Perhaps we may compare this outline to the map of the world on Mercator's projection with which so many of us began geography: the whole world was spread out flat on the page, with Japan (at the extreme right) apparently at the opposite side of the world from California. Political boundaries were marked, and perhaps nothing more. Certainly it did not look as if the shortest way from Los Angeles to London was over the North Pole. The map on Mercator's projection is, in fact, dangerously misleading: geography is more complicated than that.

So it is with Old Testament theology. The outline is needed, but we must pass on from it to more complicated statements, each of which looks at the theology of the Old Testament in a particular way. Only by studying several other maps (akin to the geographer's "vegetation," "climate," "geological," etc.) can we learn what the Old Testament world of theology is truly like.

The Theology of the Yahwist

The Pentateuch as we know it (that is, the first five books of the Bible) contains several different "theologies." The reason is that these books (Genesis, Exodus, Leviticus, Numbers, and Deuteronomy) were not written in the way modern books are written (or thought to be written, from page one to the end). Rather, each book represents a collection of stories, laws, and other material taken from a number of different sources. That is why the Pentateuch sometimes makes difficult reading—the men who put it into its present form often tried to combine contradictory versions of one and the same event.

In the story of the Flood, for example (Gen. 5-8), there are several annoying repetitions and an unbelievable confusion over dates. In modern times, we avoid such difficulties by indicating citations of different sources: we use quotation marks, footnotes, and references ("according to Moscow Radio . . . according to Western observers" . . .). Unhappily for us, the ancient writers were not so considerate: they thought nothing of putting two versions of one event side by side, and leaving the reader to sort out the discrepancies. Worse, they would even conflate into one narrative two contradictory interpretations of an event, and leave the reader to draw his conclusions; it is as if a journalist had run together into one "objective" communiqué the Communist and the Nazi versions of the Reichstag fire in 1934 and published it as a "full account," in spite of the inherent contradictions. Our present task, therefore, in this essay, is to disentangle the confusion by picking out, one by one, the different threads of thought (the different "theologies") which are practically tied in knots in the Bible. We shall begin with the oldest strand.

THE OLDEST STRAND: A GREAT SAGA

Around the time of David and Solomon (roughly 1000 to 930 B.C.) a great saga—an "epic version"—of the religious history of Israel was composed. Since it generally calls the God of Israel by the name "Yahweh," it is known as the "Yahwistic source," or the "Yahwistic tradition," and its author is called "the Yahwist." It tells the story of Israel from the creation to the conquest of Canaan, from Paradise to the Promised Land, from Adam to Joshua and Caleb. Much of this story may have been gathered together into a national epic during the early days of David's reign, before his conquest of Jerusalem. But as we find it in the Bible, it seems to have been edited by someone who was both deeply devoted to Yahweh and a loyal subject of Solomon. He would almost certainly have regarded the unprecedented glory, peace, and prosperity of Solomon's reign as the beginning of the fulfillment of the promises made to David by the prophet Nathan (2 Sam. 7). Reflecting on the goodness of Yahweh to His people Israel, the Yahwistic author set out to tell the glorious history of what God had done for them.

GATHERING AND INTERPRETING THE ANCIENT TRADITIONS

The first concern of the Yahwist was to gather the ancient traditions of Israel. These traditions comprised not only the major events such as the Exodus from Egypt, the covenant at Sinai, the wandering in the wilderness and the conquest of Canaan, but also several local traditions (for example, about Abraham's stay at Hebron) which were perhaps remembered only in a particular locality. He also included traditions about the surrounding king-

GIANT BIBLE OF MAINZ (A.D. 1452), *illuminated page from the book of Genesis*

doms conquered by David (Edom, Moab, Ammon), and interpreted them all in the light of his own view of history. All these ancient stories he saw as pointing, however remotely, toward the establishment of the kingdom of David and the glorious prosperity of Solomon's empire.

But the increased volume of trade in Solomon's day brought new problems too: along with the material goods, new ideas were being imported from Egypt and Babylon. New questions were being asked by a more sophisticated people, principally about the origin and the early history of the world. Egypt had an answer; Babylon had one. And so the Yahwist too had to provide one. He, therefore, presented the entire cosmos—the heavens and the earth—as governed in every detail by the all-embracing plan of Yahweh, the God with whom Israel had made a covenant. All nature, he taught, existed for the benefit of mankind, and all the destinies of mankind revolved around the one people, Israel, from whom a son of David would one day arise, in whom all the nations of the world would be blessed. Thus there are in his work traces of a latent and primitive messianic hope, together with a totally new awareness of the sweep of Yahweh's power over all the earth.

The Yahwist was also conscious that his own generation, just emerged from a semi-nomadic or peasant way of life, were being unduly impressed and attracted by the superior culture and wisdom of the Egyptians, with whom they were in constant contact. Many Israelites, it seems, were being tempted to desert their ancestral God for the learning, culture, and material civilization which was the glory of Egypt. The Yahwist, therefore, took immense care to explain how Yahweh's power and wisdom excelled the best that Egypt could produce, and the Exodus gave him the ideal historical setting for teaching this lesson.

AN EXAMPLE OF INTERPRETATION: THE EXODUS

The Yahwist version of the plagues of Egypt is contained in: Exodus 7:14-18, 20b, 21a, 23-25, 26-29; 8:4-11a, 16-28; 9:1-7, 13-21, 23b-34; 10:1-11, 13b-19, 23-26. It is not possible to explain here why scholars select perhaps one half-verse (for example, 7:21a) and ascribe it to a particular "source" or tradition, and it should be openly confessed that specialists do not always agree on such details. But the broad pattern is universally accepted, and the reader who will take the trouble to read just these verses consecutively will find that they give a fairly coherent story of the helplessness of the Egyptians when faced with the power of Yahweh, the God of Israel. (The most effective way of doing this is for someone to read the selected verses aloud to others who are *not* following the text in a Bible.)

The Yahwist version of the Exodus and the crossing of the Sea of Reeds (not, as older translations say, wrongly, "the Red Sea") is contained in Exodus 11:1-6; 12:21-23, 27b, 29-39; 13:20-22; 14:5b, 6, 9a, 10b, 13-14, 19b-21, 24-25b, 27, 30-31. Here again the Yahwist stresses the impotence of Pharaoh, of his wise men, and of his people in their futile attempt to prevent Yahweh from carrying out His plans for His own people. For instance, the Yahwist includes in his version of the crossing of the Sea the assertion that Yahweh "clogged" or "jammed" the wheels of the Egyptian chariots (Ex. 14:25). The terrifying effectiveness of the Egyptian chariot as a weapon of war had been newly realized precisely during Solomon's reign: it was, to the ancient, what the tank has been to our own age — something which made all the older theories of fighting out-of-date. The Yahwist therefore stressed that the power of Yahweh could make even the most modern weapons utterly futile.

ANOTHER EXAMPLE: THE STORY OF JOSEPH

Joseph is presented, in the Yahwist version, as a true Israelite who, relying solely on the charism which he receives from Yahweh, outstrips all the sages and administrators of Pharaoh's court in those very humanistic virtues for which the Egyptians were most admired (wisdom and astuteness, striking good looks, modesty, chivalry, and so on). The verses of Genesis containing this story are: 37:3a, 4, 5a, 6-21, 25-28; 39:1-23; 41:34a, 35b, 41-45, 46b, 49, 55, 56b, 57; 42:1b, 4, 7, 9-11, 14-16, 21, 23-24; 43:1-34; 44:1a, 2-34; 45:1, 4, 5a, 16-28; 46:1a, 5b, 28-34; 47:1-5, 13-26, 29-31; 50: 1-10a, 14a. These verses tell how Joseph rose from destitution to the highest place in the land, and was thanked, blessed, and honored by all the Egyptians from Pharaoh downwards.

Again, Pharaoh (Gen. 12:10-20) and the king of the Philistines (Gen. 26:6-14) are forced to recognize the sacredness of the patriarchs' wives and to acknowledge that Abraham and Isaac are men of God and therefore specially protected.

THE YAHWIST'S CONCEPTION OF GOD

The Yahwist "saga," as we have termed it, falls naturally into three parts: (1) the early history of mankind (Gen. 2-11); (2) the story of the patriarchs (Gen. 12-50); (3) from the oppression in Egypt to the arrival in the Promised Land (Ex. 1-Num. 31). The first section is the most original part of his work.

Before the age of Solomon, the Israelites seem to have thought of their God mainly as a champion in war, upholding justice, pun-

CARRYING OFFERINGS, *detail from a wall-painting, dated about 1450 B.C.*

ishing sin, and granting that fertility of soil on which their survival depended. From time to time He intervened in history on their behalf, to ensure the fulfillment of His plans. But in Solomon's day, their regular contacts with Egypt showed them a developed idea of creation itself as a divine activity. The Egyptians did not think of the creator god as one who intervenes only at isolated points in history, but as being ever present to the world he had created, governing it at all times, and breathing life into all creatures as he willed.

The Yahwist, therefore, fused together the ancient Israelite idea of a covenant God who intervenes in history and the new Egyptian concept of a creator God who is ever present to His people. With this richer vision of the divine Being, the Yahwist then perceived that God's plans for Israel did not begin with the call of Abraham, but with the creation of the world. The author saw all the forces of creation as engaged in the accomplishment of the divine plan, as at the Flood and in the plagues of Egypt: all of them were at the service of the Lord, to guide His people toward their promised homeland. There, He had planned and promised, they would dwell before Him forever in unending peace.

The Yahwist evidently thought of this God as *transcendent,* for he speaks of Him as *"coming down"* from heaven to inspect and to intervene in human affairs. "Yahweh came down to see the city" (Gen. 11:5; cf. 11:7). "I have surely seen . . . I have heard . . . I have come down to deliver . . ." (Ex. 3:8). "Yahweh came down from Mount Sinai" (Ex. 19:20), "came down in a cloud" (Num. 11:25). From His place in heaven He disposes every detail of the universe, controls the wind and the rain and the sun, and determines the fates of all peoples throughout the world (Gen. 11).

Yet, astonishingly, this same God is also *immanent,* i.e., constantly and everywhere present in the world He has created. He molds man out of the dust and breathes into his nostrils the breath of life (Gen. 2:7); He sets man in a garden (Gen. 2:15), and takes one of his ribs to form a woman (Gen. 2:22). We read of Yahweh walking in the garden in the "daytime wind" (Gen. 3:8), making coats to dress Adam and his wife (Gen. 3:21), shutting the door of the ark after Noah and his family had gone inside (Gen. 7:16), and meeting Moses during the night (Ex. 4:24). It should be plainly stated that these ideas are not (as is sometimes asserted) the product of a naive and unsophisticated mind. On the contrary, they are a reflection of the relatively advanced humanistic thinking of Solomon's reign, when for the first time men found it possible to speak figuratively about their God of the covenant. They represent a very profound insight into the nature of God.

THE SIN OF THE WORLD

The characteristic temptation of the humanist is *hubris,* a Greek term for that pride, insolence or arrogance which seeks to achieve a more than human status through knowledge and mastery of the forces of nature. This was the crime of Adam and Eve, who tried to become "like God, knowing good and evil" (Gen. 3:5), and of the men who built the tower of Babel (Gen. 11): mastery over nature is sought by evil means, or from wicked motives. The

Yahwist, therefore, teaches that true wisdom and power come from Yahweh alone, and are granted only to those who "find favor in his eyes" (Gen. 6:8) and "walk with him" (Gen. 5:22, 24) in humble obedience to His will. *Hubris*, then, is the sin of the world.

The Yahwist also has his own distinctive idea of punishment. Each time a sin is committed, the guilty are banished from an inner sphere where all is peace and harmony to an outer sphere which is cursed, where nature is hostile to man and peace is diminished. So Adam and Eve are expelled from Paradise, the sphere which yields fruit without toil, to the land of thorns and thistles which man must work "in the sweat of his brow" (Gen. 3:17-19, 23). Cain and his family are compelled to leave the tilled land, "the face of the ground," to become nomads in the barren desert (Gen. 4:12) where blood-vengeance is the rule of life (Gen. 4:15). Finally, as a punishment for the sins of mankind the whole earth is rendered uninhabitable by a great Flood, and only a tiny remnant is saved in the ark, where it is dependent on Yahweh alone for its survival.

The relevance of these stories to the humanist age of Solomon, with its sudden and intoxicating prosperity, needs no explaining.

YAHWEH'S VICTORIES OVER SIN

The first part of the saga (Gen. 2-11) is essentially *forward looking*. Thus in the Yahwist narrative of the creation (which begins at Gen. 2:4b; 2:4a is the conclusion of another account, and the Yahwist text does not begin until 2:4b), God does not look back on His creation and "see that it was very good" (2:4a). On the contrary, He continually improves it. First the earth is made, and then water to irrigate it (Gen. 2:5-6); next, man is created, but he needs companions, so Yahweh creates the animals and makes them subject to him (Gen. 2:18-19). But since none of the animals is a suitable companion, woman is created, equal to man (Gen. 2:20-24). And just when we have reached the climax of the creation story, the woman tempts man into sin, and both are banished from Paradise (Gen. 3). Yet even then a new line is founded, and when

STONE STATUE OF RAMESES II, *king of ancient Egypt, nineteenth dynasty*

Cain in turn proves a murderer, his prerogatives as first-born are transferred to Seth, and from this point onwards men "begin to call on the name of Yahweh" (Gen. 4:26).

Yet once again the human race falls into sin, but Yahweh ensures that His created world, and the predestined line now represented by Noah shall survive the cataclysmic Flood. After the Flood, Noah worships Yahweh not merely by calling on Him, but by building an altar and offering sacrifices to Yahweh from the beasts which are under his dominion. In return, Yahweh promises that He will never again "curse the ground for man's sake" (Gen. 8:20-22).

Of Noah's three sons, Shem is the one to carry the destiny, but once more sin increases and reaches a new climax in the attempt to build the Tower of Babel (Gen. 11:1-9). Once more the established order is disrupted, and the unity of language is broken forever, but from the ensuing chaos there emerges a chosen figure to carry the divine purpose a long stage nearer fulfillment—

Abraham, upon whom all the previous history of the world con-
verges.

TOWARD THE EMPIRE OF SOLOMON

In the second part of his saga (Gen. 12-50), the Yahwist seems
to have had rather different problems in mind. His first task here
was to collect the different traditions current among the tribes
(and especially at local sanctuaries like Hebron), and to weld them
into one continuous story. It was important for him not to omit
any tradition, for this might easily have alienated the sympathy
of a group to whom that particular story was sacred.

At the same time, he wanted to make the whole saga point forward to Solomon, and therefore he presented all these ancient
stories as so many foreshadowings of Solomon's accession and
reign. For example, Solomon had gained the throne by displacing
an elder brother through the influence of his mother. The Yahwist, therefore, emphasizes similar events in the lives of the patriarchs. Ephraim had received Jacob's blessing before Manasseh,
his elder brother (Gen. 48:13ff.); Jacob had displaced his elder
brother Esau, through the influence of his mother Rebekah
(Gen. 25:23ff.; 27); Isaac had been preferred to Ishmael, again at
the instigation of his mother (Gen. 21:9ff.). Still more remotely,
the Yahwist would have recalled that Abel's offering had been preferred to that of Cain (Gen. 4:4-5), and that it was the line of Seth,
the younger brother, which became the predestined line (Gen.
4:15). In the latter case, it was the mother who said "God has appointed me another offspring instead of Abel."

The ancestor of Solomon's tribe, Judah, was also a younger son,
and throughout the period of the Judges, Judah seems to have
been among the most poverty-stricken and obscure of all the
tribes. But then David had completed the conquest of Canaan by
capturing those very citites which Joshua (the Ephraimite leader)
had been unable to subdue (*see* Judges 1). The Yahwist, therefore, places on the lips of the dying Jacob a prophecy that the man
God had destined to be ruler of Israel would come from the tribe
of Judah: "The scepter shall not depart from Judah, nor the ruler's

CAIN AND ABEL, *a woodcut from the Albert Schramm collection of incunabula (1472)*

staff from between his feet till Shiloh comes" (Gen. 49:10–11). When Solomon set the seal on David's achievements by building the temple and installing there the Ark of the Covenant, it was a supreme sign that Yahweh had chosen Judah and Jerusalem as His dwelling, and had at last begun to fulfill His ancient promises in the person of Solomon.

Solomon's claims rested primarily on the promise made to David by Nathan (2 Sam. 7:10ff.), and his building of the temple was directly connected with this promise (1 Kings 8:20). But Solomon had also received two personal revelations from Yahweh, one at Gibeon (1 Kings 3:4ff.) and one immediately after the building of the temple and palace (1 Kings 9:1ff.). So the Yahwist stresses similar happenings in the lives of the patriarchs: Yahweh revealed Himself, the patriarch built an altar or shrine, and settled down beside it for a time. Abraham had responded to the appearance of God at Shechem by building an altar (Gen. 12:8); Isaac did the same at Beersheba (Gen. 26:23-25) and Jacob at Bethel (Gen. 28:13-16). Each of these stories foreshadows Solomon's act in building his house next to the final and permanent shrine where Yahweh had chosen to live forever.

The Yahwist was also intensely interested in the nations which had been forcibly incorporated into the Davidic empire. By telling stories about the ancestors of these tribes, he tries to show that Yahweh had from the first intended that the tribes should be subordinate to His chosen people, and pay tribute to them. Thus Esau, the ancestor of the Edomites, is shown to have lost his birthright to Jacob (Gen. 25:31–34); Laban the Aramean lost both his daughters to Jacob, along with the pick of his flocks and the household gods which were, so to speak, the title-deeds to all his property (Gen. 30:25; 31); Ammon and Moab were the children of an incestuous union between two daughters and their drunken father Lot (Gen. 19:30). Lot himself is as weak and greedy as Abraham is brave and chivalrous: Abraham first allows him to choose the best land (Gen. 13:8ff.) and then rescues him from captivity (Gen. 14:12ff.).

UNITY OF THEME

These various traditions, when interpreted in this way with Solomon's empire in mind, acquire an impressive unity of theme. Just as the first part of the Yahwist saga (Gen. 2-11) pointed to Abraham, so the second part (Gen. 12-50) shows the process of election narrowing down within the community of Abraham's descendants, until Jacob's final blessing goes principally to Judah. The patriarchs become, too, a visible embodiment of Yahweh's presence among men, and Yahweh demands that they should be reverenced by all others as they live out their earthly lives (*see,* for example, Gen. 12:14-20). For nothing can halt the divine plan: inexorably Yahweh achieves His purpose in spite of barren wombs and poverty and famine and old age and exile, working through younger sons of younger sons, through the tricks and ruses and deceptions of men. He is the Lord of history, and no human being can thwart His decrees.

POOL OF SOLOMON—*there are three so-called "Pools of Solomon" in the valley of Urtas near Bethlehem*

In the third and longest part of his saga (Exodus, Numbers), the Yahwist is concerned not with local traditions preserved by particular tribal groups, but with the great central "pan-Israelite" traditions of the Exodus, Sinai, and the arrival at the Promised Land. These, too, he welds into a continuous whole, and their general theme is well summed up in Exodus 34:10: "Behold I make a covenant. Before all your people I will do marvels, such as have not been wrought in all the earth or in any nation; and all the people among whom you are shall see the work of Yahweh; for it is a terrible thing that I will do with you." Thus, in this third part of the saga, the author shows the Israelites as a nation to be envied by the Gentiles—even (we can almost hear him saying) by the Egyptians, who appeared so much more powerful and civilized to his fellow Israelites during Solomon's reign.

This third section of the saga is in fact far more closely linked to the earlier parts than the present division of the biblical books might suggest. The pattern contained in the command and promise to Abraham (Gen. 12:1-3) is now applied to the entire nation descended from him. As Abraham said farewell to a Gentile land in the hope of a land which Yahweh would give him, so the Israelites said farewell to Egypt. As he in his wanderings was stripped of all support except that of Yahweh, so were the Israelites in their journey through the desert. As he received a revelation, a command and a promise, so the Israelites at Sinai were favored with a theophany, a series of commandments, and a promise which (like that made to Abraham) is reiterated at various points in the narrative (Ex. 3:8,17; 13:5; 33:1-3a; Num. 14:40). Moreover, Yahweh's intervention as described in the key passage (Ex. 3:7-8) reproduces the basic pattern of His earlier interventions in Genesis, for it is intended as the climax to them. It is found in the story of man's sin, and repeated in the accounts of the Flood, of Babel, and of Sodom and Gomorrah (Gen. 3; 6-8; 11; 18-19), and may be summarized thus. (1) Men, by their sin, resist the right order willed by God. (2) Yahweh takes a practical interest in the situation by "coming down to see." (3) He decides to intervene and to destroy the state of affairs which has been distorted by sin. (4) He puts His decision into effect. (5) He then preserves a "righteous remnant" from the general destruction, so that from it He may create a new order, in accordance with His will.

This is precisely the pattern which underlies Exodus 3:7-8, where the old, "wrong" order is represented by the Egyptian oppression of His chosen people, and the new order is achieved by destroying the forces of Egypt in the Reed Sea so that Israel may be preserved for its destiny at Sinai.

There are many other ways, too, by which the Yahwist stresses continuity with the past. For instance, the episode of Abram at Pharaoh's court (Gen. 12:10-20) refers to the "great plagues" inflicted on the Egyptians by the hand of Yahweh (verse 17): this is deliberately intended to foreshadow the plagues of Egypt at the Exodus. More important, Yahweh Himself is shown as a mysterious, powerful, and jealous God, insisting on the undivided devotion of His people (Ex. 34:14).

He uses this omnipotence not merely to destroy the enemies of His people, but also to feed, to sustain, and to guide His chosen ones. As in the history of the patriarchs, Yahweh is both transcendent and immanent—the terrifyingly holy God, yet ever near to His people. The sense of faithfulness to His promises is never far away even in texts which speak of Him as the all-powerful Lord manipulating both nature and history for the fulfillment of His plans. The great God of all the earth is always the faithful covenant God of Israel, guiding the "righteous remnant" of His people toward that Promised Land where He will establish a messianic kingdom with its Anointed King.

MOSES: A TYPE OF SOLOMON

The Yahwist's treatment of Moses also throws light on his theology as a whole. He appears to have seen Moses as in some sense a patriarchal figure, associated particularly with the locality of Kadesh, rather as Abraham is associated with Hebron, Isaac with Beersheba, and Jacob with Bethel. As a result of his close relationship with Yahweh, Moses (like the patriarchs) finds water and

THE WADI HEBRON IN SINAI

digs wells (Ex. 15:22-25; Num. 21:16-18). The circumstances in which Moses finds his wife (Ex. 2:16ff.) are unmistakably reminiscent of Jacob's meeting with Rachel (Gen. 29:10ff.). Above all, Moses is like the patriarchs in that Yahweh reveals to him His secret "counsels" and plans for the future, of which the Gentiles are totally ignorant. Like Joseph, Moses uses his private knowledge of Yahweh's intentions in order to confound the Egyptians and to predict the future, and the accuracy of his predictions is a sure sign that Yahweh is with him, giving him this wisdom and the power to implement his predictions.

But Moses is not portrayed solely as a patriarchal figure of the past: he is also a type and model pointing forward to the Davidic monarchy—a king in all but name. The story of how Moses was found in an ark by Pharaoh's daughter (Ex. 1-2:10) is quite evidently influenced by a similar infancy narrative about an early Babylonian king, Sargon of Agade; and the account of how Moses first proved his own power and authority by making his hand first leprous and then healthy (Ex. 4:6-7) is remarkably similar to a sign performed by Marduk, the god of Babylon, before the battle by which he achieved kingship over the gods.

Again, it was the glory of the Egyptian king to claim that he gave food and drink to his people, and this is precisely what Moses did for the Israelites at Kadesh. Moses, too, received the Law from God and gave it to the people: the Davidic monarch, at his coronation, received from the hand of the priest, who represented Yahweh, the "code" he was to follow and enforce during his reign. (In this, Moses' position is like that of Hammurabi, the king who received the laws of Babylon from the sun-god.) And in battle, too, Moses wins strength for the warriors of Israel by raising his hands against their opponents, the Amalekites (Ex. 17:8-15): the records of the ancient Near East often attribute a similar gesture and power to kings. These instances could be multiplied, but enough has been said to show that the Yahwist was concerned to portray Moses as a type of the Davidic king who was to come.

THE YAHWIST'S THEME

Many more examples could be cited to prove that this narrative is all orientated toward Solomon. The great stories of the Passover, of the crossing of the Sea, and of Sinai are all concerned with events which were at the center of Israel's liturgical year; and these feasts were kept in the temple.

But more important than the detail is the dominant theme. It is seen in retrospect that right from the creation onwards the whole of world history, and especially through the history of His chosen people, Yahweh has been working toward a single goal: the establishment of the kingdom of Judah under the anointed son of David. Into this theme every single detail, every story, every local tradition is integrated; and through the saga which results we are taught the basic truths concerning God and man. The Yahwistic theology is optimistic: the author never despairs of man because that would be to despair of God. It is precisely because God is not like men that He has the power, and the wisdom, to save mankind from itself.

This is the first of our "maps," tracing out the broad lines of early Old Testament theology as it was developed in the kingdom of Judah under Solomon. We must now turn to a second map of the same terrain, drawn in very different circumstances.

The Theology of the Elohist

After the death of Solomon around the year 930 B.C., the northern tribes seceded from the United Kingdom of Israel and Judah to set up the independent kingdom of Israel (*see* 1 Kings 12). This state lasted for just over two centuries, and was finally destroyed by the Assyrians in 721 B.C. Its history often makes unpleasant reading, for a long series of unstable and corrupt kings led it into material and moral disasters; and even at the best of times, the people of the North were exposed to the seductive attractions of Canaanite religion, whose moral codes were far less exacting than that of Israel.

It was against this background that the second of the great Old Testament theologies was composed. We shall call its author the "Elohist," because in the stories recorded in Genesis he uses the Hebrew word "Elohim," not "Yahweh," to denote the deity. It is not, however, implied that the author was necessarily a single individual, though he may have been.

The Elohist probably wrote toward the end of the Northern Kingdom, in those catastrophic years when it was evident to all that the destruction of the kingdom was, humanly speaking, inevitable. This would explain why the Elohist directs the gaze of his contemporaries not forward (as the Yahwist does) to a future messianic age, but back to the time of Moses and Joshua, when Israel was united not as a kingdom, but as a tribal confederation led by men of faith.

In the Pentateuch as it now stands, there is far more of the Yahwist's work than of the Elohist's: indeed, the work of the latter has

SUMERIAN TABLET, *with the liturgy of Kés,
dating from the time of Hammurabi*

frequently survived only in fragmentary form, and often has to
be disentangled from a Yahwist context in which it has been em-
bedded. This much, however, seems clear: the central idea in the
mind of the Elohist was the covenant relationship between Yahweh and Israel. For this reason his narrative opens with the story
of Abraham's vision (Gen. 15), in which the events associated
with the covenant at Horeb are clearly foreshadowed. (The Elohist calls the mountain of the covenant Horeb, not Sinai, and this
usage is one of the many clues by which his work can be detected.)
And according to many scholars, the work of the Elohist ends with
the account of the covenant ceremony at Shechem, in which the
terms of the Horeb covenant were recapitulated and ratified on
the soil of the Promised Land (Josh. 24). And to judge from the
detailed and solemn way he describes the events leading up to the
covenant at Horeb, and the ceremony performed there, it would
seem beyond all doubt that the author would have regarded this
event as the central and most important part of his work.

A basic theme of the Elohistic narrative is that Israel is a people set apart, "a people dwelling alone and not reckoning itself among the nations" (Num. 23:9). For Israel was united with its covenant God as His most precious and intimate possession. "Israel is my first-born son," Yahweh declares to Pharaoh through Moses (Ex. 4:22-23), and the words remind us irresistibly of the words of Hosea, the prophet of the Northern Kingdom (*see* Hos. 11:1; 13:13). The people voluntarily accepted this relationship at Horeb, and promised to be obedient to God's word: "All that Yahweh has spoken we will do" (Ex. 19:8; 24:3); and the same promise was renewed at Shechem after they had entered the Promised Land (Josh. 24:24).

In return, Yahweh "gave Himself" to His people. According to the Elohist author, a most significant moment in this self-giving came when God revealed to Moses that His name was "Yahweh" (Ex. 3:14), for (according to the author) no man had previously known God's true name. The interpretation given to this name in the biblical text ("I am who I am") is as mysterious as the name itself. One scholar (S. D. Goitein) has advanced a most interesting explanation. Arguing from a similar word in Arabic (*hawa*), he has suggested that the name Yahweh implies two things: that its bearer passionately demands exclusive devotion, and that he is himself passionately devoted to those that worship him. Again we meet the theme of the election of Israel.

Let us turn, however, to the rather artificial interpretation given in the Bible ("I am who I am"). Elsewhere in the Old Testament the same construction is used with many other verbs. For instance, "I will be gracious to whom I will be gracious, and I will show mercy on whom I will show mercy" (Ex. 33:19b), and "send by the hand of whom you will send" (Ex. 4:13). In these phrases the speaker either claims for himself complete freedom of choice (the first example), or gives to his hearer complete freedom (the second example). It seems only logical to suppose that a similar meaning lies behind "I am who I am": that is, God claims complete freedom to be Himself, untrammelled by man's actions, and therefore remains to men wholly mysterious and undefined. Yet

VIEW OF THE DESOLATE
ROAD FROM JERUSALEM
TO JERICHO

even this is a partial revelation of Himself, by which He makes
Himself accessible by name (Yahweh) to the one nation He has
chosen. They know His name; and therefore they can call upon
Him, and be sure of attracting His attention, whenever they
choose to do so.

GOD THE UNKNOWABLE

The Elohist uses every device at his command to present the
great God of Israel as holy, transcendent, inaccessible in majesty.
God appears at Horeb veiled in cloud and thick darkness (Ex.
19:9, 16b; 20:21), whereas in the Yahwist's account God is revealed by the presence of fire and smoke (Ex. 19:18). Again, the
Yahwist tells us that some of the elders actually ". . . saw the God
of Israel. . . . They beheld God, and ate and drank" (Ex. 24:9, 11).
But according to the Elohist God formally warned the Israelites
that anyone breaking through the darkness in an attempt to see
Him would die (Ex. 19:21; *compare* 3:6). Even Moses was only

permitted to see Him from behind (Ex. 33:23): "You cannot see my face, for man cannot see me and live" (Ex. 33:20).

For the same reason, the Elohist describes the theophany at Horeb as something not so much *seen* as *heard*. The sound of the trumpet "exceeding loud" leads to the still more terrifying climax when Moses hears the voice of God (Ex. 19:16b, 19). Yahweh is heard, but remains unseen.

This insistence on God's transcendence is strikingly at variance with the technique of the Yahwist, who said (it may be recalled) that Yahweh walked in the garden, and even closed the door of the ark when Noah was safely inside. The Elohist consistently avoids any suggestion that Yahweh "comes down" to intervene in person in this world. God, when He wishes to communicate with men, usually does so by night and through dreams, as He did with Abraham (Gen. 15:1ff., 12ff.), Abimelech (Gen. 20:3), Jacob (Gen. 28:12; 31:10; 46:2), Laban (Gen. 31:24) and Balaam (Num. 22:9,20). The Elohist's interest in dreams is abundantly illustrated in the story of Joseph.

Another way in which Yahweh's transcendence is preserved is by His using men or angels as messengers. Thus in the story of Hagar, it is God who hears Hagar's voice, but an angel who replies from heaven (Gen. 21:17). Similarly, it is an angel who calls to Abraham from heaven to prevent him from putting Isaac to death (Gen. 22:11). In Jacob's dream at Bethel angels ascended and descended the sloping ramp between heaven and earth (Gen. 28:12). And how completely these angelic intermediaries represented Yahweh is vividly illustrated by Exodus 23:20–21: "Behold, I send an angel before you to guard you on the way and to bring you to the place which I have prepared. Give heed to him, and hearken to his voice, do not rebel against him, for he will not pardon your transgression."

The human intermediaries are of even greater theological interest, but of them we shall speak later. For the present, enough examples have been quoted to show the stress given to the transcendence of God.

The text which best sums up the Elohist's notion of God in his dealing with Israel has many affinities with Wisdom literature: "Yahweh, Yahweh, a God merciful and gracious, slow to anger and abounding in steadfast love and faithfulness, keeping steadfast love for thousands, forgiving iniquity and transgression and sin, but who will by no means clear the guilty, visiting the iniquity of the fathers upon the children and the children's children, to the third and fourth generation" (Ex. 34:6-7).

For the Elohist, Yahweh is above all a God of justice and judgment. Ultimately, He is inexorable in exacting requital for every violation of His will. He reveals to Abraham that He has decided to allow the "iniquity of the Amorite" to accumulate for four generations (Gen. 15:16), but then He will exact retribution in full. In short, though sins may be allowed to accumulate over a long period, in the end they never go unpunished.

In one passage, the idea is applied to Israel itself with terrifying effect. After the episode of the golden calf, when Moses prayed for forgiveness, Yahweh replied: ". . . Now go, lead the people to the place of which I have spoken to you: behold my angel will go before you. *Nevertheless, in the day when I visit, I will visit their sin upon them"* (Ex. 32:34). Later generations often compared this sin with the setting up of golden calves for worship at Bethel and Dan (1 Kings 12:32), and it may well be that the doom pronounced in Exodus 32:34 is a prediction, by the Elohist, of the final ruin of the Northern Kingdom in 721 B.C.

Yahweh, then, is a God of justice. When He inflicted plagues on the Egyptians and decreed the defeat of Canaan, it was not merely to further the interests of His own people, but also because the sins of these Gentile nations had to be punished. "I have sinned this time," says Pharaoh, "Yahweh is righteous, and I and my people are wicked" (Ex. 9:27).

But Yahweh is also a God of "steadfast love and faithfulness" (Ex. 34:6). This is the distinctive mark of Israel's God. He guided, protected, and sustained His people before and after the covenant at Horeb. He is "the God of thy father, the God of Abraham, the

BLACK BASALT OBELISK, *this side showing King Jehu of Israel (ca. 842–815 B.C.) paying tribute to the Assyrian king Shalmaneser iii*

God of Isaac and the God of Jacob" (Ex. 3:6), constant in His devotion to the people, and (in spite of their sins) "slow to anger." The sentence which epitomizes His work most neatly occurs in the account of the covenant at Horeb: "You have seen what I did to the Egyptians, and how I bore you on eagle's wings and brought you to myself" (Ex. 19:4).

GOD SPEAKS THROUGH HIS PROPHETS

God, we said, sometimes communicates with favored souls like the patriarchs through angels, or in dreams. More commonly, and to the generality of men, He is said to speak through His prophets. (It is noteworthy how often the Elohist calls people "prophets" he uses the term of Abraham (Gen. 20:7), of Aaron and Miriam (Ex. 15:20; Num. 12:2, 6) and Moses (Ex. 4:12).

What he means by "prophet" is apparent from the episode in Numbers 11:16-17, 24-30. Yahweh imparts a share of the spirit which is "upon" Moses to the seventy elders who are to help him. Having received this spirit, they begin to "prophesy" (verse 26), i.e., show that they have the power to do the work of God. Moses himself was, for the Elohist, more than a prophet, for he communicated with Yahweh directly, and not through dreams or visions or "dark speeches" (Num. 12:6-8).

But a prophet does not merely speak to men on behalf of God: he also conveys man's words and prayers to God. Thus Abraham prayed for Abimelech (Gen. 20:7), and Moses often prayed for the people. At the climax of the theophany on Horeb, "Moses spoke and God answered him with a voice" (Ex. 19:19). He also conveyed the terms of the covenant to the people (Ex. 19:7), and the people's acceptance of these terms to God (Ex. 19:19). Yahweh, indeed, gave to Moses a fullness of authority which is almost startling: "Lo, I am coming to you in a thick cloud, that the people may hear when I speak with you and may also believe you forever" (Ex. 19:9). After that, Moses was to a unique extent accepted as the spokesman of Yahweh. A slight offered to him, a failure to recognize his authority, was a slight to Yahweh Himself (Num. 12:2-8). His position was explicitly acknowledged: "And they said to Moses: 'You speak to us and we will hear; but let not God speak to us lest we die'" (Ex. 20:19). Indeed, Moses' anger for their sin of idolatry was a projection of the fury of Yahweh Himself (Ex. 32:19b-20).

Yet it is no less important to appreciate the extent to which Moses was accepted as the intercessor for the people, with whom he identified himself even in their sin. This is eloquently stated in Exodus 32:32: "Yet now, if thou wilt forgive their sin — *and if not, blot me, I pray thee, out of thy book which thou hast written.*" He was the priest who taught them Yahweh's name (Ex. 3:13ff.) and His covenant words, thereby becoming a mediator between them and God. (Later, we shall see how the role of the priest became more "sacramental," with a stress on ritual words and gestures, though this is not be excluded entirely even from Moses' life: once at least he presided over a "liturgical" ceremony when the covenant was ratified, Ex. 24:3-8.) But the central function of Moses' mediatorship is well summed up in the counsel of Jethro, immediately before Horeb: "You shall represent the people before God, and bring their cases to God; and you shall teach them the statutes and the decisions, and make them know the way in which they must walk, and what they must do" (Ex. 18:19-20). In these words, as elsewhere, we see that the thought of the Elohist revolved around the covenant relationship between Yahweh and His people.

THE LAWS OF THE COVENANT

The covenant was intended to make the people one with God, and therefore it included a series of laws. By observing these commandments, the people would become, like God Himself, truly just and faithful and compassionate. The purpose of all these laws was, put quite simply, to direct Israel to the imitation of God.

These laws are found principally in two blocks of ancient legal tradition which the Elohist incorporated into his narrative. They are the Ten Commandments (Ex. 20:1-17) and the Book of the Covenant (Ex. 20:22-23:14). For the Elohist, the Ten Commandments state, in a very direct manner, what Yahweh wanted from the people: no idolatry (Ex. 20:3), no images (Ex. 20:4), no abuse of His holy name or of His holy day, the Sabbath (Ex. 20:7-10). The remainder of the commandments treat of right relations between men; they uphold the rights of parents to be respected by their children, and the right of each member of the community to life, marriage, property, and fair judgment (Ex. 20:12-17).

In the mind of the Elohist, the prohibition of the worship of other gods may have been especially called for, because there is ample evidence that the Israelites were tempted to worship Baal along with Yahweh (1 Kings 16:31ff.; 18:18ff., etc.). (This was particularly true of the Northern Kingdom.) Again, since the Elohist regarded Yahweh as a God whom no man could see, the prohibition of images would have had a personal appeal to him.

VIEW OF THE DEAD SEA FROM MOUNT NEBO

The keeping of the Sabbath, too, was an external confession, frequently and regularly reiterated, that man depends on Yahweh alone for all life's needs. And since the holiest of all the "words" which Yahweh had revealed at Horeb was His name, a special commandment ordered that this name must never be pronounced except with reverence and devotion. The Ten Commandments spell out in noon-day clarity the ethical consequences of the Elohist's doctrine.

The Book of the Covenant (Ex. 20:22-23:14) treats similar precepts in still greater detail, emphasizing that Israel must act as Yahweh would act. Strangers must never be wronged or oppressed, ". . . for you were strangers in the land of Egypt" (Ex. 22:21; 23:9). Clothes which the poor need against the cold of the night must not be retained as security for debts, because ". . . if he cries to me I will hear him, for I am compassionate" (Ex. 22:26). Yahweh is compassionate, and therefore will be angry with anyone who oppresses the widow or the orphan (Ex. 22:21-23). What Yahweh has done for Israel, they must do for each other. The whole Book of the Covenant abounds in similar examples, for in the ancient Near East chivalry and compassion for the poor were considered to be among the most glorious qualities any ruler could possess.

THE THEME OF THE ELOHIST: THROUGH DEVOTION AND RIGHTEOUSNESS TO PEACE

The personal relationship between Yahweh and Israel can best be summed up in three Hebrew words, each of which is so rich in meaning as to be almost untranslatable: *hesed, sedaqah,* and *shalôm. Hesed* denotes that total devotion and love which Yahweh shows to those who are in covenant with Him, and which He demands from them in return. *Sedaqah* means justice or righteousness; but it is not justice conceived of as obedience to statute law, or abstract norms. Rather, it is the virtue by which a man fulfills his personal obligations, stands true to himself and to his family — and to his covenant partner. Yahweh is the embodiment of this virtue, and calls upon all Israel to reproduce it in their lives. Finally, the term *shalôm*, usually translated "peace," stands for the state of total security, prosperity, and peace which is bestowed by God on those who uphold His covenant. Thus Israel was invited to advance through *hesed* ("devotion") and *sedaqah* ("righteousness") to the final reward, *shalôm*. This is the theme of the covenant blessings in Exodus 23:27–31.

The Elohist, therefore, turns his mind from the corrupt and degenerate age he lived in to that earlier age when the covenant was first defined and lived. He sees the age of the patriarchs, of Moses, and of Joshua as a kind of Golden Age for Israel. The Elohist had before him more or less the same stock of traditional stories as the Yahwist had, but he worked over them to give them a different interpretation. He held up the heroes of the past as exemplars of the covenant virtues, showing that their deliverance from poverty and affliction was the result of their steadfast loyalty to their covenant God.

Thus at the very beginning of his work he states that Abraham's faith (that is, his complete trust in God's word) was held by God Himself to be "righteousness" (Gen. 15:6). His principal story about Abraham tells how the patriarch was prepared to sacrifice his only son rather than to disobey God's command (Gen. 22). He shields Abraham from the charge of lying by remarking that Sarah was indeed his "sister" (as he had told Abimelech) as well as his wife (Gen. 20:2,12). Abimelech is saved from punishment because he had acted "in integrity of heart and in innocence of hands" (Gen. 20:5) and had not knowingly taken another man's wife (Gen. 20:3). And in the story of Hagar (Gen. 21:9-21) he gives a living example of Yahweh's care for the refugee and the orphan.

The same pattern is followed in this version of the life of Jacob. The old tradition told how Jacob had outwitted his brother Esau and his uncle Laban by his greater cunning. The Elohist superimposes on this a moral interpretation. Esau had lost his birthright to Jacob because of his gluttony (Gen. 25:29-34). And because Laban had cheated Jacob (Gen. 31:7,36-42), Yahweh intervened to make his sheep breed only such lambs as would fall to Jacob's lot (Gen. 31:8-12). This favor was a return for

Jacob's vow at Bethel (Gen. 31:13), and for his relying on God alone (Gen. 31:42). The Elohist was particularly anxious to show that Jacob was wholly innocent of the sin of idolatry. He tells us that *he did not know* Rachel had stolen Laban's "gods" (Gen. 31:32), and points approvingly to the episode when Jacob made his household abandon their "foreign gods" at Shechem before going up to Bethel to make an altar (Gen. 35:1-4). This was a shining example for the Elohist's own contemporaries.

PROPHETICAL THEMES

We have said that in his writing the Elohist stands very close to the prophets. The themes of *hesed, sedaqah,* and *shalôm* are most certainly prophetical themes. And the whole story is an illustration of them. Abraham, Jacob, and Joseph are all, to some extent, portrayed as types of the poor and the oppressed, whose sufferings arouse the compassion of Yahweh; and each of them, in the end, achieves happiness and prosperity because he has put his trust in God alone. And what was true of the patriarchs became true of the entire people in Egypt; they cried out to their God, and He, in His love and righteousness, delivered them from their oppressors and led them out of Egypt to a land where, if they observed His covenant, they could find peace.

The Theology of Deuteronomy

It is now generally agreed that the hard core of the book of Deuteronomy originated from men who came from the Northern Kingdom. There is still some dispute about the exact time when it was written, but the most likely theory is as follows. After the fall of Samaria in 721 B.C., a stream of refugees, among whom were many Levites, flowed southwards into Judah to escape the Assyrian occupation. These Levites, now aliens and poverty-stricken refugees, were naturally led to reflect on the unpre-

ASSYRIAN WINGED GENIUS, *dated* 884 B.C.

cedented disaster which had annihilated their homeland; and like the Elohist before them, they re-thought the history of their nation to learn new lessons from it. Thus, in Deuteronomy, we have yet a third version of the early period of Israel's history which, though it reproduces much of the legal material contained in the Elohist source, contains many additions and supplements.

As Levites, they turned quite naturally to Moses, the greatest Levite of all time, and they presented their version of the history of Israel as a "last will and testament" of Moses himself (Deut. 28:69). This was a familiar literary device at the time, and they would not have considered it odd (much less fraudulent) to place their own ideas on his lips. Indeed, the last words of any great leader were regarded as particularly solemn and sacred (*compare* Josh. 23; 1 Sam. 12), and for the Levites, therefore, the last words of Moses would have been the most solemn testament of all.

The scene is set in the plains of Moab. Moses is now an old man who has led his people out of Egypt to the edge of the Promised Land, and the long years in the desert are now over, years marked by phenomenal favors and by equally terrible punishments. What will the future be like? Moses exhorts the people to engrave the memory of the desert years so firmly on their hearts that they may never again be tricked or deceived into forgetting the God of their fathers. He reminds them that Yahweh had chosen them not for any merit of theirs — they had none (Deut. 7:7; 9:4-6) — but solely out of love (Deut. 7:8). And His love had never failed, in spite of their stubbornness and unfaithfulness (Deut. 10:15; 14:2; 32:9). He had made Israel His dearest possession (Deut. 7:6; 14:2; 26: 18), His own son (Deut. 8:5; 14:1), and the hard trials of the desert were seen, in retrospect, to have been the acts of a devoted father humbling, chastising, testing, and instructing his son so that he might "do you good in the end" (Deut. 8:15-16).

Israel, therefore, was never to forget that its ancestor had been "a wandering Aramean" (Deut. 26:5), that it had been "a slave in the land of Egypt" (Deut. 5:15). The remembrance of this past history should serve as an everlasting reminder of the need for *humility, gratitude, loyalty,* and *unswerving obedience* to all the words of the Lord. This is the mainspring of the thought of Deuteronomy.

But Moses, as he gazed into the Promised Land, also spoke of the future. It was a "good land, which Yahweh your God gives you" (Deut. 8:7), "flowing with milk and honey" (Deut. 6:3), rich in vines and corn and mineral treasures too (Deut. 8:7-9), well watered, with the vineyards and olive-groves already flourishing, with houses and cities already built (Deut. 6:10-11). As long as Israel was not beguiled into forgetting Yahweh, it could be an earthly paradise. But there was one danger. The Israelites, when they saw the Canaanites ascribing the fruitfulness of this land to their own gods, gods of fertility, might all too readily be tempted to do the same. In the desert, Israel had known Yahweh primarily as a "destroyer" God, full of fury and ready to annihilate all who opposed His commands; from now on, the people had to

SUNRISE OVER THE DEAD SEA, *viewed from the Wilderness of Judea*

learn that He was also the sole provider of fertile soil, and if they ever forgot that, He would again destroy them.

How sadly Israel failed to live up to this ideal is shown in the prophecies of Hosea (especially in chapter 2), and the book of Deuteronomy condemns idolatry ("following other gods") so frequently that we must conclude that the sin had become very widespread indeed (Deut. 6:14-15; 7:4; 8:19-20, etc.). That is why Deuteronomy decrees that the awful law of *herem* — the command to destroy *totally* — was to be pitilessly enforced not only against pagan idolaters, but against all Israelites who fell into this sin. Whole cities, with all their inhabitants, were to be destroyed, and even close relatives and loved friends were to be exterminated without pity (Deut. 13:6ff.). Every contact with the Canaanites was forbidden: no intermarriage, no sharing in their worship, or Israel would lose its soul (Deut. 12:2–3, etc.)

ONE CENTRAL SANCTUARY

Deuteronomy is definitely connected with a movement of reform, and the most distinctive of its laws is the one which orders that all worship must be carried on at a single sanctuary in the center of the land. (Probably this was a result of the danger of compromising with Canaanite worship, to which the little local shrines were particularly exposed. It would be easier to control the orthodoxy of worship in one central sanctuary.) This sanctuary is consistently referred to as "the place which Yahweh your God shall choose out of all your tribes to put his name there" or "to cause his name to dwell there" (Deut. 12:5, 11, 21; 14:23, 24; 16:2, 6, 11; 26:2). All Israel was ordered to make a pilgrimage to that shrine three times a year, for the feasts of Passover, Weeks, and Tabernacles (Deut. 16:1-17), and all their sacrifices, tithes, and first-fruits were to be offered only in this place. There alone the Levites were to receive their part of the beasts sacrificed (Deut. 18:1-8).

This is an important development. It stresses that Yahweh, while remaining transcendent in heaven (Deut. 26:15), makes Himself present at the shrine through His name and His words. His "name" dwells there, and the thought here is that He can always be called upon in this central sanctuary, where He will listen to His people, and listening, will forgive.

And yet Yahweh was present at this central sanctuary in a still more special way. The most sacred object in the sanctuary was the Ark of the Covenant. In later ages, this was regarded as the "throne of Yahweh," representing His earthly presence. But in Deuteronomy the Ark was not a throne at all, but the box or chest which contained the words of God. Moses, recalling the events of Horeb, said: "Then I turned and came down from the mountain, and put the tables [of the Law, on which the Ten Commandments were written] in the Ark which I had made; and there they are as

REAPERS GATHER THE HARVEST

Yahweh commanded me" (Deut. 10:5). The same fact is recorded in Deuteronomy 31:24-26. Yahweh's name signified His spiritual presence in the sanctuary, and the words of the Law signified His will and statutes for the people. The curses and blessings with which the covenant was concluded (Deut. 28) are merely an amplification of this idea: they spell out in greater detail what is in practice entailed by respect for the commandments.

The worship which Deuteronomy demands corresponds closely to this theology of reverence for "the name and the word." It is not to consist principally in ritual purifications and sacrifices (as in later times), but primarily and essentially in *words*. Thus the Israelite on pilgrimage is exhorted to make a "negative confession" that he is innocent of sin: "I have not transgressed any of thy commandments, neither have I forgotten them" (Deut. 26:13), and to recite a positive "*credo*" that he acknowledges Yahweh as the God who delivered Israel from Egypt, and who alone bestows fertility on the Promised Land (Deut. 26:5-9).

Thus, according to Deuteronomy, the Israelite achieved union with Yahweh not primarily or essentially through external acts of worship, but by constantly listening to God's words in his heart wherever he might happen to be. "For this commandment that I command you this day is not too hard or you, neither is it far off. . . .But the word is very near to you; it is in your mouth and in your heart so that you can do it" (Deut. 30:11, 14). This theme is repeated on almost every page of the book: Israel must listen to His voice, His words, His statutes, His judgments, His testimonies, observing and doing them with heart and soul. The whole aim of Deuteronomy is to intensify the Israelite's awareness of the words of Yahweh and to prevent him from ever forgetting them even for one moment. In Deuteronomy 11:18-19 we read the commandment about binding these words as a sign upon the hand and as frontlets between the eyes, upon the door-posts of the house, and upon the gates. As Joshua, in obedience to Moses, had inscribed the covenant words upon stone at the entrance to the Land (Deut. 27:3,8; Josh. 8:32), so the individual Israelite was to inscribe them at the entrance to his home and the entrance to his own soul.

"TODAY"

The central sanctuary was sacred because Yahweh's name "dwelt" there and because His words were contained in the Ark. Together these facts made a direct link between the generation which had stood at the foot of Horeb and the generation which found itself in exile after 721 B.C. As Moses had been the teacher and guide of the earlier generation, so the Levites from the North claimed to teach and guide their own generation, reiterating the commandments of Moses. And so throughout Deuteronomy it is stressed that Yahweh is concluding a covenant not just with one generation (that of Moses), but with all future generations, including the one present here today. "Yahweh made this covenant not with our fathers but with us, even us, who are all of us here alive *today*" (Deut. 5:3). "*Today* you are all standing before Yahweh your God . . . so that he may establish you *today* as his own people and so that he may be your God" (Deut. 29:10ff.).

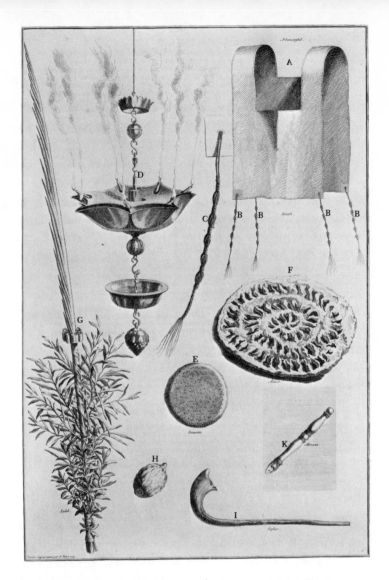

ARTICLES USED IN JEWISH RELIGIOUS OBSERVANCE

ABC: *The undergarment* (arbá kanfot) *worn daily by observant Jewish males, with its four fringes* (cf. Num. 15:37–41).

D: *A sabbath lamp.*

EF: *Two types of unleavened bread for the Passover.*

G: *A palm branch* (lulav) *with willow and myrtle.*

H: *The citron* (etrog) *used together with G during the service on the festival of Tabernacles* (Sukkoth).

I: *The ram's horn* (shofar), *sounded in the synagogue during the High Holiday Period.*

K: *The small parchment* (mezuzah), *inscribed with verses from Deuteronomy* (6:4–9; 11:13–21), *which is placed in a case and nailed to the doorposts of Jewish homes and synagogues.*

After the disaster of 721 this "today" must have had a poignant significance for the refugees who had just escaped the cruelty of the Assyrians. It must have seemed to them that they had been given, almost miraculously, one last chance of returning to those old traditions and ancient standards of the desert. It is as though the Levites of Deuteronomy were inviting them to full conversion, asking them to take up anew the spirit of total dedication with which their fathers had entered the Promised Land.

"Now that crisis and change have come upon you," the Levites seem to be saying, "become that Israel again! Resolve now, *today*, to *remember* Yahweh as He was revealed by Moses, and fill your hearts with the consciousness of His covenant words! Blot out of your minds everything that might tempt you to forget Him, and base your lives solely upon trust in Him who brought you out of Egypt, and through so many hardships and trials to this place and this hour!"

The Theology of the Priestly Tradition

It might be thought that, after the Yahwist saga, the Elohist version, and the Deuteronomic interpretation, all possible rethinking of the early history of Israel had been exhausted. Yet a disaster worse than the destruction of the Northern Kingdom was yet to come. In 587 B.C. the Babylonian army captured the holy city, Jerusalem, dismantled its walls, and sacked the temple. The population of Judah was taken into exile. The "everlasting kingdom of David" had been brought to nothing; it looked as if Yahweh had either deserted His people or had been vanquished by the gods of Babylon; and—worst of all—the people could no longer make atonement for their sins by offering expiatory sacrifices in the place where Yahweh had set His name.

It was a heart-rending test for the faith of Israel. But during the Exile (587–537 B.C.) a group of priests produced yet another

BOUNDARY STONE OF KING NEBUCHAD-
NEZZAR I

interpretation of the history of the people: their work incorporated
much earlier material concerned with the temple worship (and
later ages added other material too). Indeed, after the return from
exile, a general revision was undertaken, probably around 450-
400 B.C. The Yahwist and Elohist versions were incorporated
into the story, and thus the Pentateuch as we now know it was
formed. Here, however, we are concerned only with the distinctive contribution of the "Priestly Writers."

THE "GLORY" OF THE LORD

In contrast with the Elohist and the authors of Deuteronomy,
the Priests presented Yahweh's self-revelation as something
seen rather than heard. He manifested Himself in cloud and fire
and light on Sinai: "The cloud covered the tent of meeting and
the glory (Hebrew: *kabod*) of Yahweh filled the tabernacle. . . .
For throughout all their journeyings the cloud of Yahweh was
upon the tabernacle by day, and fire was upon it by night in the

sight of all the house of Israel" (Ex. 40:34, 38). Clearly, the "glory" here is an external manifestation of the mysterious, unseeable God.

This concept of God's glory is central to the thought of the Priestly tradition. And it is worked out in minute detail. The nearer one approaches to this "glory," the more terrifying it becomes. The whole description of the shrine in the desert turns around this idea. For in the Priestly tradition the camp in the desert was not a war camp (as in Deuteronomy) but an assembly set in order for worship, with the worshippers organized in a carefully graded hierarchy around the central shrine. We are meant to think of it as a series of courts or ante-chambers converging upon the "most holy" or "the holy of holies" at the center, that innermost "cell" where the glory of the Lord was physically enthroned, and elaborate rituals of purification are prescribed as one proceeds from the outermost sphere (occupied by the lay members of the community) to an inner one. The plan of the camp in Numbers, chapter 2, makes this clear.

Here the innermost ring is the tribe of Levi, with the sons of Aaron in the place of honor, facing the entrance to the Holy of Holies. Around them are the tribes of Israel, with the tribe of Judah in the place of honor on the east, again facing the entrance to the shrine. But in the mind of the Priestly writers, the descendants of Abraham, united in the covenant of circumcision, form yet another ring which includes the descendants of Ishmael (Gen. 25:12-18), Keturah (Gen. 25:1-6) and Abraham's concubines, though Isaac's descendants are clearly in the place of honor, for God established His covenant with them (Gen. 17:21). Vaster still is a circle comprising all the creatures which survived the Flood, where Noah and his descendants occupy the place of honor, because though this circle embraces all living creatures, God made His covenant only with men (Gen. 9:8-10). Finally, the widest ring of all is constituted by the entire created world, with Adam, the image of God, unmistakably in the place of honor (Gen. 1). Thus, in the mind of the Priestly authors, all creation is ranged in concentric circles around the shrine of the *kabod*, the presence of the covenant God.

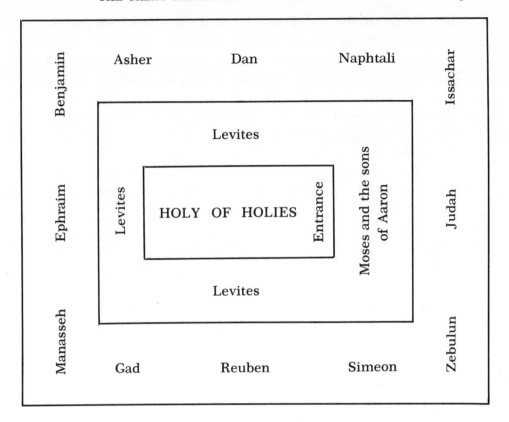

TEN GROUPS

Such is the vision of the authors, and we see the same vision repeated in the phrase "These are the generations" which occurs throughout their writing. This phrase is applied to exactly ten groups of men culminating in Moses and Aaron and their descendants. The ten groups diminish by a process of elimination, and a straight list of these references will show how they narrow down:

(1) Gen. 5:1: "this is the book of the generations of Adam" (2) Gen. 6:9: "These are the generations of Noah." (3) Gen. 10:1: "These are the generations of the sons of Noah." (4) Gen. 11:10: "These are the descendants of Shem." (5) Gen. 11:27: "These are the descendants of Terah."

It is significant that this particular group, the one which includes the first of the Israelite patriarchs, should occur at the exact center of the series. Among Abraham's descendants the next group to be designated by the phrase is:

(6) Gen. 25:12: "These are the descendants of Ishmael." (7) Gen. 25:19: "These are the descendants of Isaac." (8) Gen. 36:1, 9: "These are the descendants of Esau." (9) Gen. 37:2: "This is the history of the family of Jacob." (10) Num. 3:1: "These are the generations of Aaron and Moses."

Thus the vision of the Priestly tradition starts from Adam, and reaches its culmination in the great priests of Israel who had direct access to the Holy of Holies. This is the central notion in the Priestly tradition.

THE FOUR AGES OF THE WORLD'S HISTORY

Like many pagan authors of ancient times, the Priests regarded the history of the world as falling into four great "ages." For the Priests, these were: (1) from the Creation to the Flood; (2) from the Flood to Abraham; (3) from Abraham to the descent into Egypt; (4) from the Exodus onwards.

The second, third, and fourth of these ages were initiated by covenants made between Yahweh and representative groups of men. Although no covenant is mentioned for the first age, it is clear from the Priestly account of creation (Gen. 1-2:4a) that the general pattern of a covenant between God and man is there presupposed. Each covenant is a creative act, an irrevocable step forward in the creative process which leads up to the founding of the ideal theocratic community which was Israel. At each step, successive layers of sinfulness and profanity are stripped away: chaos is destroyed at the Creation, all sinners at the Flood, the idolaters by whom Abraham is surrounded are pushed aside, and finally the Egyptians are separated by miles of desert at the Exodus. In each instance, the "holy ones" chosen by God are set apart and preserved.

Each covenant contains a sign: the sun, moon, and stars at the Creation, the rainbow in the Noahic covenant, circumcision for the descendants of Abraham, and the sabbath day for those who shared the covenant at Sinai. Each covenant contains a blessing

CELEBRATING THE FEAST OF TABERNACLES—*the procession of the palms around the altar by (Portuguese) Jews, during the service on one of the days of the Feast* (Sukkoth)

and a promise of fruitfulness; and finally, at each covenant, Yahweh prescribes some special food for the group He has separated for Himself (green herbs at the Creation, flesh without blood for Noah, the fruits of Canaan for Abraham, clean beasts for the Israelites).

The Priestly writers also seem concerned to show that the knowledge of Yahweh deepened as the four ages of the world unfolded. During the first and second ages (that is, before Abraham), God is referred to as *Elohim*. During the third age (from Abraham to the descent into Egypt) He is called *El Shaddai*, the exact meaning of which is uncertain, but which is clearly meant to imply a closer relationship than had obtained before (it is often translated as "God Almighty"). Finally, in the fourth age, He becomes "Yahweh," and the full intimacy with Israel is estab-

lished: "And God said to Moses: 'I am Yahweh. I appeared to
Abraham, to Isaac and to Jacob as El Shaddai, but by my name
Yahweh I did not make myself known to them'" (Ex. 6:2-3).
Again we see the stress on the continuity and progress of the
revelation to mankind.

But the Priests did not see history as evolving without any set-
backs toward a better world; they were too perspicacious not to
observe that man left to himself is prone to sin. And so they de-
pict the evil consequences of sin by noting the progressive short-
ening of the human life-span throughout the four ages. In the
first age, before the Flood, the ordinary life-span is 7-10 centuries.
In the second age (before Abraham), it is 2-6 centuries. In the
third period it is 1-2 centuries, and in the fourth it becomes the
70-80 years to which the contemporaries of the Priestly writers
were accustomed. The underlying principle here appears to be
that of Proverbs 10:27: "The fear of Yahweh prolongs life, but
the years of the wicked will be short."

THE LITURGY OF ISRAEL

With the earthly temple at Jerusalem lying in ruins, it was natural that the Priests should regard its restoration as one essential in the concept of redemption and salvation. Unlike the Yahwist, they did not visualize God's triumph as the setting up of a
messianic kingdom on earth; rather, they saw it as the restoration
of a purified liturgy on earth, with all the tribes of Israel gathered
anew around the central shrine, devoting themselves to a cease-
less round of worship. They described this future liturgy as revealed by God to Moses in the desert (though it is evident that
many of the ideas are copied from the worship offered before
587 B.C. in the temple).

Much of the Priestly writing is devoted to the description of
the tabernacle in the desert and its furnishings. The underlying
idea here is that the earthly dwelling-place should be a replica
of heaven where Yahweh is enthroned. The most sacred object in
the tabernacle was, of course, the Ark of the Covenant, and it is
noteworthy that according to the Priests' tradition the Ark was

NOAH'S SACRIFICE
Bernardo Cavallino

not primarily (as in Deuteronomy) a chest containing the Law, but
a throne. It was surmounted by a platform of pure gold, called
the *kapporeth*, at each end of which were two golden cherubim,
whose wings were stretched over the *kapporeth*. The significance of this is that the cherubim who guarded and supported
Yahweh's throne in heaven had to be represented in this earthly
replica of His throne.

The description of the clothing of the high priest in Exodus 28
also merits attention, for the idea is that Yahweh, as He looks
out from the shrine, will see in the splendidly arrayed priest the
reflection of His own glory. In front of the priest's turban is a
golden flower engraved with the words "Holy to Yahweh" (Ex.
28:36–37), and around his shoulders are two precious stones each

bearing the names of six of the tribes of Israel. The high priest, therefore, stands before God as the representative of all Israel. The highly idealized account of Aaron's ordination in Exodus 29 stresses that by this ceremony Aaron is separated from all that is profane, so that he may worthily stand before Yahweh in the name of all Israel.

PRIESTS' VERSION OF CREATION

It will by now be evident that the distinctive characteristic of the Priestly writing is a preoccupation with order and symmetry and hierarchical structure. This is supremely true of the Priests' version of creation in Genesis 1-2:4a. This story was originally addressed to the exiles in Babylon who were, perhaps, dangerously impressed by the magnificence of the *ziggurats*, those enormous temple-towers built in seven storeys or tiers, on top of which was the temple proper. A Priestly writer, therefore, composed a poem showing that the whole universe is Yahweh's temple-tower, which He alone constructed by a mere word, with marvellous symmetry and order, in seven "days" or stages. The Babylonian *ziggurat* was decorated with lifeless images, but Yahweh had peopled His world with living creatures arranged in a carefully graded hierarchy and crowned, not by the lifeless image of a god, but by the living, breathing image of Himself — man.

"WHAT RETURN SHALL I MAKE TO THE LORD?"

Up to this point we have been concerned with two apparently different elements in the Priestly tradition. We have examined the basic notions underlying the narrative and historical part of the work, and (secondly) the controlling themes concerning the liturgy. These two parts of the work were not unconnected in the mind of the authors, for the thought which dominated their minds was the realization of the "glory" of the Lord. History and worship were in their minds inseparable. All creation and all history converged upon the community of Israel, whose vocation was to proclaim and to worship the Creator and Lord of all. How

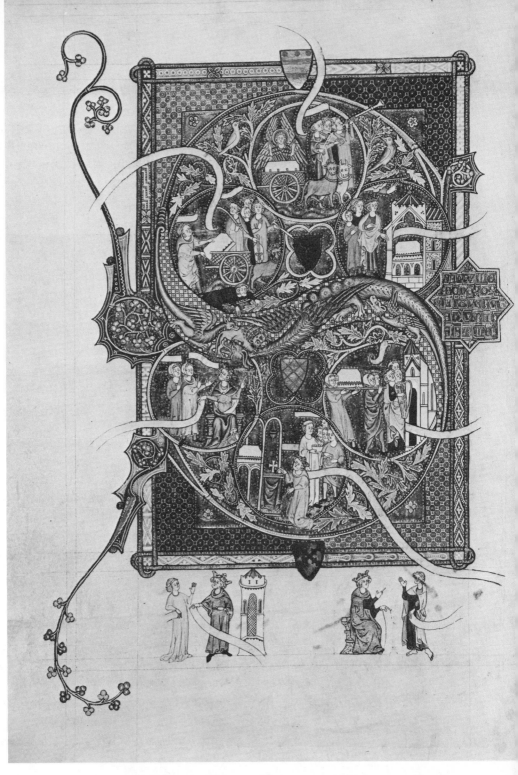

ILLUMINATION FROM THE TICKHILL PSALTER (14th century): *David transports the Ark to Jerusalem*

was Israel to give this great God that worship which would acknowledge His majesty?

The Deuteronomists asked Israel to worship by prayer and by
word. For the Priests, the supreme act of worship consisted in
sacrifice, by making over as gifts to God the most precious things
that man possessed. Hence an elaborate system of sacrifices is set
out in the "Law of Sacrifice" (Lev. 1-7).

The basic idea of sacrifice in ancient Israel was that, by destruction, a thing was transferred from "this world" (where man
might use it) to "that other world" where God would receive it.
There is a parallel here in the customs of certain ancient societies
of Egypt and Mesopotamia. When a highly placed person such as
a king died, several of his servants and animals were killed and
buried with him (along with food and utensils), so that by their
destruction they might be transferred to the realm beyond the
grave and there continue to be of use to him. Though this custom
was not followed in Israel, the underlying notion of destroying
animals so that they might "pass over" into the realm of the
divine is essentially the same.

A second concept must also be mentioned. It was taken for
granted in the ancient Near East that, in order to secure a great
man's favor, he should be approached with gifts. Such gifts would
make his face "light up" (as we would say) or "shine upon" the
one who sought his favour. Hence the Israelite who came to
entreat God's favor would approach the sanctuary with a gift, and
(since it was commonly believed that the gift of blood was pecul-
iarly pleasing to Him, for it betokened a *total* giving) the gift
would often be a beast just slaughtered.

And yet a third notion was sometimes involved in sacrifice. In
the so-called "communion-sacrifice" the flesh of the victim was
divided between Yahweh, the priests, the offerer himself, and his
family. The abdominal fat and (with sheep) the fat tail were
simply burnt, because they were regarded as the choicest parts,
and therefore to be given to Yahweh (Lev. 3:3-5). One breast and
one thigh were given to the priests, who by accepting it, accepted
it on behalf of Yahweh. The remainder was shared by the offerer

and his family, who received back their gift from Yahweh as a token that He was well pleased with their offering. Such communion sacrifices were made as a visible expression of praise or thanksgiving, sometimes simply out of devotion and at other times in fulfillment of a vow. But they all had the same fundamental purpose: to express and to intensify the bond of union and love between Yahweh and His people.

Finally, we must mention sacrifices offered in expiation of sin. When such a sacrifice was offered to expiate the sin of the entire people, or of the high priest, the whole offering was burnt; when it was offered for the sin of an individual, he himself received no share, but the priests received a portion. The rules for these sacrifices are set out in Leviticus 4:1-7:10.

RITES OF PURIFICATION

Israel's response to Yahweh, therefore, consisted mainly, according to the Priestly writers, in seeking ever closer union by sacrifices. And because the union was achieved by taking things from "this profane world" into "that other world where Yahweh dwells," those who sought to offer sacrifice had to take every possible precaution to ensure that they were undefiled by anything profane. That is why the book of Leviticus devotes so much space to prescribing rules about ritual purity. Death and the first symptom of man's mortality, disease, were alien to the Lord of life: therefore anyone who had been in contact with a corpse was debarred for a while from the sphere of the holy, and (characteristically) the Aaronite priests were forbidden ever to incur this defilement except when a member of their immediate family had died (Lev. 21:1–3). But the high priest himself was forbidden to touch the dead bodies of his own parents (Lev. 21:10ff.). Similar laws are laid down about contact with lepers, with unclean beasts, and even about the use of sex. The theme is always the same: that which is "of this world" must be kept at a distance from that which is holy.

We need not go into detail about these rites of purification, for enough has been said to illustrate the dominant theme in the

SAMARITAN CHIEF PRIEST, *leaning on staff, and eating the Passover sacrifice on Mount Gerizim*

Priestly source of the Pentateuch. Israel is holy to the Lord, chosen by Him, loved by Him; and the vocation of Israel is to remain steadfast in loyalty, resisting the allurements of the magnificent liturgies of Babylon, and remembering that the Lord will one day restore to its former glory that earthly sanctuary of Jerusalem. "His anger will not last forever."

THUS WAS THE PENTATEUCH FORMED

During or after the Babylonian exile, the Priests who collected and edited this version of Israel's history took over the ancient history books of their people — the Yahwist, the Elohist, and the Deuteronomic versions — and incorporated them into their own scheme. No doubt a number of versions were made, the later ones adding supplements to the earlier editions; and thus the Pentateuch as we know it was formed. It must have been completed in its present form by 400 B.C., for by that time the Samaritans were already regarded as a sect apart from official Judaism, and they accepted the Pentateuch as we have it. Some scholars would dispute this argument, but it is fairly safe to say that no significant additions were made after this date.

The Theology of Second Isaiah

"Comfort, comfort my people, says your God. Speak tenderly to Jerusalem, and cry to her that her 'forced service' is ended, that her iniquity is pardoned, that she has received from the hand of Yahweh double [punishment] for all her sins" (Is. 40:1-2). With these words the second part of the book of Isaiah (chapters 40-55) open. It is nowadays acknowledged by all that these chapters were written by an anonymous prophet (commonly referred to as Second Isaiah) living in Babylonia just before the end of the Exile (537 B.C.). Cyrus, the king of Persia, was sweeping victoriously through country after country, and the end of Babylon was clearly in sight. In the words of the prophet "victory greeted Cyrus at every step he took" (Is. 41:2), and the coming of the Persians brought deliverance and humane government to many subject nations.

THE HOME-COMING FROM BABYLON

The prophet, therefore, was profoundly certain that he and his people were standing at the threshold of a new age, an age in which Israel would know Yahweh's *everlasting* love (Is. 54:8), his *everlasting* salvation (Is. 45:17) and *everlasting* joy (Is. 51:11). Yahweh was about to set His irrevocable seal on a new covenant, a covenant of peace (Is. 54:9-10).

The prophet, reflecting on past history, declares that Yahweh has not merely foretold everything: He also *caused* it: "The former things I declared of old, they went forth from my mouth and I made them known; then suddenly I did them and they came to pass" (Is. 48:3). This is a warning to Israel not to be deceived into thinking that the idols of Babylon had for a time gained the mastery over Yahweh: He who had decreed the Exile, had now decreed their return: "Arise, O captive Jerusalem! Loose the bonds from your neck, O captive daughter of Zion" (Is. 52:2). The idols of Babylon were worthless blocks of metal and wood, representing nothing: there was no being in the "other world" to which they corresponded.

Cyrus, the conqueror of Babylon and liberator of God's people, was to a limited but real extent Yahweh's anointed one; he was the Lord's chosen representative in a far more positive sense than was Nebuchadnezzar, who, as Yahweh's agent, had punished Judah fifty years before. It was Yahweh who had raised him up (Is. 44:28), guided him by his right hand (Is. 45:1), led him to tear down the gates of Babylon (Is. 41:2-3, 25; 45:2; 48:14), to issue an order for the rebuilding of Jerusalem (Is. 44:28), and to send the exiles home (Is. 45:13).

In ancient times Yahweh had fought against the Gentiles to deliver His people from Egypt. Now a still more glorious exodus was in prospect: Yahweh leading His people home without battle. In lyrical ecstasy the prophet pictures the home-coming as a new Exodus, not through the sea but over the desert, along a highway from which all obstacles have been removed (Is. 40:3-4; 49:11), where darkness has been turned into light (Is. 42:16) and streams and springs have made the desert into a garden (Is. 41:18-19). Indeed, nature itself (represented by the mountains, hills, and trees) is presented as singing for joy at the return of the exiles to Zion (Is. 55:12–13), for this new Exodus was not a hurried flight from deadly enemies, but a solemn festal procession to the earthly home of God in Jerusalem (Is. 52:11–12).

The triumphant journey home would, the prophet proclaimed, force the Gentiles to recognize the God of Israel, and to reverence His people. "They will make supplication to you, saying: 'God is with you only, and there is no other, no god besides him'" (Is. 45:14). Indeed, the farthest countries of the world would see His law as " . . . a light to the peoples" (Is. 51:4), and seek salvation

Grand Pretre

קדש ליהוה
Lame
Sainte

ARTIST'S CONCEPTION OF A HIGH
PRIEST

from Him alone. "The coastlands wait for me, and for my arm
they hope" (Is. 51:5). So Israel would achieve its destiny as
Yahweh's witness (Is. 41:10; 44:8), servant (41:9; 42:18ff.), and
mediator to the Gentiles (Is. 45:14).

And all this had been achieved by Yahweh's word alone. Compared with that word, the power of all the empires on earth was as
flimsy and transient as the grass or flowers which wither away
under the sun. "The grass withers, the flower fades . . . but the
word of our God will stand forever" (Is. 40:6–8). Time and time
again we read in Isaiah 40–55 that Yahweh speaks a word, and the
effect follows—inevitably, because He is the creator of the world,
the first and the last. "Before me no god was formed, nor shall
there be any after me. I am Yahweh" (Is. 43:10–11).

The Elohist and the Deuteronomists had described Yahweh's
presence among His people as a presence through His name and

word. The Priestly tradition had presented it rather in terms of a visible manifestation of His glory. But during the exile there was no Ark containing the words of the Lord, no temple in which His glory was physically present. And so Second Isaiah had to ask himself how Yahweh could be present to His people far away from the Promised Land, beside the rivers of Babylon. For it was all too evident that the people might think their God had abandoned them in their distress.

With an originality of thought that is unique even in the old Testament, Second Isaiah summoned his fellow-Israelites to hope for a future even more glorious than anything they had known. He tells them that the deliverance from Babylon will be an event even more astounding than the Exodus from Egypt, that the rebuilding of Zion will be like a new creation (Is. 43:15-21; 44:23-28; 45:1-13). Previously, the Israelites had tended to worship Yahweh as the God who was master of their nation's history; Second Isaiah tells them bluntly that He is master of the destinies of *all* the nations of the world. He brings one age of history to an end, as He had put an end to the history of Assyria in 612 B.C., to the history of the kingdom of Judah in 587 B.C., and to Babylon in 538 B.C. And by the same token, He initiates a fresh age. Therefore the prophet looked forward to a "new age" in which the God of Israel would make all things new.

As Lord of all time, then, Yahweh is uniquely transcendent. Elsewhere in the Old Testament, this transcendence of God is pictured (so to speak) spatially and vertically: He looks down upon creation from a remote dwelling-place high up in the heavens. This image of God "in heaven above" is not foreign to Second Isaiah, for he tells us that Yahweh sits "above the circle of the earth" and looks down on its inhabitants like grasshoppers (Is. 40:22). But the prophet tends rather to express the transcendence of God in a "horizontal" image of the flow of time. Yahweh is "the first and the last." He *was there* before creation began, and He *will be there* after it has ceased. It is in this concept of "before" and "after" that Yahweh's distance from all creation is most fully expressed. He is "the Eternal."

A VIEW OF THE EUPHRATES RIVER, *from a palm grove, in Iraq*

THE BEGINNINGS OF ESCHATOLOGY

Second Isaiah foretells that a new age of everlasting peace is about to come to Israel. In earlier prophecies, and especially in Deuteronomy, Israel had been confronted with a choice: *either* to obey Yahweh and live, *or* to disobey Him and die. " . . . I have set before you life or death, blessing and curse. Therefore choose life that you and your descendants may live" (Deut. 30:19). By its sin Israel had chosen the path of death, but now that the time of its punishment was over, God was again offering life. Second Isaiah has, in effect, changed the "either-or" of Deuteronomy into a "before-after."

It has been plausibly argued that it was precisely this change from an "either-or" religion to a "before-after" faith which was the root of Old Testament eschatology. For it is here in Second Isaiah that we first encounter the idea of two successive ages radically distinct from each other, in which the second "new" age is incomparably more glorious than the first. Israel's history had told of the first creation, and of the first great act of redemption at the Exodus; but (according to Second Isaiah) the second creation and the second redemption were to be still more astounding. For in the new age the blessings of law, justice, and deliverance would no longer be confined to Israel, but would extend to the Gentiles also (Is. 51:4–5): they were to share in the salvation of Israel (Is. 51:8). Israel would indeed remain the first of many nations, the teacher of the world, but the whole of mankind would pronounce it blessed for the lessons it had taught the world about the God of heaven and earth (Is. 45:14).

As a summary of Second Isaiah's message, therefore, we might suggest this. Yahweh is about to use His vast wisdom, skill, and power as Creator to inaugurate a new and permanent age, in which He will create a new world order, where the Gentiles will be happy to serve and adore the God of Israel. Cyrus is His chosen instrument to initiate this work. And the realization that all past prophecies (both of woe and of ultimate redemption) have been fulfilled is a sure guarantee that the "new things" also, now declared for the first time, will most surely come to pass.

The Suffering Servant of the Lord

It is now universally recognized that four of the most important passages in Second Isaiah are poems or "songs" composed independently of the rest of Isaiah 40-55, and later interpolated into this part of the book. The four poems are: Isaiah 42:1-4; 49:1-6; 50:4-9; 52:13-53:12; and they are all concerned with a "Servant of Yahweh." Many interpretations have been put forward, and not everyone would agree with the interpretation suggested here. But no discussion of the great theologians of the Old Testament would be complete without some treatment of these texts, for they play a crucial part in the understanding of the New Testament.

THE SERVANT AS A PROPHET SUFFERING FOR THE PEOPLE

The description of the Servant and of his mission represents a fusion and a development of several distinct themes. First, the Servant does seem, by his vocation and mission, to be portrayed as a *prophet*. The title "Servant of Yahweh" is used elsewhere in the Old Testament of prophets, particularly with reference to Moses and to David. This itself indicates that the "Servant" mentioned in Second Isaiah has a prophetic role, a Mosaic role, and a messianic or Davidic role.

The Servant, as a prophet, meets the fate of so many prophets. Like Elijah, he was to undergo suffering and rejection in the course of his ministry (1 Kings 19:2ff.); like Jeremiah, he was mocked and persecuted by those to whom he was sent (Is. 50:6; 53:3-5; Jer. 11:19; 20:7-8). Like Jeremiah, he was consecrated for his office from his mother's womb (Is. 49:1, 5; Jer. 1:5), and in his failure and despondency looked to Yahweh alone for vindication (Is. 49:4; 50:7-9; 53:12; Jer. 11:20; 18:19ff.; 20:7, 12). So impressive are these similarities that several authors have argued that the poems actually refer to Jeremiah.

There is, however, a most significant difference. In the prophecies of Jeremiah, the fact of the prophet's sufferings is stated, but not explained, while in the Servant Songs the meaning of this suffering is carefully elaborated as a *positive element* in Yahweh's plan for the redemption of mankind. And to explain the worth of these sufferings, the author has recourse to concepts and expressions which are undoubtedly derived from a context of worship. For instance, it had been prescribed in the Law that the priests should "bear the iniquity of Israel" (Num. 18:1, 23); and the priest Ezekiel himself undertook to "bear the iniquities of the house of Israel and of the house of Judah" (Ezek. 4:4). The Servant, too, is said to "bear the iniquity" of those to whom he is sent (Is. 53:11).

Again, in the law of worship it was commanded that the priests

KING DAVID, *an illumination from fifteenth-century Psalter for Cistercian use*

should make sin-offerings on behalf of their fellow-Israelites (Lev. 5:14-16). The Servant himself becomes a "sin-offering" on behalf of the Gentiles who have offended God (Is. 53:10). Thus what the priests accomplished by their ritual offerings of animals on behalf of the chosen people, the Servant accomplishes by his own personal righteousness on behalf of the whole world.

THE SERVANT AS A NEW MOSES AND A NEW DAVID

A second strand of tradition woven into the poems is the Mosaic theme. Like Moses, the Servant is sent by Yahweh to convey not merely a prophetic message, but a message of justice (Is. 42:1, 3,4), that is, to proclaim right religion both in worship and in morality, as we read in Isaiah 49:6 and 53:11. Like Moses, he is "to re-establish the tribes of Jacob" (Is. 49:5-6). Like Moses, he is a mediator between Yahweh and those to whom he is sent, speaking to them for Yahweh, and interceding for them, suffering on their account and dying prematurely because of their sins (*compare* Deut. 3:23ff.; 4:21-22; 9:18ff., 25ff.).

But this is not his only role. It has frequently been observed that the Servant is presented as a royal, and perhaps even as a messianic, figure. Thus he is described as "a young plant . . . a root" (Is. 53:2), metaphors which are very close indeed to those used of the stock or stump of Jesse in Isaiah 11:1. Again, when we read that " . . . he shall prolong his days . . . he shall divide the spoil" (Is. 53:12), we are inevitably led to think of the messianic king triumphant in battle.

More specifically, the description of the Servant runs extremely close to the descriptions of the Messiah in Isaiah chapter 7 and in chapter 9 where the future king is called a "Wonderful Counsellor." The Servant's task is essentially that of a "Wonderful Counsellor," implementing Yahweh's plan or counsel, bringing forth true judgment and law, and establishing it – by peaceful means – among the Gentiles (Is. 42:3-4); *compare* 9:6). And therefore Yahweh bestows His spirit on the Servant, as on the Counsellor (Is. 42:1, 11:2), so that he may be a light to the Gentiles, opening the eyes of the blind (Is. 42:7; 8:23–9:1). The Servant, by his preaching, would " . . . bring out prisoners from the dungeon, and those that sit in the darkness from the prison house" (Is. 42:7), just as the messianic King was to break " . . . the yoke of his burden, the staff on his shoulder, the rod of his oppressor" (Is. 9:3). But whereas the messianic King would bring the gift of freedom by breaking the yoke, the Servant would achieve his mission by more peaceful means, by carrying their griefs and sorrows as his own burden (Is. 53:11). The achievement would be the same, the means very different.

It can be seen that many of the functions attributed before the Exile to the messianic King have been transferred, by Second Isaiah, to this primarily prophetic figure, the Servant of the Lord. Several strands of tradition are here woven into one fabric, and the pattern alters. It is no longer a question of an Israelite warrior-king dominating the Gentiles, but of a poor and humble and suffering prophet being acclaimed by the Gentiles. As a new

Moses, he brings God's law and religion not to one people only, but to all the nations of the world; as a new David, he conquers them not by the sword but by the words of his mouth; and like a new Solomon, he is the "Wonderful Counsellor" of a universal empire of peace.

The Theology of the Wisdom Books

We turn now to the last era of Old Testament theology – that represented by the Wisdom books (chiefly Job, Proverbs, Ecclesiastes or Qoheleth, and the deutero-canonical books of Wisdom and Ecclesiasticus). It is notoriously difficult to give a single theme which would show forth the unity of thought inherent in these books. We may commence, however, with the suggestion that "wisdom" is the *knowledge which gives control*, using this notion in the widest possible sense.

What is wisdom?

At one extreme, the word "wisdom" is used to denote the omniscience of God which enabled Him to create, and which enables Him to control all that exists in heaven and earth. At the other extreme, the word is used for that "worldly wisdom" which enables a man to control his environment and his circumstances, living in peace and harmony with his fellowmen, and avoiding what is evil.

But the word has many other meanings in the Bible, and includes all the following senses. (1) It is used for what we would call *cunning*, the capacity to outwit others, whether this cunning is used to trick others dishonestly (as Jacob tricked Esau, Gen. 27) or from highly commendable motives (as the Hebrew midwives tricked the Egyptians, Ex. 1:16-21). (2) It is used for *craftsmanship*, that skill with materials which was so evident in those who constructed the tabernacle and the temple (Ex.

THE RIVER JORDAN, *an aerial view looking north from above the Allenby Bridge*

35:30-36:1; 1 Chr. 22:15). (3) It is applied to *administrative skill and foresight* such as Joseph showed in Egypt (Gen. 41: 47-49). (4) It also means that *knowledge of religious and moral principles* which lead to a virtuous (and therefore happy) life for the individual. This is the idea which predominates in the Wisdom books of the Old Testament. (5) *Esoteric knowledge of revealed truth*, especially of the Law, is also called "wisdom," for by such knowledge a man can live according to God's will. (6) Arising out of this is *the ability to judge all earthly things* like suffering, death, the prosperity of the wicked, and the feebleness of man in the light of eternity.

One of the basic axioms of wisdom theology is that the good life leads to happiness, and the evil life to misery. To live a good life is therefore wise, to live an evil life is folly. And yet perhaps the basic problem of human existence is that in practice this principle is constantly belied. This is the problem with which the Wisdom books are mainly concerned.

WISDOM AS THE GIFT OF GOD

If the description of wisdom given above really penetrated the concept to its inmost depths, then the authors of the Wisdom books might reasonably be accused of a shallow utilitarianism. This is, in fact, exactly the impression which a superficial reading of this literature conveys. The notion, however, reaches much deeper, for the controlling theme is that God Himself has imposed upon the entire universe a certain harmony and order. Creation was planned by the eternal wisdom of God before it was made (Prov. 8:22-31): nature and history, and the moral and social laws proclaimed by God are meant to regulate everything in proper order.

The Old Testament writers repeatedly insist that there is a parallel between the physical order of creation and the moral order to be observed by man. This accounts for the frequent parallels between natural phenomena and moral behavior. For instance, in Proverbs 25:23 we read: "The rain is born of the north wind; the ravaged face of a backbiting tongue," and in Proverbs 26:20: "No wood, and the fire goes out; no tale-bearer, and the quarrelling dies down." The task of the wise man, therefore, is to see that every detail of his moral behavior corresponds with that harmony of creation which God has made. Such wisdom is, of course, a gift and grace bestowed by God (Prov. 3:13ff.), and it is normally imparted to men through a counsellor or teacher who has already, by humble study and prayer, learned the ways of the Lord.

From the time of the Exile onwards, wisdom becomes increasingly identified with the Law, which is presented as an infinitely superior alternative to the secular "philosophies" of the

JOSEPH INTERPRETING PHARAOH'S DREAM
Lazzaro Bastiani

Gentiles, the product of merely human minds. In the introduction
to Deuteronomy (a part which was prefixed to the book after the
Exile), the people are exhorted to observe the Law on the grounds
that it ". . . will be your wisdom and your understanding in the
sight of the peoples, who, when they hear all these statutes, will
say: 'Surely this great nation is a wise and understanding people'"
(Deut. 4:6). This identification of wisdom with the Law is carried
much further in the writings of Jesus the son of Sirach (Ecclesiasticus). Thus, immediately after the long discourse of
Wisdom personified (Ecclus. 24:1-31) we read: "All these things
are the book of life, and the covenant of the Most High, and the
knowledge of truth" (Ecclus. 24:31).

PROVERBS AND JOB

It is in the Wisdom books (and especially in Proverbs) that the
Old Testament reveals most clearly how deeply Israel was influ-

enced by its neighbors. Egypt and Mesopotamia, Phoenicia and Canaan all produced more or less similar literature, and the author of Proverbs drew liberally upon these foreign sources. Thus the rather primitive notion of wisdom as "cunning" (such as we find in the stories of Jacob and Samson, Judg. 14-16) was gradually replaced by a more sophisticated concept.

The dominant influence here was undoubtedly that of Egypt. We have already remarked (in writing of the Yahwist) that from the time of Solomon, Egyptian influence and culture began to be felt in Israel. The development of trade with Phoenicia and Canaan no doubt made its effect felt also; and then the people came into daily contact with the Babylonians, and finally with the Persians and the Greeks. All these foreign cultures had a contribution to make to civilization, and Israel tried to absorb from each of them all that could be reconciled with, or made positively to contribute to Israel's own indigenous faith.

So collections of proverbial sayings were made, many of which seem intended for the upbringing of boys and young men, if we may judge by the frequent use of the phrase "My son." The outlook and the attitude of the speaker is that of an older and more experienced man teaching the young and immature about the pitfalls of life and warning them to be on guard against what seems superficially attractive. Thus the natural experience of age and maturity is presented as "the teaching of the Lord" to guide the young along the right paths.

The type of society envisaged is almost invariably a monarchy, and warnings are issued even to the king (Prov. 16:10, 12; 31:4). Most of the teaching, however, is directed to the ordinary citizen, who is exhorted to flee from pride, avarice, lust, adultery, anger, and sloth. The choice of friends, and above all of a good wife (Prov. 31:10-31), is a matter of particular concern. A wife should be chosen not for her beauty but for her wisdom; children should be well-disciplined and well instructed, for their own future happiness. Servants should not be pampered or spoiled, but should most certainly be well cared for. In regulating his life with this divinely-given wisdom, a man will find happiness and true peace.

Bas relief of Mede carrying vase, *dated about 400 b.c.*

Yet the plain fact is that a virtuous life does not always and inevitably lead to happiness. This is the problem discussed in the book of Job.

Although important differences can be discerned in the arguments of Job's three friends, still (as a group) they are trying to uphold the justice of God's providence by stating the old, conventional ideas of Israel. Their arguments rest on two basic axioms. The first is that good deeds lead to happiness, and that misfortune can only be the result of sin. The second is that when a man finds himself in distress, he has only to repent of his sins, acknowledge his guilt, and plead for forgiveness; then God will surely hear his prayer and rescue him. The friends simply apply these axioms to the case of Job: they are the champions of the conventional attitude.

Job's speeches, on the other hand, represent a radical questioning of this point of view. What he yearns for is not forgiveness or deliverance, but death (Job 3:21-22; 6:9; 7:16; 9:21) or (alternatively) the chance of a confrontation with God (though he recognizes the futility of this desire). He seems to argue with confidence that if he could somehow meet God "on equal terms," he would win the argument! It is clear that Job's longing to "take God to court" (Job 13:3ff.; 16:18ff.; 19:23ff., and especially chapter 31) is the direct opposite of that patient acceptance of punishment and confession of guilt which orthodoxy prescribed. He persists in protesting that he is innocent, that to admit guilt would be hypocrisy and lies, and he calls confidently on God as though He was the avenger in a blood-feud, with a sacred duty to exact requital for injuries done to a friend or relative (Job 16-17). Indeed, he even summons God to be a witness or advocate defending him against his friends and against unjust condemnation by future ages (Job 19).

A BASIC FALLACY

Now it is clear that behind the arguments of the friends and of Job there lies a single basic fallacy. Both sides assume that "just treatment" is something readily comprehensible to man, and that God's actions (as well as those of men) can be measured by human

JOB AND HIS FRIENDS, *sculpture on a tomb in the crypt of St. Peter's in Rome*

standards. It is as though "justice" were an abstract ideal circumscribing the actions of God Himself, a norm by which God could be judged. Thus both the friends and Job fail to realize that to men the mind of God must remain eternally a mystery. Their sense of "holiness," of God's "complete otherness," has failed at a crucial point.

This explains the apparently irrelevant answer which God makes to Job in chapters 38-41. Job wants an answer to the question "How can my sufferings be reconciled with your justice?" God does not answer this question, but instead demands to know by what right Job dare challenge Him to argue the case. Hence a major element in the reply of God is the ironic invitation to Job to have his wish, and to enter into a legal argument: "Gird up your loins like a man, I will question you, and you shall declare to me" (Job 38:3).

God's ironic question to Job asks whether he, with his human wisdom and power, can produce anything to match the immensity of God's works, of that creation which is a manifestation of divine wisdom and divine power. True wisdom never diminishes man's sense of the divine; on the contrary, it enhances it, and makes a man genuinely humble. To demand an explanation of God's ways is to say goodby to the essential attitude of a creature before its creator: humble love and loyal faith. The purpose of God's answer to Job, therefore, is to re-awaken in him the sense of the divine, to show him the insolence of calling into question God's ways. Basically, it is the same answer that St. Paul gives to the same question: "Is there injustice on God's part ? . . . But who are you, man, to answer back to God: Will what is molded say to its molder, 'Why have you made me thus?' " (Rom. 9:14, 20). Job, too, is brought to realize that his questioning of God springs not from wisdom, but from a false substitute for wisdom, a spurious "enlightenment" which makes him expect to understand God's ways, and makes him indignant when he cannot.

The book of Ecclesiastes

The problem which confronted the author of Job was also the problem which worried the "Preacher," the writer of Ecclesiastes (Qoheleth). How *does* one reconcile human suffering with the justice of God? The conventional answer that men receive their deserts in this life is daily contradicted by experience: "In my vain life I have seen everything; there is a righteous man who perishes in his righteousness, and there is a wicked man who prolongs his life in evil-doing" (Eccles. 7:15).

Job had tried to understand why he was suffering. The Preacher tried to work out, from his experience, in what human happiness consisted. In a deliberate and controlled exploration of all possible sources of happiness (Eccles. 2), he finally concludes that all is vanity, that all human happiness and enjoyment is so limited and transient that it can never satisfy the heart of man. The pursuit of earthly pleasures is empty delusion.

This is true even of wisdom itself, in acquiring which the author has spent his life. Even this, he now realizes, is futile, "for in much wisdom there is much vexation, and he who increases knowledge increases sorrow" (Eccles. 1:18). This is chiefly be-

VIEW OF THE JORDAN AND
THE PROMISED LAND, *from
the heights of Moab*

cause the amount of wisdom that can be acquired in a lifetime of
study is so fragmentary and incomplete: "I said, 'I will be wise,'
but it was far from me. That which is, is far off and deep, very deep,
who can find it out?" (Eccles. 7:23-24). It is also because fools and
wise men alike have the same destiny—death: "one fate comes
to all" (Eccles. 9:3).

Yet even the limited amount of wisdom which man can achieve
is infinitely preferable to folly. "Wisdom excels folly as light
excels darkness. The wise man has eyes in his head, but the fool
walks in darkness" (Eccles. 2:13-14). For the essence of wisdom
lies in the recognition of man's limitations, that he cannot comprehend the work of God (Eccles. 8:17).

It is precisely this negative recognition of man's limitations
that prepares the way for the Preacher's ultimate declaration of
absolute faith in God: "I know that I cannot comprehend," he
seems to be saying, "nevertheless, I believe." In spite of God's
incomprehensible ways, the author firmly trusts that his God is

just in the end: "Though a sinner does evil a hundred times and prolongs his life, yet I know that it will be well with those who fear God.... But it will not be well with the wicked ... because he does not fear God" (Eccles. 8:12-13). In default of any positive doctrine of a life beyond the grave, this is the highest happiness attainable by man on this earth.

THE BOOK OF WISDOM

We may pass over the book of Ecclesiasticus, for it contributes very little that is not found in earlier sources, and its author is content to recommend to those seeking wisdom the study of the ancient traditions of Israel. We come, then, to the last book (in time) of the Old Testament, the Wisdom of Solomon, which was written in Greek at Alexandria around 50 B.C.

As might be expected, a book written in Greek in Alexandria at that time was bound to be profoundly colored by Platonic thought. Thus the idea (deriving from Plato) that the soul was imprisoned in the body lies behind much of its philosophy; and the consequence of this was a firm belief in the immortality of the soul after the death of the body: "The souls of the righteous are in the hand of God ... they are in peace ... their hope is rich with immortality" (Wis. 3:1, 3, 4).

This writer, then, firmly believed in the survival of the soul after death: in that after-life the righteous would be united with God in everlasting happiness, while the wicked would be cast from His presence into eternal misery. On the basis of this belief he finds it comparatively easy to resolve the problem of evil, which had so perplexed the author of Job and all others who had no clear ideas about retribution in the after-life. For the author of Wisdom, the sufferings of the righteous constitute a brief period of testing, after which those whom God has proved worthy of Himself are admitted to His presence for all eternity (Wis. 3:5ff.). Even the case of those who die prematurely is explained on similar grounds: "He has been carried off so that evil may not warp his understanding or treachery seduce his soul" (Wis. 4:11).

However, it is important not to exaggerate the influence of Greek thought on this writer. The central part of his book is deliberately and intensely traditional—a long meditation on the wonders of salvation as recorded in the Bible (chapters 10-19). For the author, true wisdom is practically identified with God Himself, for it is "a breath of the power of God, the pure emanation of the glory of the Almighty . . . a reflection of eternal light, an untarnished mirror of God's active power, an image of his goodness" (Wis. 7:25-26).

LOOKING TO THE FUTURE

The book of Deuteronomy pictures Moses standing on the frontier of the Promised Land, looking out across the Jordan towards the country of his dreams—the country of the future. And as we conclude this study of the great theologians of the Old Testament, it is not fanciful to see the author of Wisdom as standing on the frontier of a new age, looking to the future. Like all his predecessors in the Old Testament, his eyes were fixed on "the God of our fathers" who had been faithful to every promise throughout the ages. Very soon, that same God who had spoken in many fragmentary and varying utterances to their fathers through the prophets, would speak to them the final message of salvation through His Son.

Kingdom and Messiah

Dermot Ryan

In His preaching Jesus proclaimed that "the kingdom of God is at hand"; He told Pilate, "I am a king." What did He mean? To answer this question we must, first, understand the various implications "king" and "kingdom" had for the people Jesus preached to, His contemporaries, who were schooled in the language of the Old Testament. Secondly, we must understand that, while making use of Old Testament language and ideas, Jesus purified and perfected the expectation of the Old Law and inaugurated God's reign in the New.

King David
Bernardo Ciuffagni

Patriarchs and Kings

In Mark's Gospel (1:15) Jesus opens His preaching with the proclamation: "The kingdom of God is at hand." His very first words link Him with a kingdom. At a later stage in His public life, the crowds seeing His miracles wished "to take him by force to make him king." But "Jesus withdrew again to the hills by himself" (John 6:15). Yet when Pilate asked Him: "Are you the king of the Jews?" (John 18:37), Jesus replied: "I am a king" (John 18:37). What then is the meaning of "kingdom" on the lips of Jesus? In what sense is He a king? Why in fact did He choose to speak in such terms? In an age characterized by the diminishing popularity of kings, such questions demand an answer if Christ's message is not to be obscured; it might even seem irrelevant in the newly structured society of many modern states.

In search for answers, we must first recall that when Jesus spoke to His contemporaries, He aimed to make His message intelligible. There was, therefore, little point in inventing a totally new terminology to convey His meaning; it would be more a hindrance than a help. Since He spoke about God and religion, He used the current religious vocabulary of His fellow countrymen. He had learned it in His prayers at home and in the synagogue services, as well as in the temple at Jerusalem. It was, for the most part, the language of the Old Testament, the Sacred Scriptures or Bible of the Jews, and it is to it that we now turn for enlightenment. From its pages, we can learn the implications of "king" and "kingdom" in the religious vocabulary of Jesus' contemporaries, and, by contrast, appreciate what is new in the teaching of Jesus.

The patriarchs

The Jews have always looked on Abraham as their father (Is. 51:2). It was he who was called by God in the first instance to become the mediator of God's blessings, first to his own people and then to all mankind (cf. Gen. 12:1ff.; 17:4-5; 18:18, etc.). He lived about 1800 B.C. in a group which, by reason of the fact that they rarely stayed long in any one place, is usually described as semi-nomadic. Since this group was organized on a tribal basis, the patriarch, or eldest family head, exercised authority within the group. He was also the religious head who performed religious functions in the name of the tribe, even to the extent of offering sacrifice.

Since the life of this group centered on the rearing of cattle and sheep, their movements were determined by the availability of water and pastures. The resultant insecurity made the building of temples impracticable: men simply worshipped God where they happened to be — on mountains (Gen. 22), at wells (Gen. 21:33), or under the shade of a tree (Gen. 12:6) — and they addressed Him in terms of the tribal structure with which they were familiar. This practice is reflected in their proper names, which often included a reference to the divinity under the title of "father," "brother," "uncle." God was father, brother, and uncle to the tribe and its members.

DID THEY THINK OF GOD AS KING?

Did these people think of God as king? Since they were not ruled by kings, one might even ask if they thought of kings at all. Taking the second question first, it is clear from the Bible that the patriarchs moved in areas of the Middle East where monarchy was a well established institution. In travelling from Ur to Haran (Gen. 11:31–32), Abraham passed through Mesopotamia (the land between the two rivers, the Tigris and the Euphrates) where city states and limited empires had been ruled by kings for centuries before Abraham was born. The Bible recounts his conflict with the kings and his subsequent meeting with Melchizedek (Gen. 14), and his short visit to Egypt was said to have brought him into conflict with the Pharaoh (Gen. 12:10ff.).

The office of king was, then, nothing new in the Middle East of the patriarchs' period. They would have been familiar with the

EXCAVATION UNCOVERING TOMBS
IN THE CEMETERY AT UR

powerful monarchies of Egypt and Mesopotamia, as well as with
the less imposing kings of Palestine's city states. There is no clear
evidence, however, that they chose to use the title of king in the
worship of God. The intimate relationships of their tribal life provided a terminology which adequately expressed their intimacy
with God. Their use of the terms "father," "brother," "uncle" for
the divinity should not, however, leave the impression that God
for the patriarchs was no more than a distinguished member of
the family with no greater power than such a person might wield.
There is evidence that the patriarchs worshipped God under the
title of "Maker of heaven and earth," which implied an appreciation of the mastery which He exercised over the whole of creation. Of this, the descendants of Abraham would later have experience in Egypt.

Israel and the Exodus from Egypt

Israel's experience of monarchy in Egypt was initially a happy one, but they learned to regret the might of the Egyptian king and the absolute authority he exercised over his subjects. They were reduced to the level of slaves and were employed by the Pharaoh in his massive building projects (Ex. 1:8ff.). From their slavery and their sorrow, the Israelites called on the God of their fathers to help, "and God remembered his covenant with Abraham, with Isaac, and with Jacob" (Ex. 2:24f.). In the account of the plagues which led up to the departure of Israel from Egypt, one is left with the impression of a violent conflict between two kings with mighty forces at their disposal. As Lord of creation, Yahweh exercised a truly royal power on behalf of His people: He summoned His creatures to their aid, and, like a king at the head of His people (Ex. 13:21), He led them to safety.

Awareness of Yahweh as king

It is not surprising to find in this context an early expression of awareness on the part of Israel that Yahweh, her God, was truly her king. Although the snatch of lyric in Exodus 15:21 does not use the word "king," it commemorates Yahweh's triumph over Pharaoh in terms which reflect His royal dignity and power (*see* a similar chant in 1 Sam. 18:7). At a later stage in Israel's history, the ideas of this lyric cry were expanded in the chant of Exodus 15:1–18, which in verse 18 includes a more specific reference to Yahweh's royal rule. The Exodus gave Israel her first experience of Yahweh's effective control as He set about implementing His will for Israel and ultimately for mankind.

If modern scholars are right, yet another indication of Israel's realization that Yahweh was her king is implied in the covenant of Sinai which bound Israel to her God. In its simplest form, this covenant or agreement could be stated: "I shall be your God, and you shall be my people" (e.g., Lev. 26:12). But, in its more extended form, it contained references to the events which led up to the making of this agreement, details of the consequent obligations of the contracting parties, and a listing of curses and blessings to guarantee the implementation of the agreement. The agreement was ratified by various ceremonies (cf. Ex. 19-24; Deut. 5 and 27-28).

Similar features occur in treaties between Hittite kings and subject monarchs of the 15th century B.C. If, then, the covenant of Sinai is cast in the form of a royal treaty, it was as if Yahweh had rescued His people from Pharaoh to make them His own people. He now invited them to accept the terms under which they could enjoy the benefits of His rule. It was He who took the initiative, He who made the offer; He was the one who had something to give. If Israel wished to share in His love, they must keep the commandments which were the expression of His will (Ex. 20:5-6). Israel was being called to implement God's will that His reign might be established on earth.

ANCIENT ROYAL TREATIES AND THE TABLES OF THE LAW

The laws by which Yahweh declared His will for His people are similar in some respects to the law codes of great monarchs of Mesopotamia, like Lipit Ishtar (*ca.* 1865 B.C.), and Hammurabi (*ca.* 1728-1686 B.C.), which, like the ten commandments, were written on stone and have survived the hazards of the centuries. Like them, Yahweh wished to ensure peace and contentment for His people: it was only to be found in doing His will. Unlike these kings, however, Yahweh's rule was not limited to a kingdom, to a specific territory. His kingdom involved rather a royal care for the people that would do His will (cf. Ex. 19: 5-6).

The ancient royal treaties were usually deposited in the royal shrine as a constant reminder of the sacred obligations which had been contracted. In line with this tradition, the Israelites put

TABLET WITH PORTION OF THE CODE OF HAM-
MURABI: *"the first of the laws has not been known
before"*

the stone tables of the Law in an ornate chest which was variously
called "the Ark of the Covenant of Yahweh" (Num. 10:33), "the
Ark of the testimony [or commandments]" (Ex. 26:33), or simply,
"the Ark of the Covenant" (Josh. 3:6), and was located in the tent,
(Ex. 40:21; the Deuteronomic tradition does not connect the Ark
with the tent; such a connection is not, however, excluded by
the texts).

The Ark was not just a container for the tables of the Law; it
was also a symbol of the presence of Yahweh. He was, as it were,
enthroned on the cherubim, which rose above the Ark. The cherubim, part human and part animal, resembled the winged sphinxes
which sometimes flanked the thrones of ancient Oriental monarchs. Here they provide a throne for Yahweh, the king of Israel.

Although there is some difficulty in dating the texts, there is little doubt that the Ark was already a symbol of the kingship of Yahweh before monarchy was introduced into Israel (cf. de Vaux, *Ancient Israel*, pp. 297ff.).

In all this work, Moses was the chosen representative of Yahweh, exercising authority in His name and mediating between Him and the people. Yet at no stage in the account of the Exodus is he given the title of king, nor is there any record of any wish on the part of the people to make him king. Circumstances, however, would change and new experiences would suggest that Israel might benefit from such a ruler.

The Monarchy

On their way from Egypt through Transjordania, the Israelites met with resistance from the kings of the Edomites, the Moabites, and the Ammonites. Nor were they allowed to forget the effectiveness of these leaders during the period which followed the conquest of the Promised Land. The Canaanites still controlled the plains, the highways, and several great fortress cities, so that the tribes of Israel were often isolated, one from the other, and were forced to bear the brunt of attacks from their enemies without much help from their friends. The Moabites (Judg. 3:12ff.), the Canaanites (Judg. 4:2ff.), the Midianites (Judg. 6:1ff.), the Ammonites (Judg. 11:4ff.), and the Philistines (Judg. 13:1ff.) in their turn afflicted Israel. To meet the crisis in each case, God raised up a special leader on whom God's spirit rested (cf. Judg. 6:34; 11:29, etc.). They were given the title of "judge" although their role was rather that of a military leader.

These charismatic leaders tend to pass from the pages of biblical history when the time of crisis has come and gone. Called as they were to deal with a localized disturbance, they showed no great eagerness to build on their success whether by founding

Samson Slaying the Philistine, *a bronze by*
Baccio Bandinelli

a dynasty or by extending their control over neighboring tribes. There was, however, an exception: the book of Judges records the attempt of Abimelech, the son of Gideon, a judge, to win acceptance as king; it also describes his ignominious end (Judg. 9). As yet, Israel was unwilling to have a king, a situation of which both Gideon (Judg. 8:23) and Jotham had a better understanding than the foolhardy Abimelech. The attitude of Jotham is recorded in the first parable in the Bible (Judg. 9:7-20).

THE REQUEST FOR A KING

During the 11th century B.C., the Philistines were the source of greatest danger to the Israelite tribes, as is clear from the exploits of Samson (Judg. 13–16) and the conflicts recorded in the early chapters (4-7) of 1 Samuel. The failure of the sons of Samuel to reproduce the virtues of their aging father (1 Sam. 8:1-3) accentuated the weakness of Israel at a time when she should act in unison. Lack of stable authority gave free reign to the forces of disorder: "In those days there was no king in Israel; every man did what was right in his own eyes" (Judg. 17:6). In this situation, the elders of Israel approached Samuel with the request: "Appoint for us a king to govern us like all the nations" (1 Sam. 8:5).

The observant reader may find chapters 8-12 of 1 Samuel a little disconcerting. Obviously their purpose is to tell how Israel came to have a king, but the story is told with what seems to be little regard for consistency. One group of texts (9:1-10:16; 11) favors the introduction of the monarchy, while another (8; 10:17-27; 12) is opposed to it. Here it is not possible to consider in detail the problems created by the juxtaposition of these texts, but the way the author of Samuel has interwoven the two accounts which he found in his sources shows us his readiness to admit that from the start, there was a difference of opinion about the advantages of monarchy, particularly in the context of Israel's worship of Yahweh. In passing, it may be noted that neither account is complete; they may reflect different stages in the introduction of monarchy and can be used to complement one another. In any event, on a number of important points they are in agreement.

THE KING IS YAHWEH'S CHOSEN REPRESENTATIVE

Both accounts leave no doubt that Yahweh was the real king in Israel; the human king was His chosen representative, in one case, granted grudgingly (cf. 1 Sam. 8:7-22), in the other, selected by divine initiative (1 Sam. 9:16-10:16). In the latter case, a divine reservation is entered through the emphasis on Israel's remaining Yahweh's people: "You shall anoint him to be prince over *my* people Israel...he shall save *my* people....It is he who shall rule over *my* people" (1 Sam. 9:16-17).

Although the king was Yahweh's chosen representative on earth and was charged with the care of His people, he could make no claim to divine sonship as the Egyptian monarchs did, nor could he become a law unto himself. He was a member of the covenant people and bound by their obligations to Yahweh. His unique position among the people carried with it additional burdens of which the king and the people were bluntly reminded by the prophet Samuel when he gave them their first king (1 Sam. 10:25; cf. Deut. 17:14-20).

In both accounts of the origin of the monarchy, Samuel the prophet, God's messenger who declares His will to His people *and* to His king, is very much in control. This was the source of the conflict which resulted in the rejection of Saul. This conflict would never fail to be prominent in the history of Israel's monarchy as the prophets of Yahweh praised, condemned, advised, and encouraged the kings of Israel on the basis of the divine will made known directly to them. The king who neglected the will of Yahweh could scarcely mediate the blessings of God's reign to His people. Saul failed in obedience to God's will and was rejected for his failure (1 Sam. 15ff.).

YAHWEH'S ANOINTED

When Samuel was sent to choose David as successor to Saul, it is said that "he took the horn of oil, and anointed him" (1 Sam. 16:13). Saul had likewise been anointed; Solomon in his turn would receive a similar consecration. In Hebrew, the verb "to anoint" is *mashah* from which is derived *mashiah* meaning "anointed." This latter word is known to us in the form "Messiah" (or Messias) which acquires a technical meaning in the course of centuries; but initially, it was used of the king who was described as "Yahweh's anointed" (1 Sam. 24:7). It is from the time of David that the concepts of messiah and messianism begin to be formed; it was then that the monarchy enjoyed a success on which a vision of the future could be built.

DAVID'S REIGN

What, in fact, were the merits of David's reign? In the first place, he succeeded in welding the tribes of north and south into a co-

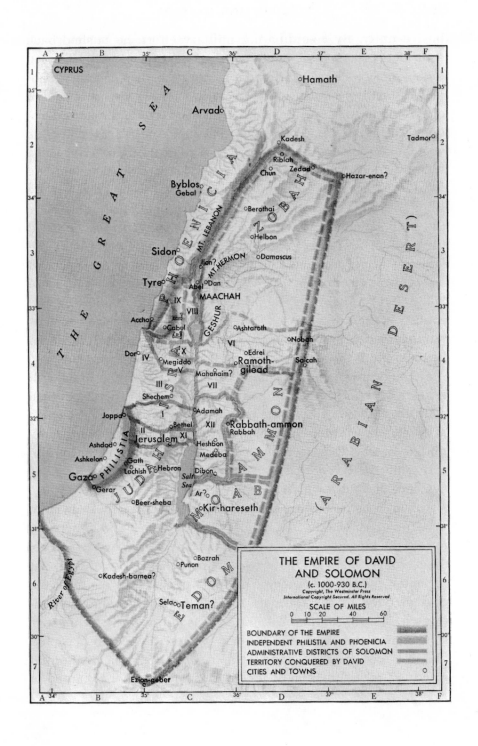

THE EMPIRE OF DAVID
AND SOLOMON
(c. 1000-930 B.C.)
Copyright, The Westminster Press
International Copyright Secured. All Rights Reserved.

SCALE OF MILES
0 10 20   40   60

BOUNDARY OF THE EMPIRE
INDEPENDENT PHILISTIA AND PHOENICIA
ADMINISTRATIVE DISTRICTS OF SOLOMON
TERRITORY CONQUERED BY DAVID
CITIES AND TOWNS

hesive unity. By co-ordinating military effort, he pushed back
from the borders those enemies which had for so long harassed
Israel, and by carrying the attack into their own territory, sub-
jected them to his control. He gave his people a worthy capital
city by capturing Jerusalem and focused on it their religious devotion by bringing the Ark, with its ancient memories of the Exodus
and the accompanying presence of God, within the city walls.
What was in the first instance the capital city of the kingdom, the
royal residence of the king, also became the dwelling place of the
King he represented. By bringing the national shrine to rest in
the royal sanctuary, David paid tribute to the fact that he owed
his position to Yahweh, and that the continued success of the
king, resulting in peace and prosperity for the people, depended
on Yahweh's continual care. By the close association of royal
house and royal shrine, the people were invited to put king and
country in their prayers to Yahweh, while the king had a constant
reminder of the presence of the God he represented, before whom
he must plead for his people, as well as for himself.

Although much of this is admirable, has it anything to do with
religion? David seemed to combine military skill with political
acumen, and many an astute politician has appreciated the value
of religion in winning united support without himself being committed. In David's case, however, one can scarcely doubt his sincerity, and, in the context of a limited revelation, he at times gives
evidence of a faith which is remarkable.

Although he was aware that he had been chosen by Yahweh to
take the place of Saul, he displayed a reverence and generosity
toward the king, which, from a human point of view, were scarcely
deserved. He made no move to anticipate the wishes of God, but
patiently awaited the outcome of Saul's decline. His courage was
characterized by his faith in Yahweh in whose name he confronted Goliath (1 Sam. 17:45). If he was guilty of the meanest of
sins, he was also capable of generous sorrow; he readily accepted
the just rebuke of his conduct and submitted in a penitential
mood to God's punishment for his sins. He was not ashamed to

WALL OF THE JEBUSITES AND THE
REMAINS OF THE TOWER OF DAVID

express in public his enthusiasm for his God as he danced before
the Ark (cf. 2 Sam: 6:16-23).

GOD'S PROMISE TO DAVID

It was David's devotion to the Ark which made him wish to see
it suitably housed: "I dwell in a house of cedar, but the Ark of
God dwells in a tent" (2 Sam. 7:2). Yahweh made known through
His prophet Nathan that He accepted the good will for the gift
and postponed the building of the temple. He did, however, reward David's intention of building a "house" (temple) by giving
him a "house" (dynasty) whose kingdom He would establish forever (cf. 2 Sam. 7:5 and 11ff.). He would regard the kings of the
dynasty as His sons, but He added the sober reminder that they
would be subject to chastisement if they sinned. Though called
His sons by God, no king of Israel could lay claim to divinity. The
God of Israel was one, and the king was His representative,
chosen to implement His will; his performance was subject to
scrutiny, and many of David's sons would feel the rod of God's

anger. It will be in accordance with this law that God will later suspend their rule until a worthy successor to David should appear.

The success of David in politics and war, combined with his religious fervor, had the advantage of demonstrating that monarchy as such was not necessarily incompatible with the worship of Yahweh. Initially, the reign of Solomon helped to consolidate this viewpoint, particularly by the building of the temple and the development of a cult to match the splendor of the buildings. The labors of David had borne fruit; they had been endorsed by God's promise to David (2 Sam. 7; *see above*).

From now on, the hopes and aspirations of Israel would be focused on the dynasty of David. With the birth of this hope that a son of David would realize the unfulfilled promise of his reign, one has the beginnings of messianism in Israel. This is not to suggest that before the time of David there was no awareness of a God-given destiny. From the days of Abraham, the eyes of his people were on the future. But it was in the context of a monarchical society that their aspirations for the future were concentrated on the anointed king, the Messiah, the Son of David.

THE KINGSHIP'S ENORMOUS INFLUENCE

A number of features now combined to give the king a position of enormous influence: he was the representative of Yahweh on earth, chosen by Yahweh Himself, endowed with His spirit, enjoying the inviolability of the sacred without being himself divine. As mediator between Yahweh and the people, he communicated God's blessing to His flock; as mediator between the people and Yahweh, he presented the tribute of their devotion. As leader of the hosts of Israel, he was their savior and he brought salvation from their enemies. If he gave peace on their borders, he also made peace at home; he judged with the justice of Yahweh, and divine wisdom guided his choice. As son of David and heir to God's promise, he incorporated Israel's hopes for the future. To many it seemed that Israel's destiny was one with the destiny of David's son. His success was Israel's glory, and his failure her shame.

The Royal Psalms

As they recount the history of the monarchy, the books of Samuel and Kings abundantly illustrate the central role of the Israelite king. It is, however, in the Psalter that one can feel Israel's affection for her king: how much he was part of her life, and particularly of her religious life. It would, in a sense, be true to say that the Psalter grew rather than that it was written. Its growth was spread over centuries, from the time of David (*ca.* 1000 B.C.) to the post-exilic period (*ca.* 400 B.C.) when Israel no longer had a king. Many of its prayers were used in the temple of Solomon until it—and the monarchy—came to an end in 587 B.C.

This association of the Psalms with the royal sanctuary led some scholars to regard it as a royal prayer book and to identify the "I" of the psalms with the king. While it is likely that the psalms were in more general use, it is not entirely fanciful to think that the king would have used such prayers as he prayed for himself, for Israel, and for Sion; as he sought deliverance from his enemies, from slanderers, and from sickness; as he affirmed his faith in God, praised His great glory, or sought His pardon when he sinned. Such prayers, we have seen, were part of David's life and would fittingly be found on the lips of his successors, but it is particularly to the "royal psalms" as such that our attention is now directed.

VICTORY THROUGH YAHWEH

Psalm 20 was probably used in a service to implore God's blessing on the king as he set out for battle (cf. verses 4-5). It is only through Yahweh that victory can be achieved (6-9), and it is from the royal sanctuary on Sion that help will go out (1-3). The people will share in the joy of success (4-5). Psalm 21 might be the sequel to 20, an act of thanksgiving for victory achieved. The king's request has been granted (2), and the psalmist recalls with pleasure that the length of days has been given to the king. It is an assurance of a period of stable government, which is based on the king's trust in Yahweh (7). With Yahweh's support, he has nothing to fear from his enemies.

In Psalm 144, the king himself asks for victory, opening with praise of Yahweh's power which contrasts with the weakness of man (verses 1-4). He calls on Yahweh's power as Creator to destroy His deceitful enemies (5-8), and rejoices in victory (9-11). He concludes with a prayer for fertility, prosperity, and peace, so that the psalm becomes an all-embracing prayer for the welfare of the people which depends particularly on the success of the king.

A similar linking of prosperity with the effectiveness of the king's rule is found in Psalm 72 (verses 15-16) which is cast as a prayer for the king. Particular emphasis is laid on the justice of his rule (cf. also Psalm 101), and his care for the poor and the needy. It is the psalmist's wish that this care for the lowly should be accompanied by universal rule (8), the respect of the monarchs of the earth (9-11), and everlasting peace (7). It is through this son of David that the patriarchal blessings (cf. Gen. 12:1-3, etc.) will be mediated (17).

ROYAL WEDDING AND ENTHRONEMENT

The concern for the continuation of the Davidic dynasty and the joy of a royal wedding are reflected in Psalm 45. The king's rule is based on justice (verses 6-7) and there is consolation in the thought that through this union the line will be continued (16).

In view of the importance of the king, it would not be surprising to find psalms associated with his enthronement. Most probably Psalms 2 and 110 belong to this category. Psalm 2 harks back to the prophecy of Nathan (2 Sam. 7; *see above*) when it states Yahweh's decree of the king's appointment in the words: "You are my son, today I have begotten you" (7). The newly crowned king is promised possession of the nations which think they can do without God (1-5); they are warned to submit in time lest they perish (10-11).

DAVID COMPOSING THE PSALMS, *an illumination from Greek Psalter in St. Catherine's Monastery at Mount Sinai*

A like control over enemies is promised to the king in Psalm 110, and the link with Sion as the source of his power is re-affirmed (verses 1–2). A surprising feature of the Psalm is the declaration that the king is "a priest forever after the order of Melchizedek" (4). Ultimately this implies that Sion is heir to the ancient cultic traditions which go back to Melchizedek, king of Salem (an ancient name for Jerusalem; cf. Gen. 14:18), but it is not at all clear what were its implications for the individual king. David (2 Sam. 24:22-25) and Solomon (1 Kings 3:4) offered sacrifice on occasion, but even in their time the sanctuary was served by priests. It was the normal function of the king to ensure that the temple was supplied with victims and in a general way to maintain the cult. He would also be present in the temple on the greater feasts. In this way he exercised what might be broadly called a priestly role of mediation, representing Yahweh to the people and the people to Yahweh, but the details of the cult were usually the concern of the priestly class.

Attempts have been made to involve the Israelite king in a pattern of worship which included a new year festival. This festival was celebrated in Mesopotamia to ensure the return of vitality to nature at the beginning of a new year. By a series of ritual acts in which the king played the part of the rising god, he mediated for the country and people the life-giving forces which would result in the revival of nature. Scholars who take this view understand the phrase "Yahweh reigns" in Psalms 93,95–99 to mean "Yahweh has become king again." Through the ritual involving the king, Yahweh's power is again made effective in nature.

There is, however, no certain evidence for such a new year festival in Israel, nor any support for the view that Yahweh was at anytime deprived of His throne and dominion; in no sense can He be regarded as a dying and rising god of the fertility myths. It is much better to understand these Psalms (93,95–99) as a hymnal expression of faith in Yahweh's kingship which, as we have seen, is the theological basis for the king's position in Israel, and is never far from view in any of the royal psalms.

SOLOMON'S STABLES, *under the Dome of the Rock in Jerusalem*

THE TRANSFER OF THE ARK TO JERUSALEM

David's transfer of the Ark to Jerusalem was decisive in the history of this holy city. It had long been a center of worship (cf. Melchizedek, Gen. 14:18), and the settling of the Ark on Sion implied Yahweh's taking possession of this ancient shrine. Here the Israelites could venerate the God who was their Savior from Egyptian toil, and, in doing so, they may have drawn on more worthy elements of the cultic traditions of Melchizedek.

In view of the importance of this event, it is not improbable that it was commemorated in the liturgy of the temple—whether in an annual feast or not, it is hard to say. Some such commemoration would provide a suitable context for Psalm 132 (perhaps also Psalms 24 and 47) which draws together the traditions concerning David's intention to build a temple (verses 2-5), the transfer of the

Ark to Jerusalem (6-8), Yahweh's oath to David (11-12), and His choice of Sion (13-18), and sets them in a liturgical context (cf. verses 1,6–7,8,9,10).

It is this choice of Sion by Yahweh which makes it the source of salvation, and explains the lyrical tones of the "Psalms of Sion" (e.g., 84,87,122, etc.). Yahweh and His earthly representative the king are working from Sion to bring salvation to men. Although many of the generations that used it may have felt that not all its suppositions were verified, nor all its prayers answered, yet it was open to fulfillment in an unexpected way.

The Divided Kingdom

The development of the Psalter received its initial impulse from the building of Solomon's temple and the organization of cult. Not all of Solomon's efforts, however, had such a happy outcome. He inherited from David a kingdom that was secure, and this freedom from anxiety in the military field gave him scope for the development of trade. His success was such as to provide revenues for the building of the palace and the temple, but his ambition outran his income, and the weight of taxes and enforced labor extinguished the good will which David had won, particularly from the northern tribes.

NORTHERN TRIBES BREAK AWAY

On Solomon's death (about 930 B.C.), the ten northern tribes broke away from Judah and Benjamin (cf. 1 Kings 12ff.). The subsequent history of the monarchy is shared between the kings of Israel (the North) and the kings of Judah. Jeroboam I, the founder of the northern kingdom, set up shrines at Bethel and Dan (cf. 1 Kings 12:25ff.) to woo the people from Jerusalem, but in spite of this often condemned act of schism the North was not abandoned by Yahweh. It is, in fact, remarkable that some of Yahweh's greatest prophets (Elijah and Elisha) were active in the northern kingdom, where even at its worst there were seven thousand people who had not bowed the knee to Baal (cf. 1 Kings 19:18).

The monarchy of the North, however, was greatly lacking in stability, and its whole history (1 Kings 12–2 Kings 17) is marked by frequent and violent dynastic changes. Such an experience of monarchy, particularly during the last twenty-five years of the northern kingdom (745-721 B.C.; cf. 2 Kings 15:8-17) makes intelligible Hosea's discontent with kings: "They made kings, but not through me; they set up princes, but without my knowledge" (8:4). The northern kingdom would soon be destroyed and "in the storm, the king of Israel shall be utterly cut off" (10:15).

A MYSTERIOUS CHILD OF THE HOUSE OF DAVID

In Judah, on the other hand, God's promise lent stability to the monarchy, and one member after another of David's line ascended his throne. Not indeed that all were models of virtue and representatives of increasing perfection! Like the kings of the North, the Davidic kings were subject to the strictures of the prophets, but faith in the family of David shone brightest when the immediate outlook was darkest. When Ahaz (*ca.* 735-715 B.C.) ruled in Jerusalem, he was condemned by Isaiah for lack of faith in his God (Is. 7:3ff.), and showed this was justified by dangerous association with Assyrian worship (2 Kings 16:10ff.). Yet it was during his reign that Isaiah pinned the hopes of the people on the birth of a mysterious child of the house of David:

> The people who walked in darkness have seen a great light:
>   those who dwelt in a land of deep darkness, on them light has
>   shined . . . .
> For to us a child is born, to us a son is given;
>   and the government will be upon his shoulder,
>   and his name will be called
>   "Wonderful Counsellor, Mighty God, Everlasting Father,
>   Prince of Peace."
> Of the increase of his government and of peace there will be no
>   end, upon the throne of David . . . [Is. 9:2-7; cf. Is. 7:10ff.].

This son of David will be equipped with the fullness of God's spirit:

> There shall come forth a shoot from the stump of Jesse,
>   and a branch shall grow out of his roots.
> And the spirit of the Lord shall rest upon him,
>   the spirit of wisdom and understanding,
>   the spirit of counsel and might,
>   the spirit of knowledge and fear of the Lord. . . .
> He shall not judge by what his eyes see,
>   or decide by what his ears hear;
> But with righteousness he shall judge the poor,
>   and decide with equity for the meek of the earth . . . [Is. 11:1-4].

The result of this king's rule will be universal justice and peace, a return to the happiness of paradise which becomes possible because all will know God:

> The wolf shall dwell with the lamb,
>   and the leopard shall lie down with the kid. . . .
> They shall not hurt or destroy
>   in all my holy mountain:
> For the earth shall be full of the knowledge of the Lord
>   as the waters cover the sea [Is. 11:6-9].

This passage does contain a reference to what one might call the aggressive tendencies of the future king (verse 4): "He shall smite the earth with the rod of his mouth, and with the breath of his lips shall he slay the wicked." There is, however, an overriding emphasis on the king's moral and spiritual qualities which derive from the abundant presence of the spirit of Yahweh. His delight is "in the fear of Yahweh," a term which might be said to embrace all the best attitudes of Old Testament religion. The outcome of his intimacy with Yahweh is a universal sharing in the knowledge of God and an awareness of His goodness and mercy which evoke the same qualities in men.

MICAH'S FAITH IN THE DYNASTY OF DAVID

Micah, who was Isaiah's contemporary in Judah, also shared his faith in the dynasty of David. He looks to the future glory of Bethlehem, the birthplace of David, when another great king shall emerge from this otherwise insignificant village:

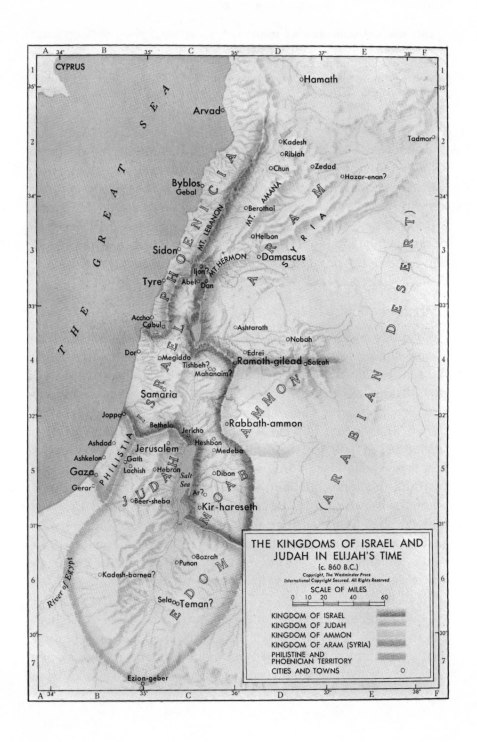

THE KINGDOMS OF ISRAEL AND
JUDAH IN ELIJAH'S TIME
(c. 860 B.C.)
Copyright, The Westminster Press
International Copyright Secured. All Rights Reserved.

SCALE OF MILES
0   10   20   40   60

KINGDOM OF ISRAEL
KINGDOM OF JUDAH
KINGDOM OF AMMON
KINGDOM OF ARAM (SYRIA)
PHILISTINE AND
PHOENICIAN TERRITORY
CITIES AND TOWNS   o

But you, O Bethlehem Ephrathah,
  who are little to be among the clans of Judah,
from you shall come forth for me
  one who is to be ruler in Israel,
whose origin is from of old,
  from ancient days [Mic. 5:2].

Isaiah and Micah were witnesses of the fall of the northern kingdom and of the events which left Hosea disillusioned with northern monarchs. They must also have witnessed the appearance in Jerusalem of refugees from the northern capital (Samaria). With their own city gone, they sought refuge under the protection of the Davidic king in the city where Yahweh had chosen to dwell. But Jerusalem would in turn be unfaithful and share in the fate of her sister (cf. Jer. 3:6ff.; Ezek. 23).

JEREMIAH

To judge by Jeremiah and Ezekiel, whose prophetic activity spanned the years from 626 to 580 B.C., there was little in the conduct of the Davidic kings to justify the earlier optimism of Isaiah and Micah. According to Jeremiah, they failed in those very virtues which were to be characteristic of Isaiah's king (cf. Jer. 22:1-8; 8:1-3, etc.; Is. 11:3-4); they had failed to shepherd their flock (Jer. 23:1-4) and their kingdom would shortly be destroyed. It was precisely in this time of failure that the prophet professed his faith in David: "Behold, the days are coming, says the Lord, when I will raise up for David a righteous Branch [cf. Is. 11:1] and he shall reign as king and deal wisely, and shall execute justice and righteousness in the land. In his days Judah will be saved and Israel will dwell securely. And this is the name by which he shall be called: 'The Lord is our righteousness'" (Jer. 23:5-6).

The crumbling kingdom and the smug complacency of both rulers and people (cf. Jer. 7; 8:8-12) highlighted the shortcomings of the covenant of Sinai, and Jeremiah outlined the features of a new covenant which would create a firmer bond between Yahweh and His people (Jer. 31:31-34). In addition to an abundant for-

VIEW OF BETHLEHEM

giveness of sin, this covenant will be characterized by a knowledge of God which will be universal and deeply sincere. As we have seen, this was also to be a feature of the reign of Israel's messianic king: "No longer shall each man teach his neighbor and each his brother, saying, 'know the Lord,' for they shall all know me, from the least of them to the greatest, says the Lord" (Jer. 31:34; cf. Is. 11:9). In this prophecy the work of the messianic king is brought into the context of the new covenant.

EZEKIEL

Ezekiel's condemnation of the shepherds of Israel (chap. 34) produces the dramatic assertion that Yahweh Himself will come to shepherd His people: "Ho, shepherds of Israel who have been feeding yourselves . . . but you do not feed the sheep. . . . There-

THE MARRIAGE OF DAVID, *a silver disk dated 6th–7th century* A.D.

fore . . . because my sheep have become a prey . . . since there was no shepherd. . . . Behold, I, I myself will search for my sheep, and will seek them out" (34:1ff.).

This message of hope was immediately relevant to the return of the Israelites from exile, but it clearly stated the principle that Yahweh Himself would come to save His people lest they perish utterly through the failure of His human representatives. Once again the figure of the Davidic king appears in the context of God's saving activity: "I will save my flock. . . . And I will set over them one shepherd, my servant David, and he shall feed them and be their shepherd. And I, the Lord, will be their God, and my servant David shall be prince among them" (Ezek. 34:22-24). As in Isaiah, peace will ensue: "I will make with them a covenant of peace and banish wild beasts from the land" (Ezek. 34:25).

In his vision of the new Jerusalem (chaps. 40-48), Ezekiel refers to the privileged position of the prince (44:2-3; 45:7-8, 17,

22; 46:2,8,12,16; 48:21). Being himself a priest (1:3), Ezekiel depicts the restoration in terms of a renewal of the cult in a rebuilt city and temple. The effectiveness of life-giving worship in the sanctuary is represented by the streams of fresh water flowing from the temple (47:1-12), healing the salt waters of the Dead Sea, and giving life to trees whose "leaves will not wither nor their fruit fail, but they will bear fresh fruit every month, because the water for them flows from the sanctuary. Their fruit will be for food, and their leaves for healing" (47:12). In this effective cult, the prince, although he is not described as a priest, has a leading role to play. In fact, without him, the cult would scarcely exist (cf. 45:17,22; 46:15).

The Exile and the Suffering Servant

The fall of Jerusalem and the Exile in Babylon were a shattering experience for Israel. Deprived of her king, her country, her capital city and her temple, she was left to reflect in exile on the meaning of her destiny, to which in faith she still adhered. The absence of a human monarch led Israel to review the role of the Davidic king. The text of Isaiah chapters 40-55, the work of the great prophet of the Exile (sometimes called Second Isaiah), places renewed emphasis on the kingship of Yahweh almost as if to say that the Davidic king served his purpose as long as he rendered more effective the kingship of Yahweh. The faults of these kings had brought disaster (43:28) and they were powerless to deliver Israel from captivity. Their failure might even tempt some to doubt the sovereignty of Yahweh and to give allegiance to the Babylonian gods. But Yahweh had a purpose in forsaking His people, and when it was accomplished, her deliverance would come (40:1-2). As in the days of Egypt, it is Yahweh, the Creator, Israel's king, who will accomplish her deliverance (43:15; cf.

40:3ff.). Again it is on the basis of His being Creator that Yahweh lays claim to the title of king (cf. 45:1-13).

THE PROMISE TO DAVID IS NOT FORGOTTEN

Yet the promise to David is not forgotten; and in conjunction with a reference to a new "everlasting covenant," the prophecy of Nathan is recalled. The kings of the Davidic line may have sinned, but the God they represented was merciful: "In overflowing wrath for a moment I hid my face from you, but with everlasting love I will have compassion on you" (Is. 54:8). The new representative of the line of David will be heir to the nations:

> I will make with you [plural] an everlasting covenant,
>   my steadfast, sure love for David.
> Behold, I made him a witness to the peoples,
>   a leader and commander for the peoples.
> Behold, you [singular] shall call nations that you [singular] know
>   not, and nations that knew you [singular] not shall run to you
>   [singular],
> because of the Lord your God, and of the Holy One of Israel [Is.
>   55:3-5; cf. Ps. 2:8ff.; Is. 11:10ff.].

Even in the desolation of exile, the figure of David is a rallying point for the hopes of Israel.

THE SUFFERING SERVANT

The Babylonian captivity led to what might be called a national examination of conscience. What had gone wrong and why? The prophetic preaching which had often been ignored in their lifetime was re-read in the light of events. The exiles of Israel now turned from these texts with regret that their warnings had gone unheeded and with a deeper awareness of sin. They and their fathers had sinned; they had offended a good, merciful, and faithful God and they now bore the consequences of their sin. This consciousness of sin—both national (Is. 53:6) and individual (cf. Jer. 31:29-30; Ezek. 18)—was borne in on Israel in a way not hitherto experienced. It brought with it a desire to be delivered from sin and the accompanying realization of the incapacity of Israel to achieve this deliverance, laden as she was with sin.

HIEREMIAS

JEREMIAH
Michelangelo

The prophetic message of Isaiah (chap. 52:13-15 and chap. 53) gives hope of relief from this situation. This unique passage in Old Testament prophecy describes with great pathos the sufferings of one who is "righteous," who has "done no violence" or "deceit"; he bears the sins of Israel in accordance with the will of Yahweh (53:6,10) and "makes many to be accounted righteous" (53:11). He is called by Yahweh "my Servant" (52:13; 53:11), but who, in fact, is he? With his coming, a new idea appears in Israel's religious thinking, that of vicarious satisfaction, the idea that another, particularly a just man, can render satisfaction to God for the sins of his fellow men. Who in Israel could accomplish this on such a scale as to make many righteous?

WHO IS HE?

Scholars have searched the pages of Israel's history in their efforts to identify "the Servant." Moses, David, and Jeremiah, who suffered in their time for their people, have all been suggested, but they and others from Israel's past are excluded by the setting of the Servant's work in the future.

Reference to the other Servant Songs (Is. 42:1-9; 49:1-6 and 50:4-11) complicates the problem of identification. In 49:3, the Servant is clearly identified with Israel; and although 49:1-6 and 50:4-11 suggest his identification with the prophet himself, 53:1ff. seems to associate the prophet with the sinners who benefit by the Servant's sufferings, and is therefore distinct from him.

Without deciding whether all four songs refer to the same "Servant," it is worth recalling at this point what has already been said about "corporate personality" in relation to the king. Although an individual, he summed up in his person the hopes and aspirations, the success and the failure of his people, who must suffer for his sins (2 Sam. 24:15), even if they do benefit by his virtue (cf. 1 Kings 6:12-13). Many scholars hold that the same principle is helpful in understanding the Servant Songs, in which the author moves from a collective to an individual Servant and back again. He passes from Israel's experience in exile, when she suffered to expiate her guilt, to the ideal concept of the sinless one expiating the sins of others. He returns to the collectivity in thinking of how a group will be associated with the Servant in the sharing of his hard won "spoil" (cf. Is. 53:10–12). If it is said that the prophet had no specific individual in mind, it must also be said that he had no intention of excluding one. In presenting this new mission of Israel the just, namely, to suffer for the sins of men, he had no wish to exclude the role of an outstanding member of the people, no more than he would wish to exclude David from a consideration of the kingdom.

If the problem were not complicated by the reference to "Israel" (Is. 49:3), the remaining songs could refer without difficulty to a single individual; and, since the work of the Servant is primarily a work of salvation, attempts have been made to see in him the messianic king of the Davidic dynasty. The Servant is primarily a person whose fate astonished kings (52:15) and who, in his restoration, is associated with the great (53:12). He can represent the people before God, as did the king, and his satisfaction works their salvation (53:10). His sufferings are God's will for him, a decision he accepts without murmur (53:10,7). Such perfect fulfillment of God's will, as we have seen, is to be characteristic of the messianic kingdom. The Servant will labor to blot out sin and thus prepare the way for the new covenant (cf. 53:5,10ff.; 49:8; Jer. 31:24).

The Period after the Exile

The foregoing are some of the points which suggest a link between the Suffering Servant of Yahweh and the messianic king of the Davidic dynasty, but it is a curious feature of Israel's history that, in spite of this passage in Isaiah (chap. 52:13-15 and chap. 53), we have no evidence that the concept of a suffering Messiah was ever accepted by Israel in the Old Testament period.

GENEALOGY OF CHRIST, *an illumination from the Book of Kells, showing a portion (Jorim-Sala) of the genealogy in Luke's Gospel (3:29–32)*

In fact, on their return to Jerusalem from exile, some Jews hoped for a revival of the ancient glories of David in the person of Zerubbabel (cf. Hag. 2:20-23; Zech. 3:8; 4:1-5a, 10b-14; 6:9-15, where in verse 11, Zerubbabel should probably be read instead of Joshua) to whom they applied the earlier prophecies (Is. 11:1; Jer. 23:5) concerning the messianic Son of David.

HOPE IN DAVID'S LINE REMAINS

We have no record of what became of Zerubbabel, but the Jews were quickly made aware of their position as a province of the Persian empire. Militarily and politically, they were of no significance, and even for a religious undertaking like the rebuilding of the temple and the restoration of the cult, they required the sanction of the Persian authorities (cf. the books of Ezra and Nehemiah). In these circumstances, there was no room for a Davidic prince in the traditional mold. This is not to imply that David's Son had been forgotten.

Sometime during the 4th century B.C., the books of Chronicles (to which Ezra-Nehemiah are to be joined) were composed with – among other aims – the purpose of exalting the role of the temple and the cult. In the process, David is presented in such an idealized way as almost to represent a messianic figure. The hopes of Israel were still attached to his line. At the same time, these hopes found formal expression in the cult, where the royal Davidic psalms continued to be recited, and Psalm 89 gives eloquent expression to the longing of the post-exilic community for the restoration of the Davidic monarchy. With such prayers on their lips, the faith of Israel in David could not die.

The Jewish community was now concentrated around Jerusalem and its temple, and in the absence of a Davidic king, the high priest assumed a number of features which earlier belonged to the king (cf. de Vaux: *Ancient Israel*, pp. 400ff.). This would explain how the name of Joshua came to be substituted for Zerubbabel in Zechariah 6:11.

A RELIGIOUS CRISIS

With the coming of the Greeks (332 B.C.), Israel failed to improve her position, and after Alexander's brief reign (he died 323 B.C.), she became the plaything of the Seleucids in the North and the Ptolemies in the South, being subject sometimes to the one and sometimes to the other. Both, however, mediated Greek influence to Palestine in such a way as to produce a religious crisis. Having lost her political importance, greater efforts were made to preserve the religious traditions of Israel; and when Greek ways of thought threatened to undermine these traditions, there was cause for a double revolt, against the Jews who were willing to tolerate Greek influence, and against the political authority which was ultimately the source of this influence.

The Son of Man

In the time of the Maccabees, the political authority was represented by Antiochus IV Epiphanes (175-164 B.C.), and one can follow the twofold revolt, mentioned above, in the books of Maccabees. One might have expected that, at this critical juncture, the thoughts of the Jews would have turned to the long promised Davidic king; and Ecclesiasticus (or Ben Sirach), composed between 190 and 180 B.C., bears witness to the survival of traditional attitudes at this time (cf. 45:25; 47:1ff., particularly verse 22; 48:15; 49:4). There is, however, little trace of such thinking in Maccabees 1 and 2, which have nothing of messianism and do not mention the name of David. The author is concerned primarily with the struggle between Israel, the chosen people of God, and the Hellenists with their pagan influence.

APOCALYPTIC LITERATURE

This was a dramatic struggle, and it is not altogether surprising that the period witnessed the development of a dramatic form of literature called "apocalyptic," which reflects the phases of the struggle between God and the powers of evil, culminating in the ultimate victory of God and the establishment of His reign. It was characteristic of this literature to present its message in the form of revelations (apocalypse = revelation) communicated through visions of the future.

The visions are described in a dramatic way and make abundant use of symbols whose meaning is often lost on present-day readers. The general tone is of urgency as the outcome of the conflict is awaited, and readers are invited to be ready for a share in God's final victory by fidelity to His will in a time of trial. By these means the writers impressed on their readers the

DANIEL IN THE LION'S DEN
Peter Paul Rubens

real issues that were at stake, and bolstered their wavering courage as the struggle became more intense. The use of symbols served to heighten the drama and also to conceal the real nature of the writings from all but the initiates.

DANIEL: THE COMING OF THE KINGDOM

It is to this category of writing that the book of Daniel belongs. In a series of narratives (chaps. 1-6) and visions (chaps. 7-12), the author presents what might be called a theology of history. In chapter 2, and particularly in the visions of chapters 7-12, he passes in review the great empires of recent centuries (Babylonian, Median, Persian, and Greek, *ca.* 600–170 B.C.), and presents as the climax of this historical process the coming of the kingdom (kingship, dominion, reign) of God. Before Him all kings must yield, and all the kingdoms of the earth will be subject to His sway. For the author, God is clearly the Lord of history, and the movement of history is toward the establishment of His universal and everlasting kingdom (cf. Dan. 2:44, 7:18,27, etc.). Inaugurated by a dramatic intervention of God in history (cf. 2:34), it would transcend earthly frontiers and embrace all the just who would do God's will (7:14,27). The good would rise from the dead to share in the blessings of the kingdom; the wicked would rise to rejection (12:2). Although there is considerable growth in awareness of the spiritual nature of God's kingdom, it still belongs essentially to this world.

In each of the kingdoms which succeeded one another to be finally displaced by the kingdom of God, a single nation had exercised a dominant role; in the kingdom of God, it was intended that the Jews (the just, those who observe God's law, who do His will, the "saints," cf. 1:15ff.; 7:27ff.) should be in control. As God's own people, they could mediate His will to the world and share with mankind the benefits of His rule.

Is a leading role assigned to any individual?

Yet the author of Daniel referred not merely to great nations; he also referred to their kings upon whose greatness the success of the empires was built. In view of the hopes earlier attached to the Davidic line, one might expect the name of David to occur in the context of the coming kingdom. To say that his name is not mentioned leads one to ask if his place has been taken by someone else. Does the author of Daniel attribute a leading role to any *individual* when assigning the kingdom of God to the care of the Jews? Here the opinions of scholars are divided. Some take the view that the "one like a son of man" (7:13), to whom the kingdom was given, symbolized the people of Israel in accordance with the explanation offered in 7:27.

Other scholars are prepared to concede this point, but insist that the symbolic value of this man-like figure does not exclude a reference to an individual. The ease with which the writer elsewhere passes from the kingdom to the king and back again is a warning to the reader not to interpret his symbol in an excessively literal way.

RUINS OF JERICHO, *showing excavation of the ancient city wall in Joshua's time*

The use of the concept of corporate personality (cf. above on Isaiah 53) can then help to unfold the implications of the "one like the son of man" in Daniel. But when one seeks to determine more exactly the nature of this figure, one is hampered by the vagueness of the text. It does not clearly state that it was a man; it merely says it was like a man (the phrase "son of man" in Aramaic means: "an individual of the class called 'man' "). By this it was distinguished both from the beasts representing the pagan nations and the powers of evil, and from men, because of its divine commission or origin (cf. 2:34 for the divine origin of the kingdom of God). The "clouds of heaven" which were a feature of theophanies (Ezek. 1:4; Ps. 18:11) also emphasize the divine origin of this figure.

HEAVENLY CHARACTER OF THE SON OF MAN

In Daniel 8:15; 10:16,18, angels are described as having the appearance of men; while in 9:21 Gabriel becomes "the man Gab-

riel," and another angelic figure is simply called "a man" in
10:5. This usage leads some commentators to argue that the
"one like a son of man" is an angelic rather than a human figure.
This need not imply a total separation from the human sphere,
since Genesis 1:26ff. and Psalm 8:4ff. see in man the likeness
of God, particularly in man's capacity as a ruler (cf. Ps. 80:17
where "son of man" may refer to the king).

However one understands the celestial character of the "one
like a son of man," he is identified with the "people of the saints
of the Most High" on earth in Daniel 7:27. His relationship with
the human and the divine, with the heavenly and the earthly, is
not too clearly defined, or indeed definable.

Insofar as this individual is identified with the establishment of
God's kingdom, he belongs to a messianic context. It is not at all
certain, however, that he was identified with the Davidic Messiah
or with the Servant of Yahweh by the Jews of the pre-Chris-
tian period.

EXTRA-BIBLICAL LITERATURE

The Son of Man also appears in extra-biblical literature, as,
for example, in the book of Enoch, 2 Esdras, 3 Baruch, and the
Sibylline Oracles. It would, however, take us too far afield to
consider the teaching of these books. The matter is complicated
by the problem of dating the literature. The passages in Enoch
which refer to the Son of Man are reckoned to be Christian
insertions by some scholars. The fact that they have not been
found among the many fragments of Enoch at Qumran may well
support this view. The books of S. Mowinckel (*He that Cometh*)
and D. S. Russell (*The Method and Message of Jewish Apocalyptic*) should be consulted for a fuller discussion of these questions.

Qumran's Expectation of the Messiah

A few decades after the writing of the book of Daniel, a group of Jews settled at Khirbet Qumran, a monastery on the shores of the Dead Sea, and their teachings have become known to us in recent years through the Dead Sea Scrolls. In the Manual of Discipline it is written that they lived in expectation of "a prophet and the Messiahs of Aaron and Israel" (9:11). (Scholars have some difficulty in understanding the words and speculate whether the sect at Qumran expected two or three Messiahs, or perhaps just one who would represent three streams of messianic tradition.) The "prophet" can be traced back to Deuteronomy 18:15, and although this text was generally applied to the prophet who would prepare the way for the Messiah, there is evidence in the Gospels (e.g., John 6:14), as well as in Qumran, that it was understood by some in a directly messianic sense.

THE MESSIAHS OF ISRAEL AND AARON

The "Messiah of Israel" is the kingly Messiah of popular expectation. The sectaries of Qumran did not attempt to spiritualize this title in applying it to the Messiah. They were preparing for the final apocalyptic battle in which they were willing to fight and to die under the leadership of the messianic king. They even prepared a handbook to train them for this conflict (i.e., the Scroll of the War of the Children of Light with the Children of Darkness), and when the time for revolt against the Romans came, they shed their blood in defense of their convictions.

The "Messiah of Aaron" may come as a surprise to readers of the New Testament, especially when it seems that at Qumran he was given precedence over the Messiah of Israel. The Qumran

PORTION OF ONE OF THE DEAD SEA SCROLLS: *"The War of the Sons of Light with the Sons of Darkness"*

community was made up of laymen and priests, but the priests were leaders of the group, which may have resulted in the expectation of a messianic leader from the priestly line. In the time of the monarchy, as we saw, the king did have some functions in relation to the cult, and he was regarded as a savior and mediator of his people, but the priesthood was a separate institution. In the post-exilic period, however, with the extinction of the monarchy, the high priest arrogated to himself many of the trappings of royalty, including that of anointing. The Messiah of Aaron may well be a projection into the future of this post-exilic development. The priests at Qumran would naturally give prominence to the idea which subordinated the Messiah of Israel to the Messiah of Aaron. It was their reaction to the Hasmonean princes who took to themselves the office and functions of the high priest, and they looked to the day when the Messiah of Aaron would restore them to their rightful position of authority.

Christ Purified and Perfected the Expectation of the Old Law

Having traced the origins and development of various streams of messianic thought, we may now conclude by briefly reviewing the way in which Jesus, the Christ (i.e., the Anointed, the Messiah), made use of this ancient material to reveal Himself and His Father's will for mankind. While it is true that in the post-exilic period, generally, lack of interest in the Davidic line was due to the political situation of the Jews, subject as they were in turn to the Persians, the Greeks, and the Romans, nevertheless, the weight of the Roman yoke and the material afflictions of subjection aroused their longing for a military leader of David's caliber. The result was that while, in some circles, "emphasis came to be laid increasingly on the kingly rule of God Himself in the coming kingdom and on the prime necessity of keeping His holy Law" (D. S. Russell, *The Method and Message of Jewish Apocalyptic*, p. 310), in others, flaming revolt was preached and practiced in the expectation of the Son of David. It was against this background that Christ presented His message.

SON OF MAN AND SUFFERING SERVANT

In showing a personal preference for the title "Son of Man," Christ emphasized certain aspects of His person and mission, and played down those features which made the other messianic titles more popular with the people. "For Jesus, the Jewish messianic idea was the temptation of Satan, which he had to reject" (Mowinckel, *He that Cometh*, p.450; cf. Mark 8:27–33; Matt. 4:1ff.; Luke 4:1ff.).

Reference has already been made to the heavenly aspect of the Son of Man in the book of Daniel, and this was verified in Christ in two ways: through His pre-existence with God (as in John 3:13) and through His subsequent exaltation (as in Matt. 26:64 and parallel passages). The use of the term in Ezekiel (2:1, etc.) and Psalm 8:4 suggests a more humble view of the Son of Man which was exploited to the full by Christ when He insisted—in the face of Peter's resistance—that the Son of Man must suffer and be put to death (Mark 8:31ff.). The Son of Man was also the Suffering Servant (cf. Is. 53).

SON OF DAVID

The people hailed Christ as king (cf. John 6:15), and He accepted this title (cf. Luke 19:38; John 19:21) while protesting that His kingship was not of this world (John 18:33ff.). In calling Him the "Son of David," the people looked to Him as their Savior, who would rescue them from the Romans and inaugurate an empire in which the nations would pay homage to Yahweh and His people in the city and temple of Jerusalem. But Christ repudiated the means by which David extended his kingdom (cf. Matt. 26:52-53), emptied the title "Son of David" of political significance, and opened up His kingdom to the outcasts of society, the poor, the sick, and the sinners; He invited them to share in its blessings by doing His Father's will. For Him, the real enemy was sin, and insofar as He was Savior of His people it was from sin that He saved them. The leading role of "the prince" in organizing the cult (Ezek. 44:3; 45:17) and in acting as mediator for the people (Jer. 30:21) was taken over by Christ when, as priest and victim, He gave His life on Golgotha for the remission of sins (cf. Is. 53:4ff.), and sealed the new covenant in His blood (Jer. 30:21-22; Matt. 26:28f.).

SON OF GOD

God had addressed the king in Israel as His son (cf. Ps. 2:7 and 2 Sam. 7:14), and Christ accepted the title "Son of God" from those who believed in Him. On their lips, the words may not

THE CRUCIFIXION
Pietro Perugino

have been more than a messianic title (cf. John 1:49; 11:27), but in His teaching Christ made more explicit claims to divine sonship in the literal sense (John 10:33). At His trial, He was accused of blasphemy (John 19:7); He died and rose again to bear witness to the truth of His claim.

A sincere concern for justice, a care for the weak and the poor, and a universal zeal for the knowledge of God were features of the messianic kingdom in the prophetic writings. The king was to be the embodiment of these ideals and their most zealous promoter. Christ's contemporaries fastened on the title "Son of David" and, interpreting it in a narrowly nationalistic and political sense, they became spiritually blind. By blending in an unexpected way the figures of the Son of David, the Son of God, the Suffering Servant and the Son of Man, Christ purified and perfected the expectation of the Old Law and inaugurated God's reign in the New.

The Psalms

David J. Bourke
and John McHugh

The book of Psalms is the hymn book of ancient Israel. It is an extremely varied collection, containing hymns written by different people, at different times, and on different themes. Most frequently, however, the psalms express an uncompromising devotion to Yahweh, the Lord and Savior, and were sung mainly at the great sanctuaries of Israel, especially the temple in Jerusalem. The apostles and the early Christians constantly prayed with the psalms, and if some of us today find them unsatisfying perhaps we are not sufficiently conscious of certain truths to which the early church was keenly alive.

Davɪᴅ Wʀɪᴛɪɴɢ ᴛʜᴇ Psᴀʟᴍs, *Spanish miniature,
dated about 1430–1440* ᴀ.ᴅ.

The Hymn Book of Israel

THE CHRISTIAN who uses the book of Psalms in his private devotions often finds himself bewildered, and now that the psalms are more frequently used in parish services also, private uneasiness is inevitably giving place to vocal criticism. What *is* the Christian to make of ancient Hebrew war-songs, and of texts like Psalm 109, where the plea is that his enemy's wife may be a widow and his children orphans? Many priests, too, wonder whether they derive from the Divine Office any benefit proportionate to the effort it entails. In the past, this might have been attributed to a lack of familiarity with Latin; this was especially true before the publication of the New Psalter in 1944, for the old breviary Psalter was sometimes meaningless, and even at its best exceedingly difficult for all but specialists in the Latin of the early church. But now priests, sisters, and layfolk who recite the Office in English are brought face to face with the real problem: can the book of Psalms ever be the staple diet of a Christian's daily prayer?

To resolve these problems and to dispel the uneasiness, one must look first at the book of Psalms as a part of the Bible, and then as it is used by the church.

A VARIED COLLECTION OF HYMNS

The book of Psalms is the hymn book of ancient Israel, and like our own hymn books, it contains items written over several centuries on all manner of themes. Modern hymn books include translations of ancient Latin hymns written 1600 years ago, original compositions like "Praise to the Holiest" which stand in the classical tradition of English writing, and perhaps even Negro spirituals which, though of an entirely different cultural ancestry, are not less impressive in the simplicity and sincerity of their faith.

The book of Psalms is no different. It is an extremely varied collection, made up of hymns written by different people at different times and on different themes, and eventually put together into five books in a way we can only guess at. The compilers of the Psalter would have spared future generations much trouble if they had arranged their hymns by themes, as modern editors do ("Christmas," "Easter," "Saints," "During Mass," "For the Young," etc.). Unfortunately, they did not, and it is sometimes very difficult to work out from allusions the occasion on which a particular psalm was meant to be sung.

It is equally difficult to say when any particular psalm was written, for the evidence is rarely sufficient to enable us to assign a precise date. For centuries, the traditional view was that the bulk of the psalms came from David (73 of the 150 bear his name). When modern critical scholarship began to question this tradition, it went at first to the other extreme, saying that almost all of them belonged to the period after the Exile (after 519 B.C.), and many to the time of the Maccabees (say, 170 to 150 B.C.). The best contemporary scholarship holds a middle view, that most of the psalms were composed during the period of the kings (roughly 1000 to 587 B.C.), when worship flourished around the temple of Jerusalem. It seems reasonable to believe that David himself was one of those responsible for developing this form of worship among his people, for no man achieves a reputation for poetry if he never writes a poem at all.

REVISION AND EDITING

Our own experience tells us, too, that a congregation is instinctively conservative about hymns. When a new edition of a hymnal appears, in which the editor has modernized one or two lines, or omitted a verse, there are always congregations which prefer to sing the old tunes. It was no different in ancient Israel. Thus Psalm 53 (in the Second Book of Psalms) is a "new version" of Psalm 14 (in the First Book), with the word "God" substituted for "Yahweh" or "Lord." Similarly, Psalm 108 (in the Fifth Book of Psalms) is just a combination, slightly re-touched, of Psalm

ILLUMINATED PAGE FROM
DUTCH PSALTER, *dated*
1470

57:8-12 and Psalm 60:7-14 (in the Second Book). This duplication of the same hymns is proof that the Five Books of the Psalter were compiled separately, and each of them contains psalms covering all manner of themes. Indeed, it can be taken as certain that whoever compiled each of these books incorporated into his own collection small groups of psalms which had existed previously as little collections. For example, the psalms with which Book 2 opens (Pss. 42-49) are all ascribed to "the sons of Korah," and Psalms 73-83 (with which Book 3 begins) are all "Psalms of Asaph."

The history of the Psalter is fascinating, but much further research is needed to throw light on what is today obscure. When the results of this research become available, they will no doubt teach us a great deal about the meaning and the message of the psalms. For the present, however, it is enough to say that the psalms have known the fate of all hymns—revision, editing, grouping, re-writing. And because the book of Psalms is a hymn book, it is necessary to say something about the pattern of hymns in the ancient Semitic world.

Babylonian hymns

The sequence of thought which we find in the Hebrew psalms was probably derived, in its broad outlines, from the pattern of psalms in the Babylonian world. Thus a typical Babylonian psalm opens with an *address*, in which the god to whom the prayer is directed is called upon by name. This is followed by a long section of *praise*, in which the god's attributes and activities are described. The Babylonian psalmist then moves on to his *complaint*, in which he enumerates his sufferings in considerable detail, and with all the eloquence at his command. Intermingled with this complaint is an *entreaty* or *prayer* for a favorable hearing, for deliverance and help. The psalm often closes with what is sometimes called a *"vow to praise"*: the psalmist promises that if his prayer is heard and he is rescued from his suffering, he will spend the rest of his life praising the god who has delivered him from trouble.

These, then, are the essential constituents of a Babylonian psalm—address, praise, complaint, entreaty, and the promise of future praise—and broadly speaking, they tend to occur in this sequence. But whereas in Babylonian psalms all these five themes generally occur in a single all-embracing prayer, in the Hebrew psalms it is different. The Israelites usually took *either* the first two elements (address and praise) *or* the last three (complaint, entreaty, promise of praise), and made out of them a single prayer. If the psalm consists of address and praise, scholars term it a *hymn* (with them, the word "hymn" is a technical term for a psalm of praise). If the psalms consists of a complaint, etc., they term it a *"lament."* This distinction between "hymns" and "laments" is the fundamental division in the Psalter.

Hymns of praise

In the Semitic world, as in our own, God was praised either for what He was in Himself, or for what He had done for men. He was praised for His power, His goodness, His readiness to forgive; and He was praised for the benefits He had given to men, and for delivering them from trouble. The former is sometimes termed "descriptive praise," the latter "commemorative praise." In the Babylonian psalms, descriptive praise predominates, but (as has often been pointed out) the religion of Israel is fundamentally historical: God revealed Himself to Israel in history, by the astounding feats He performed for His people. Hence the praise of Israel is chiefly commemorative; descriptive praise is less frequently found, and where it does occur, it often seems to have been introduced as a result of foreign influence.

Thanksgiving is a special instance of commemorative praise. It is worth noting that the psalmist does not "thank" God for the gift of creation, or for what He did in the past of Israel, though he may "praise" Him for these things. But when the psalmist "thanks" God and makes a "promise of future praise," it is for something which God has done in his own life-time, from which the psalmist as an individual has benefited. "Thou hast turned for me my mourning into dancing; thou hast loosed my sack-cloth

TERRA COTTA PLAQUE OF A
MUSICIAN, *dated 2025-1764*
B.C.

and girded me with gladness, that my soul may praise thee and
not be silent. Yahweh, my God, *I will give thee thanks forever*"
(Ps. 30:11-12).

The *Royal Psalms*, too, may be considered as special instances
of commemorative praise. They are basically concerned with the
covenant which Yahweh made with the house of David, and with
the favors which He bestowed on the first two kings, David and
Solomon. Although these psalms do contain a strong element of
entreaty on behalf of the reigning king, their primary purpose is
to praise Yahweh for having fulfilled His past promises in him.

The same attitude of commemorative praise underlies many of
the so-called *Didactic Psalms*, where the excellence of Yahweh's
laws and the wisdom embodied in them is praised.

PSALMS OF LAMENT

The *Psalms of Lament* form much the largest category in the
Psalter, and it is immediately evident that they embody an at-

titude of "weeping before Yahweh." Among them we must count not only penitential psalms such as the "Miserere" (Ps. 51) and the "De Profundis" (Ps. 130), but also the psalms in which a man curses his enemies (for example, Ps. 109) or protests that he is innocent (for example, Ps. 26 – the "Lavabo"), or proclaims his utter trust in God (Ps. 71). All these psalms are easily recognizable, but it is interesting to note how regularly the threefold pattern of "complaint-entreaty-promise of praise" recurs. Two great psalms which are much used in the New Testament, 22 and 69, provide splendidly clear examples of this structure:

	Psalm 22	*Psalm 69*
Complaint	1-18	1-8
Entreaty	19-21	9-29
Promise of praise	22-31	30-36

(It will be noticed that the complaint and the entreaty are, as has been mentioned, to some extent intermingled in each of these two psalms.)

The Religious Background of the Psalms

So far, we have discussed only the literary characteristics of certain psalms. Something must now be said about their religious inspiration, for this is just as essential as literary genius for a man who would write a hymn of praise. The sentiment most frequently and clearly expressed in the psalms is that of uncompromising and heartfelt devotion to Yahweh, the Lord and Savior. The psalmist speaks of fleeing to God (Ps. 91:4), his "rock and fortress" (Ps. 18:2), his only refuge (Ps. 31:4). He "clings" to God (Ps. 91:14) and to His commandments (Ps. 119:31), "waits anxiously" for Him (Ps. 25:3,5,21), earnestly "longs to see" His

WADI FEIRAN, *near Mount Sinai*

glory (Ps. 63:1-2) and "yearns for him" with all his soul (Ps.
102:1). He strives to draw closer to God by "pondering" day and
night His ways, His laws, His judgments, in which His will is
expressed (Pss. 1:2; 77:13). In intensity of devotion and earnest-
ness, the psalms of Israel stand light-years away from the psalms
used by the Babylonians, and it is reasonable to ask why this was
so. Was it a mere accident?

PRAYERS OF ISRAEL

A devout Israelite was deeply conscious of the fact that his
race was united to God by a solemn covenant: "You shall be my
people, and I will be your God" (Jer. 11:4). Because of this belief,
the psalms of Israel are shot through with a unique spirit of hope
and trust in the attentiveness and responsiveness of Yahweh. He
is the psalmist's own covenant-God—how then can He fail to

respond? He condescends to regard the prayers which His people address to Him as deeply important; He allows Himself to be moved by them, to be delighted, appeased or roused to action on behalf of those who pray, provided only that they have been true to the terms of His covenant. For the psalms are prayers which well up from the heart and mind of a man who, through conscious meditation on the covenant, lives face to face with His God.

The theme of the covenant-union between Yahweh and Israel pervades and dominates the Psalter. It involves three ideas. (1) Israel is Yahweh's chosen people, chosen out of pure love, without any particular merit on its part, but thereafter bound to Yahweh by a covenant in a way no other nation is. (2) Israel had been chosen by the Most High God for a mission—to be His instrument in leading all the nations of the world to acknowledge Him as Lord. (3) This exalted vocation was to be maintained and intensified through unswerving loyalty to His commandments. The covenant was therefore *exclusive*; it had a *purpose*; and it called for a *response in action*. As one would expect, these ideas were stressed in the hymns sung during the liturgical ceremonies of Israel.

PSALMS IN THE LITURGY

It follows from this that psalms were sung mainly at the great sanctuaries of Israel, and especially at the temple in Jerusalem. Naturally enough, many of the psalms were composed for the great feasts celebrated in these sanctuaries, and therefore they cannot be fully understood unless one knows something about the conduct of worship during the great feasts. Indeed, it seems that throughout the Semitic world the basic types of psalm were fixed and established in the context of sacred places, sacred times, and sacred ceremonies.

The very title of the book of Psalms in Hebrew, *tehillim*, suggests that these prayers were meant to be shouted aloud at a shrine by an assembly of people. We should imagine throngs of worshippers shouting out these chants in unison, led perhaps by Levites or temple singers. Exhortations such as "Shout!" (Ps.

47:1), "Cry out for joy!" (Pss. 33:1; 81:1), "Play!" (Pss. 33:2;
66:1) clearly call for a clamorous response, and the same sense of
explosive noise is present in the term *hallelu* or *hallelujah*. Often
this clamor would have been intensified by the use of musical
instruments of the louder sort, such as drums, tambourines,
cymbals, horns, trumpets, lyres, and castanets (*see* Pss. 81:2–3;
33:2; 43:4). Physical gestures, too, played a significant part in
this form of worship, for we read of raising the hands to heaven
(Ps. 134:2) and clapping hands (Ps. 47:1). Lastly, it may be noted
that several of the psalms were intended to be sung in the course
of a procession around the city, the temple, or the altar. Any
modern Christian who wants really to understand the psalms
must be continually alert for such allusions to the sacred ceremonies of ancient Israel.

Many of the psalms reflect the situations and activities for
which they were composed. Thus Psalms 100 and 122 are clearly
psalms to be sung by groups of pilgrims as they arrive at the Holy
City or the temple. The title of Psalm 100 suggests that it was also
intended to accompany a thanksgiving sacrifice, and many other
psalms seem to have been composed for thank-offerings, sin-offerings, offerings of first-fruits, the fulfillment of vows, the bestowal
of blessings or the acknowledgement of sin. Others again are
designed for particular occasions, like Psalm 30, which is said
to be "for the dedication of the temple." Of course, not all the
psalms can be placed as precisely as the ones just mentioned, but
it is quite certain that the liturgy of Israel played a decisive role
in inspiring the various types of psalm.

FOREIGN INFLUENCES

The Bavarian Catholic who landed in New York on March 17
might be forgiven for wondering whether the church in the
U.S.A. observed the same liturgical calendar as his own. Did they
keep Easter late, and was this some pre-Lenten *Fasching*? Thus
even in the Roman Catholic Church, where the liturgical calendar
is today so uniform, there have to be exceptions when the people
want them. The Society of St. Vincent de Paul and the Young

DAVID PLAYING THE HARP FOR KING SAUL
Rembrandt

Christian Workers each have their particular style of meeting and prayers, and the style is often marked by the national characteristics of the country where the society originated. Similar influences were felt in Israel.

Thus the court circles in Judah, the men close to the Davidic king, composed and introduced into the temple liturgy psalms which stressed the divinely ordained role of the king in society: he was the source of blessings, of security and peace, the dispenser of justice within Israel, and the conqueror of the Gentile nations "around about" it. These ideas come to the fore in the Royal Psalms (Pss. 2; 18; 20; 21; 45; 72; 89; 101; 110; 132; 144). The court would have been more open to foreign influence than the rest of the people, and we can see a certain preoccupation with alien gods in these psalms. Yahweh is called "the high God" to whom all other gods are subject (Pss. 96:4; 97:7,9), the "king of glory" (Ps. 24:8–10) and "lord of all the earth" (Ps. 97:5). These terms may well have been introduced under Canaanite or Jebusite influence.

Similarly, in the "Songs of Zion" (Pss. 46; 48; 76; 84; 87; 132), Mount Zion is portrayed in colors which seem to have been partly borrowed from an old Semitic myth about a mountain-home of the gods in the north of Syria (rather like the Greek myth about Mount Olympus): there is a very clear example in Psalm 48:2. These themes may well have originated among sections of the people which were particularly attracted by the mythology about Jerusalem which the Jebusites had accepted in the days before the Israelite conquest. There is a close parallel in a hymn in the Roman Breviary for the Ascension where God the Son is said to have come down "from the height of Mount Olympus." It is worth mentioning that the Second Vatican Council has decreed that all such references to pagan mythology should be expunged from the hymns of the Breviary (*Constitution on the Sacred Liturgy*, no. 93), and it can be taken as fairly certain that the temple priests who edited our book of Psalms were not less possessed by reforming zeal. Thus few direct references have survived, but we can detect a trace of the old beliefs in phrases like that of Psalm 76:4, where Zion is said to be more glorious, more majestic than "the everlasting mountains," the home of the ancient gods.

MANY REJECTED FOREIGN INFLUENCE

By contrast, there were many in Israel who adhered strictly and exclusively to their own national traditions, rejecting all foreign influence. These people would have regarded their feasts and institutions as part and parcel of Israel's native inheritance. For such as these, the feast of Tabernacles or Tents may well have been a festival at which the covenant promises were to be renewed; others may have regarded it as a New Year feast, celebrating the beginning of yet another year of Yahweh's eternal reign; and yet a third group may have regarded it as an anniversary celebrating the choosing of David and of Zion. The spectrum of

CHANT FOR THE BEGINNING OF THE DIVINE OFFICE, *published in Venice, 1549*

Israelite religion is broad enough to have included these and many other differences of emphasis and interpretation.

Finally, it must be stated unequivocally that not all the psalms were written for great ceremonies on major feast-days. Many of them show unmistakably that they were written for other occasions, or for private recitation by individuals far from any sanctuary.

The God the Psalmists Adored

In spite of these variations of context, outlook, and emphasis, an underlying unity of theme can easily be discerned in all the psalms. The creation, and still more those miracles of deliverance and constant protection which marked God's favor for Israel's ancestors during their migrations from Mesopotamia to Egypt, and from Egypt to Palestine, supplied Israel with abundant themes of praise and inspired its prayers. New psalms on the same themes were written after the return from the Babylonian exile (Ps. 126). And in the Psalter the presentation of these "mighty deeds of the Lord" generally conforms to a single pattern.

Creation, deliverance, the crushing of enemies, renewal of life, and prosperity are all presented as so many instances of God's saving power. The situation in which Yahweh intervenes is almost always one in which the forces of sin and death are threatening to gain the mastery over the forces of goodness and life. The evil forces are sometimes identified with the waters of chaos menacing the order of creation (Ps. 104:6-7), sometimes with the enemies of Israel—particularly the Egyptians at the Exodus—who threaten to destroy the chosen people (Pss. 77:14–15; 105:26ff.), and sometimes with the "ungodly" men within Israel, those "workers of iniquity" who are so often represented as plotting against the life of the psalmist himself. And in a similar way the forces of goodness and life may be embodied in the fertile earth which Yahweh has created (Ps. 104), or in the chosen people as God's servants on earth, or in the "true of heart" who stand fast by His commandments.

In all these cases Yahweh's intervention tends to occur in the same pattern. At the very moment when the fertile world, the chosen people, or the "true of heart" are on the point of being destroyed forever, Yahweh intervenes and overthrows the forces of chaos and evil, rescuing His chosen ones and bestowing on them new blessings. Thus Yahweh's "saving power" becomes a central, unifying theme throughout the psalms.

THE NAME OF GOD

One of the supreme moments in Israel's history was the occasion on which Yahweh revealed His name to Moses and to Israel (Ex. 3:13-17). To the Israelites a name was a symbol of the personality: to know a person's name was to be able to attract his attention, to engage in conversation with him and therefore to be able to build up close friendship with him. All this applied in the highest degree to Israel's knowledge of Yahweh's covenant name. His name was loved and reverenced, so that the people relied on it alone to defeat their enemies. "Some trust in chariots, others in horses, but we trust in the name of Yahweh our God" (Ps. 20:7). Israel's most earnest hope was that this name should be acknowledged by the Gentiles (Ps. 83:18), "praised to the ends of the earth" (Ps. 48:10) "for all ages, as long as the sun endures" (Ps. 72:17).

In the Semitic world, a name stood for that which, later, Scholastic theologians call the nature or essence of a thing. Hence to the Gentiles, the name of Yahweh (what St. Thomas Aquinas might have called "the nature of Israel's God") was terrifying, so much so that it is never found upon their lips. But for the Israelites it signified not merely God's majesty, but also a passionate tenderness toward their race, and a readiness to respond to every need (Pss. 36:6-8; 57:10; 63:3). So the psalmist writes: "I glorify your name forever; your love for me has been so great ... Lord God,

MOUNT SINAI, *with peaks covered by a smoky mist*

you who are merciful and tenderhearted, slow to anger, always loving, always loyal" (Ps. 86:12–13,15).

Yahweh's honor, too, was bound up with His name, and therefore with the fortunes of His people, who were called to uphold it. "Yahweh, for the sake of your name, keep your promise to save me; protect me from oppression, love me, kill my enemies, destroy my oppressors, for I am your servant" (Ps. 143:11-12). The appeal to Yahweh's honor (of which this text is one instance) is also a major theme in the psalms. If Yahweh fails to rescue His covenant partner, His name (that is, He Himself) will be derided. His enemies (who are also the psalmist's enemies) will say that He fails to act either because He is too weak or (such is the unspoken implication) because He is not prepared to honor His pledged word. If, on the other hand, He does intervene, then the very hopelessness of the Israelite's plight will only underline the fact that deliverance was the work of Yahweh alone; thus the saving of His servant will bring all the greater honor to His name.

GOD THE WARRIOR

The terror which Yahweh inspires is a favorite theme of the psalmists. His coming is described in terms like those which describe the theophany of Sinai—cloud, smoke, and earthquake (Pss. 18:9–15; 50:3), fire (Pss. 11:6; 21:9; 46:9), and, as the most terrifying of all, the death-dealing roar of the divine voice (Pss. 18:13; 29) which is often identified with the sound of thunder. When Yahweh speaks His voice is destructive of all that seems mighty enough to contest His rule or to assert its own independence. "The voice of Yahweh shattering the cedars! Yahweh is shattering the cedars of Lebanon! He is making the Lebanon buck like a calf, Syrion like a buffalo steer!" (Ps. 29:5-6).

To the covenant people, however, the voice of Yahweh was anything but a destructive and death-dealing roar. It was creative and life-giving, uttering words which they could understand and to which they could respond. For they were able to communicate with the Creator, this God of terror, in question and answer, in appeal and response. For them, the words He uttered spelt life and protection. So His commandments and judgments (Pss. 19:8 ff.; 111:7-8; 119) became, like the divine Name, an object of praise. Again and again Yahweh is praised for the wisdom, integrity, and steadfastness of His "ways" (Pss. 18:31; 25:10). Here, too, the underlying idea is that Yahweh, the covenant God, determines in detail the course His people's lives must follow to achieve His glory and their happiness.

Yet while the people of Israel plead for the coming of Yahweh, the rest of the world recoils before Him in terror. He is ". . . terrible to the kings of the earth" (Ps. 76:12). The waters of chaos, and the Gentile kings, with all their armies and chariots, flee before Him, or cringe at His feet (Pss. 104:7ff.; 68:13; 2:11-12). At His approach the whole earth is thrown into convulsions, and the most stable and immovable parts of it, like the mountains and

CHRIST PANTOCRATOR, *mosaic in the famous cathedral at Monreale in Sicily*

hills and the foundations of the earth, are seized with trembling (Pss. 18:7; 29:6; 114:4,6,8) or melt like wax before Him (Ps. 97:5). Thus Yahweh subdues the mightiest forces in nature and history alike, disposing of them exactly as He pleases.

YAHWEH THE JUDGE

After each conquest of these forces of evil, Yahweh is pictured as presiding in judgment (Pss. 75:3–9; 82:8; 105:7) as a "great king . . . a high king over all the gods" (Ps. 95:3). The psalmists represent Him as seated on a throne high above the heavens (Ps. 104:3), and sometimes the throne is said to be supported by the winged colossi known as cherubim (Ps. 80:1). He even has to stoop down to see what takes place on earth (Pss. 14:2; 33:13-15; 102:19; 113:4-6), and the clouds and the wind are like a chariot in which He descends from this throne (Pss. 18:10–11; 104:3). More usually, however, He manipulates the forces of nature from His heavenly throne (Pss. 105:32; 135:7; 147:16–18), thus bestowing prosperity and fertility on His creatures (Pss. 65:10–13; 104:10–18,27–28), peace and blessing on His chosen people (Pss. 29:11; 37:11). Several psalms contain allusions to the glory, majesty, and splendor of His appearance (*see* especially Ps. 45:3ff.), and one of the most telling lines in the Psalter is that in which God is described as "clothed with the light" (Ps. 104:2). In the effort to describe the indescribable, the psalmist speaks of God's *eyes* as piercing into the very heart of man and observing his innermost thoughts (Pss. 11:4; 33:18; 66:7), of His *nostrils*— symbol of His anger—as snorting fire (Ps. 18:8,15), and of His *breath* as giving life (Pss. 33:6; 104:30).

Since everything that exists was created by Him, it is utterly dependent on Him; and since from His heavenly throne He sees all things, He cannot be cheated or deceived. His word decides all things. His power is revealed, therefore, not only in the regular processes of nature, but also in the miracles whereby He from time to time suspends the laws of nature on behalf of His people (Pss. 78:12–31; 105:27ff.). The all-powerful Creator is ever ready to intervene as a judge.

Indeed, the quality which the psalmists praise above all others is Yahweh's chivalry toward the poor and the afflicted. To them He is a rock (Pss. 18:2,31; 28:1), a refuge (Ps. 14:6), a strong tower (Ps. 9:9), a deliverer (Ps. 72:4), an avenger (Pss. 3:7; 18:41), and an advocate (Ps. 43:1). "He does not forget the cry of the afflicted" (Pss. 9:12,18; 77:9), but gives judgment in their favor from His heavenly throne.

And the king of Judah, the heir of David, was the viceroy of Yahweh upon earth. His primary task and vocation was to ensure that the law of Yahweh was observed, especially in securing justice for the oppressed and protection for the lowly (Ps. 72). He was to ride out in glory and majesty, his sword at his side, in the cause of justice and truth (Ps. 45:4). The king's court of justice was, from a religious point of view, part of the complex of the

temple of Zion, to which the tribes of Israel made pilgrimage and
where they found "the thrones of judgment, the thrones of the
house of David" (Ps. 122:4-5).

LORD OF THE WORLD

This God who made the world has "declared his word to Jacob,
his statutes and ordinances to Israel; he has not dealt thus with
any other nation" (Ps. 147:19-20). The psalmist, therefore, felt
that he and his nation (or at least those among them who were
"true of heart") held a wholly privileged position among the
peoples of the world, for they had been called to assist in the
accomplishment of God's plan, and to manifest His glory.

This conviction underlies the first element in the formal structure of the Hebrew hymn, that is, what we have called the "summons to praise." Very frequently, this is addressed to the chosen
people as a whole (Pss. 105:6; 149:2), or to particular groups
within it, such as the priests (Ps. 134). Still more frequently, however, it is addressed to those among the chosen people who by
their piety and devotion are considered most fitted to sing His
praises. Thus the call is directed to God's "devoted ones" (Pss.
30:4; 145:10; 149:5), to the "true of heart" (Ps. 32:11), "the
righteous" (Pss. 68:3; 140:13), "those who love the name of
Yahweh" (Ps. 5:11) and "those who seek him" (Pss. 22: 26;
40:16; 105:3). And this is understandable enough: the covenant
emphasizes the need for unswerving devotion to its statutes, and
therefore those who kept the covenant loyally would naturally be
led to sing the praises of their God.

There is, however, a whole series of hymns in which the psalmist is preoccupied with the power of Yahweh as the sole and absolute Lord of creation. In these hymns, the summons to praise
is addressed not to Israel alone, but to all the earth and its inhabitants (for example, Pss. 33:8; 66:1,4), to all creatures (Ps.
145:10) and indeed to everything that breathes (Ps. 150:6—the
last line of the Psalter). Even the inanimate forces of the universe
are summoned to join in the hymn of praise: "Let the heavens be
glad, let the earth rejoice, the sea thunder and all that it con-

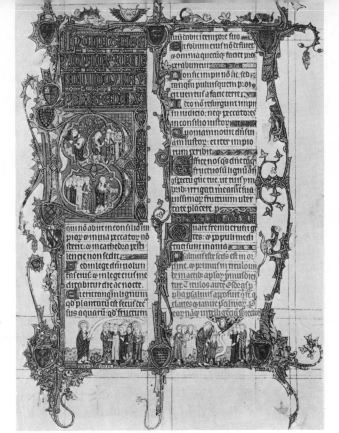

INITIAL PAGE OF THE BOOK OF PSALMS, *an illumination from a fourteenth-century Psalter*

tains" (Ps. 96:11). Still more frequently, the summons is addressed to the Gentile nations who are to be compelled to acknowledge Yahweh as their absolute Lord. Thus "all peoples and nations" (Ps. 47:1; 66:8), "all kings" (Ps. 72:11), and even Yahweh's enemies (Ps. 66:3) are commanded to bow down before Him. Finally, in several hymns the psalmist directs his attention inward upon himself, addressing the summons to praise to his own soul. "Bless Yahweh, my soul, and all that is within me, bless his holy name" (Ps. 103:1).

This attempt at a composite portrait of Yahweh as the psalmists see Him is based upon certain broad, central themes that appear to run through the whole Psalter. It does not, of course, pretend for a moment to cover all aspects of Yahweh's relationship with Israel and the world, and perhaps it goes too far in smoothing out the various inconsistencies which do undoubtedly appear in the psalms. Nevertheless, it seems reasonable, if one is looking for a dominant theme in the Psalter, to begin by trying to present a description of Yahweh Himself.

What Is Man that You Are Mindful of Him?

We have just explained in general terms how the Israelite saw Yahweh and endeavored to respond to Him in the psalms. But how did he want Yahweh to see him? To answer this question, we must turn mainly to the "Psalms of Lament," a category so large that it has been rightly described as "the backbone of the Psalter."

We have seen that Yahweh's compassion is aroused by the suffering of the humble, the innocent, and the poor. Hebrew has a special word to describe this class of people—they are the *'anawim*. The Israelite therefore spared no effort to present himself before Yahweh as one of the *'anawim*, a man sunk in the furthest depths of misery and unhappiness.

An Israelite would prepare for his prayer at the temple by fasting and penitential prayer (Pss. 69:11; 25) over a period, and with typical Oriental hyperbole would stress how weak and emaciated he had become as a result of this long preparation. "My knees are weak through fasting, my body has become gaunt" (Pss. 109:24; 102:4-5). Then he would dress himself in the garb of a mourner, a cloak of coarse black goats' hair (translated "sacking" in the English versions, Pss. 35:13; 69:11), and smear himself with dust and dirt until his face and hands and feet were utterly filthy (Pss. 38:7; 42:10). In this dress he would then approach the sanctuary with his head bowed low on his breast (Ps. 35:14), and sometimes would prostrate himself on the ground (Ps. 38:6).

These external gestures would be accompanied by words describing them, as if to make sure that God would notice the wretched condition of His servant. Thus we read verses like "my soul cleaves to the dust" (Ps. 119:25), "I eat ashes for food and drink tears" (Ps. 102:9). All this would be accompanied by loud groans, by the raising of the hands toward the sanctuary, and

PRAYER ON THE HOLY ROCK AT SUMMIT OF MOUNT GERI-ZIM, *during the Samaritan celebration of Passover*

even by copious tears. The psalmist hoped that by exhibiting these external signs of affliction, he would attract the attention of Yahweh in heaven, and rouse Him to pity.

PROPER APPRECIATION OF EXTERNAL GESTURES

These gestures and prayers seem to Western minds rather extreme, if not ludicrous. To appreciate them aright, it is essential to keep in mind that Oriental peoples, even today, are less worried by inhibitions than we are. The blind beggar in the street would consider it normal to exaggerate his truly pitiful lot in order to excite the compassion and charity of passers-by; certainly, it would never cross his mind to minimize his plight out of a false sense of vanity and a desire to show that he did not need help or money. The psalmists were only adopting toward God the attitude which the poor adopted toward men. And perhaps the very hyperbole of their language may bring home to Western minds, as nothing else could, the fact that we are in truth wretched, poor, sin-soiled, blind, deaf sinners begging for pity before the throne of the All-Holy.

And yet another fact must be borne in mind. The psalms are poetry, and we should not think that they were always accompanied by the kind of gesture described above. The Catholics in the United States have repeatedly been urged by the church, on Ash Wednesday, to "put on sackcloth and ashes" and "to weep before the Lord"; but it would hardly be fair to describe the liturgical practices of the United States simply from the texts of the Roman Missal. Similarly, in ancient Israel, metaphor was part of the stock-in-trade of a psalmist; we should beware only of going to an extreme position and thinking that whatever we would think a mere metaphor was merely a metaphor for the Israelites. Moslems prostrate themselves for prayer and raise their hands to heaven; and there can be no doubt that external gestures of humility played a great part in Israelite liturgy also.

Nor should one forget that there is a deep significance in these external actions. The psalmist was concerned to point out to the Lord of life that he was far advanced on the way to death. For to the Hebrew mind, life and death were not sharply demarcated zones — all light on one side, and all darkness on the other. "Life" for them included and embraced happiness, peace, prosperity, security, and the blessing of a family; "death," by contrast, began on this side of the grave with the onset of misery, childlessness, material misfortune, and bodily sickness — each of which was yet another step on the road to death.

Hence to pass out of the land of the living into the underworld (what the Hebrews called *Sheol* or "The Pit") was merely to pass the last frontier station, the point of no return, into the realms where death was undisputed king. Thus the psalmist, whatever his misfortune, frequently couches his cry for help in terms of mortal danger. "Save me, O God, for the waters have come up to my throat" (Ps. 69:1), and indeed, the title of Psalm 102 might well be prefixed to all of the "Laments of an Individual." It runs: "It is the prayer of one who is afflicted, when he is faint and pours out his soul before Yahweh." This same concept is vividly conveyed in Psalm 88:3–6, where the writer represents himself by anticipation as already in the grave, so heavy are his sorrows. "My soul is all troubled, my life is on the brink of Sheol; I am numbered among those who go down to the Pit, a man bereft of strength, like one forsaken among the dead, like the slain that lie in the grave, like those whom thou dost remember no more, for they are cut off from thy hand. Thou hast put me in the depths of the Pit, in the regions dark and deep."

CERTAINTY OF A HEARING

The miseries just described are so extreme that many a reader must be wondering whether they are truly representative of the "Psalms of Lamènt." Here, then, it is well to state that the Old Testament psalms do swing between two moods of extreme ex-ultation and extreme gloom. One moment the psalmist is en-larging on his griefs in the most extravagant terms, and the next moment he is triumphantly praising and thanking the Lord as though his prayer had already been answered and his troubles ended. This abrupt transition from loud lamentation to high ex-ultation has been called "the certainty of a hearing" (*compare* Pss. 31:18–19; 69:29–30). Many think that there was a pause between the "lamenting" section of a psalm and the subsequent verses, and that during this pause a priest would deliver an oracle assuring the suppliants of a favorable hearing. This is possible, but it cannot be proved. The psalmist, however, certainly thanks Yahweh immediately, thereby showing his utter confi-dence that his prayer is already heard. Sometimes this section of confident thanksgiving was expanded into a psalm of its own, detached from any lament, and so the "Psalms of Trust" were formed (Pss. 3; 23; 27:1–6; 121; 131).

Why was the psalmist so certain of a hearing? Because he was deeply conscious of being in a covenant with the God to whom he prayed. This is why we find that the psalmists are extremely bold in the form of their address. Usually, God is addressed by

"THE LORD IS MY REFUGE, MY FORTRESS IN WHOM I TRUST"

His covenant name, Yahweh, and in the imperative: "Yahweh, make haste to help me" (Ps. 70:1). The audacity and simplicity of this command is all the more striking when we compare it with Babylonian psalms: the Babylonians thought it advisable to begin the invocation of their gods with elaborate and ingratiating praises, and only afterwards to introduce their petitions. The Hebrew psalmists, by contrast, call upon the name of God as if they had a right to His attention because He had revealed to them what we might call His "personal name," Yahweh.

CONFIDENCE IN YAHWEH'S FIDELITY

The Israelite never doubted that Yahweh would listen to his prayer, because it was unthinkable that Yahweh could be unfaithful to His covenant promises. To suggest that Yahweh might fail to stand by His word was blasphemy. And Yahweh was the Lord of all creation, and ready, therefore, to turn the whole world upside down if necessary, in order to help His covenant partner. Yahweh, when called upon by name, would immediately and inevitably respond.

The only factor which could cause Yahweh to withhold His help was infidelity on the part of Israel. And so when the psalmist feels that his afflictions have been caused by Yahweh, he acknowledges his guilt and begs to be forgiven (Ps. 51). At other times he may, like Job, protest that he is innocent, asking Yahweh to probe into his soul and to see that there is no hidden evil there (Pss. 26:2; 139:23). This protestation of innocence may take the form of a "negative confession," as in Psalm 7:3–5: "Yahweh, my God, if I have done wrong, if I have ill-gotten goods in my hands . . . may the enemy trample my life to the earth. . . ." Yet even when the psalmist confesses his own guilt, or bases a prayer on his own innocence, we find him in the end appealing most of all to the mercy and compassion of Yahweh for the poor and the afflicted.

For the psalmist was always aware that he himself was piteously small and far away from Yahweh. "*From the ends of the earth* I cry to you . . . bow down your ear" (Pss. 61:2; 86:1). He is so small. Yahweh is so great. How can a mere man hope to attract Yahweh's attention, and to rouse Him to action unless he bases his prayer on the fact that he is a member of the covenant people? Then, with the voice that thundered order into the primeval chaos, with the breath that was the origin of all life, Yahweh of the covenant answers: Because down there in the darkness one small Israelite is for one moment of the world's history, alone and frightened and in pain.

THE PSALMS OF CURSING

For the Hebrew, the world was made up of friends and enemies. Misfortune was never impersonal; it was always due to some person, known or unknown, human or supra-human, who was actively attacking a man. Thus the psalmist attributes his sufferings to the ill-will of enemies trying to destroy him.

In many cases, the enemies would have been his fellow-men, but there are a few instances in which the psalmist seems to have thought that evil spirits were responsible for his plight. In either case, his only hope was to ask for the help of his God. Curse therefore had to be met with counter-curse, hatred with counter-hatred. It would be dishonest to play down or to explain away the intensity of the hatred displayed in certain of the psalms (for example, Ps. 110). Positive and intense hatred of evil is a necessary part of Christian love, and in the imperfect religion of the Old Testament, no real distinction is drawn between evil and the evil-doer. Thus the Israelite utters his harsh curses against his enemies in the conviction that Yahweh must hate what is evil, and will therefore listen to his prayer.

PSALMS OF THANKSGIVING

Midway between the Hymn of Praise and the Lament stands the Psalm of Thanksgiving. It is like a Hymn in that it sings joyfully of Yahweh's love; it is like a Lament, in that it is rather self-conscious, dwelling on what Yahweh has done for the individual Israelite. It is not always easy to distinguish a Psalm of Thanksgiving from a Hymn of Praise, but the distinctive characteristic of the Hymn is that it is wholly God-centered, and contains no explicit reference to the psalmist's own person, whereas the Thanksgiving Psalm must contain some such reference.

In the Thanksgiving Psalms the Israelite sees himself as caught up by the kindly hand of God in the sublime moment of a new creation. He feels that he has experienced the impact of God's holiness not on the world, nor on the history of his own people, but on himself. "Yahweh, my God, I cried out to you and you healed me! Yahweh, you drew my soul out of Sheol! You made me live, instead of going down to the Pit" (Ps. 30:2-3). The psalmist therefore feels that the new life Yahweh has given him must be dedicated unreservedly to proclaiming the glory of

St. John at the Foot of the Cross (*detail from* The Small Crucifixion)

Matthias Gruenewald

his Deliverer. This accounts for the declaration of intention which frequently occurs, in virtually the same words, at the beginning and end of the Thanksgiving Psalms. "I will extol thee, Yahweh . . . I will give thanks to thee" (Ps. 30:1,12). Thus the psalmist begins and ends his thanksgiving with an act of self-dedication.

The psalmist then turns to "those who love Yahweh" (Ps. 30:4), for any individual who has received a favor from Yahweh may expect all the other servants of the Lord to join with him in praising the God who saves them all. And the psalmist stresses the inward significance of his experience: through his agony and suffering, Yahweh has in fact been glorified. This glory must therefore be proclaimed—the man's friends and all who know Yahweh must share in the experience. Therefore the psalmist describes what it was like to see life ebbing away, to cry to Yahweh as to the last hope, and to be delivered to start life once again. All the suffering must be traced to its roots in evil, and the sin which provoked it must be publicly and humbly acknowledged. So the psalmist re-lives his misfortunes with all the drama and intensity of an Oriental story-teller. He cries out to Yahweh once again, with the last despairing cry which he uttered in his extremity. He perpetuates in his prayer the sacred moment of rescue when he was caught up from unimaginable horror into the safety of Yahweh's hand. In that moment of terror he had vowed to dedicate his life, if it was restored to him, to praising Yahweh, and the Psalm of Thanksgiving shows him fulfilling this vow of everlasting praise.

The Psalms as Prayers of the Christian Church

By now the reader may be saying to himself, "This is all very interesting, and informative, but it does not begin to help me to use the psalms for my own prayers. Has not the time come for a real *aggiornamento*, for a frank recognition that most of the Psalter is not much use to us Christians?" Against this, we may observe that the apostles and the early Christians constantly prayed with "the Psalms of David," and if our own age finds them unsatisfying, it may be that we are not sufficiently conscious of certain truths to which the early church was keenly alive. A rediscovery of these truths might lead us back to the psalms, to find in them that guidance and consolation which the first Christians found.

"COME, LORD JESUS"

In reading the New Testament, no one can fail to perceive the intensity and the urgency with which the church hoped and prayed for the Second Coming of our Lord. The long course of history has made us less sensitive to this truth, although we profess it so often with our lips: *He will come again in glory.* Our lives are so busily occupied in building up the church of God in this world that we sometimes forget the building is only meant to be a temporary one; the church militant will not endure for ever — only "until He comes."

"We are eagerly awaiting a new heaven and a new earth, as he promised, in which justice dwells" (2 Pet. 3:13), when "God himself will dwell with us, and will wipe away every tear from our eyes, when death and grief, sighing and sorrow, shall be no more" (Rev. 21:3–4). This vision of the book of Revelation is the same as that presented by innumerable psalms, especially by those we

DAVID'S TOMB

have termed the "Royal Psalms," dealing with the reign of God on earth (Pss. 96; 97; 98; 99). But all over the book of Psalms we are confronted with this holy impatience, this refusal to be content with the world as it is, this urgent prayer for the coming of the kingdom of peace.

If we pretend that this is simply an "Old Testament attitude" expressing a longing for the Messiah, we shall miss the whole point of these psalms. The apostles did not regard them as outdated once the Messiah had come; on the contrary, they became all the more anxious to see the remainder of the messianic promises fulfilled. *"Come, Lord Jesus!"* Perhaps, when we think of "the church," our thoughts linger too readily on the new building for which we have to pay, or upon the bishops gathered in council, instead of turning, at least sometimes, to the church as it will be in eternity. When present anxieties dishearten us, the psalms can console us by helping us to adjust our scale of values. In praying with heart and mind for the coming of the kingdom, in the words of the ancient psalms, we can fix our attention, at least for some time each day, on that glorious future when the New Jerusalem, glorious as a bride, will be achieved in all its splendor. Then indeed we shall celebrate the final defeat of all God's enemies (1 Cor. 15:24–28), the ultimate triumph of the Prince of Peace (Ps. 72).

"JESUS IS LORD"

In New Testament times the mark of a Christian was that he confessed Jesus as Lord (1 Cor. 12:3). The Douai Bible, until Bishop Challoner's revision, retained this profound apostolic insight into the unity of the Old and New Testaments by frequently translating *Dominus* in the Old Testament as *"Our Lord."* So we read, in the original Douai Old Testament (1609): "The earth is Our Lord's, and the fulnesse thereof . . ." (Ps. 24:1), and "One thing I have asked of Our Lord, this wil I seeke for, that I may dwell in the house of Our Lord al the dayes of my life" (Ps. 27:4)

To read the psalms with Jesus Christ in mind whenever we meet the word *Dominus* or *Lord* is not to falsify their meaning. That is exactly what the early Christians did when they, as a general rule, assigned one divine title (God) to the Father, and another one (Lord) to Jesus Christ. "Thou art worthy, *Lord,* to receive the book . . . for thou has redeemed us to *God* in thy blood" (Rev. 5:9). Once they had made that application, the whole book of Psalms took on a new meaning; it became Christological and Trinitarian. The hymn book of the temple became the prayer book of the new Israel of God.

WE ARE MEMBERS OF HIS BODY

Of all the marks which distinguish that civilization which is common to English-speaking lands, probably the most distinctive is respect for the individual. We do not like "regimentation," we are instinctively suspicious of government interference in the lives of the citizens, and we love the privacy of our homes. Un-

Come, let us sing joyfully to the Lord!

fortunately, this stress on individualism can restrict the scope of our prayers unless we keep a careful watch over it. We find it easy to pray for our own needs, for our families and friends, and for all whom we know as individuals. But, unlike the more "regimented" or socially-minded nations, we do not *instinctively* pray for the church universal; we have to remind ourselves of this duty.

Yet the plain fact is that we do not know as individuals the vast majority of those who need our prayers most, and who are relying upon us for those prayers. The church here on earth goes hungry and starving; it knows persecution which breaks, not just the bodies, but even the minds of its priests and layfolk. In a thousand villages whose names we do not know, it witnesses every day the triumph and taunts of God's enemies saying, "Where is thy God?" (Ps. 42:3). Every day the church sees hatred for God and for the Crucified planted in the hearts of the very young: some readers

WE SHOULD JOIN OUR PRAYERS TO
THE PRAYERS OF THOSE WHO MOST
NEED OUR HELP

may remember pictures of little Chinese children compelled amid
their tears to cheer the imprisonment or expulsion of priests and
sisters who had been mother and father to them for all the life
they could remember.

Christians in Chinese prisons or working in the labor-camps
of Eastern Europe would not consider the Psalms of the Exile
out of date today. Their churches are destroyed or abandoned:
"O God, the heathen have come into thy inheritance; they have
defiled thy holy temple; they have laid Jerusalem in ruins" (Ps.
79:1). They themselves are prisoners doomed to die: "Let the
groans of the prisoners come before thee; in thy great power,
preserve those doomed to die" (Ps. 79:11). Even the memory
of what their life used to be is a source of deeper sorrow: "These
things I remember, as I pour out my soul: how I went with the
throng, and led them in procession to the house of God, with glad
shouts and songs of thanksgiving, as the multitude kept the feast-
day" (Ps. 42:4). The least we can do is to recite the psalms in the

name of all those who can no longer publicly praise and thank God, to pray for all those who are too ill to pray, or who do not know how to pray. For we are all members of the same body, and when we pray we do so, not primarily in our own name, but "through Jesus Christ, our Lord" in behalf of the whole church.

Last Centuries Before Christ

John J. Greehy
and Philip Lane

In the past, religious instruction in the schools usually went no further than the year 587, B.C., when most of the inhabitants of Judah and Jerusalem were carried into exile in Babylonia. Consequently, many Christians have little knowledge of the important five centuries between the Exile and the coming of Christ. The following account of the history of the Jews, and of the political and theological developments within Judaism during that period will help toward a better understanding of the world into which Jesus was born and the situation within which Christianity had its roots.

RUINS OF THE TEMPLE OF JUPITER AT BAALBEK

Historical Outline

FEW CHRISTIANS grasp fully the connection between the Old and the New Testaments. This is not surprising since biblical study has tended to be rather lop-sided: religious instruction in schools often deals with Israelite history as far as the fall of Jerusalem (587 B.C.), but goes no further. Consequently, the world of the Old Testament and the world of the New may be divorced from each other in people's minds by five centuries. At the time of the Exile (when the Israelites, after the fall of Jerusalem, were carried off to Babylonia), the people of Israel were ruled by a well established monarchy, and their theological thinking was sometimes fairly primitive. By the time of Christ, entirely new political forces had arisen, belief in immortality and bodily resurrection was widespread, a highly complex angelology and demonology had been developed.

Of course, by treating the two periods as separate, it is possible to remain undisturbed by the extraordinary differences they display. The New Testament situation is taken for granted: how many Christians, for example, could give an account of the Pharisees, their origins, and religious beliefs? If it were found that only a few had any ideas on the subject, it would hardly be surprising, for the answer lies in those lost centuries between the Exile (587–538 B.C.) and the birth of Christ. It is obviously important that the gap be closed. First of all, therefore, some attempt must be made to grasp the historical outlines of the period; for it is only in their historical context that political and theological developments become fully intelligible.

The year 539 B.C. is the turning-point in later Jewish history. At the battle of Opis the Babylonian empire was destroyed, and the exiled Jews found themselves under Persian rule. No doubt they welcomed this as a change for the better: such is the habit of subject peoples. This time, however, their hope was well-founded, for King Cyrus turned out to be the most enlightened of ancient despots, pursuing a policy of tolerance toward the culture and religious beliefs of those under his sway.

In 538 B.C. a royal edict was issued authorizing the return of the exiled Jews to their homeland, and the restoration of their cult in Jerusalem. Under Shesh-bazzar and Zerubbabel, both princes of the royal house of David, a small number of exiles returned from Babylon and work was begun on rebuilding the temple. However, their early enthusiasm soon waned; for the neighboring peoples were hostile, and many of the Jews who had escaped captivity and remained behind in Judah were suspicious, if not openly unfriendly. Work ground to a halt and it was not until 515 B.C. that the new temple was completed.

Even the exhilaration over this accomplishment was shortlived. With the Persian empire in apparent difficulties, the prophets Haggai and Zechariah foretold the imminent rule of a messianic king in Jerusalem and the destruction of Judah's traditional foes. Such talk was inflammatory and dangerous, and when Darius had established himself as the Persian ruler he made sure that the Davidic line should cease to rule. Zerubbabel was deposed, perhaps killed – the facts are not clear. Never again was the seed of David to rule as God's representative in the city of Sion.

NEHEMIAH AND EZRA

Nevertheless Cyrus' policy of toleration was continued as long as the Persian empire lasted. For the next seventy years the Jewish community continued to exist under the guidance of the high priests; but its morals were lax and intermarriage with the neighboring tribes was common practice. Then in 445 B.C. Nehemiah, a Jewish official at the Persian court, was appointed governor of Judah with a commission to re-establish the political structure of the country.

Using his powerful personality to rally the people from their despondency, Nehemiah rebuilt the walls of Jerusalem in spite

MOSES RECEIVING TABLES OF THE LAW
Raphael

of the delaying tactics of the Arabs and the Samaritans. Nehemiah
was a Jew of the old stock, a religious purist, strict and undeviating
in his loyalty to Yahweh — naturally enough the religious and moral
laxity which he found saddened and angered him. Yet his plead-
ings and rages only met with limited success.

Another Jew, Ezra, was sent from Babylon with a purely religious commission to bring about the change of heart which was
necessary for any reform. He, too, was faced with apathy and re-
sentment; but after a fine public display of emotion, when he
wept for the sins of the people before Yahweh, a sudden sense of
shame came over the Jews, and after a few months of investigation and deliberation all foreign partners were divorced.

Ezra's guide and source of inspiration was the book of the Law,
a copy of which he had brought with him from Babylon: it was
this love and respect for the Law which he tried to pass on to the
Jews. The highlight of his career, therefore, not only from his

own point of view, but, in retrospect, from the point of view of the Jewish people, was the day when with solemn ceremony the men of Judah were reconstituted as a community on the basis of the Law.

The importance of this event cannot be overemphasized. From this time onward a Jew was a Jew because he observed the Law of Moses, not because he lived in Palestine and worshipped at the temple in Jerusalem. As a result of this, all those Jews of the Diaspora, or Dispersion, no matter where they lived—in Babylon, Egypt, Greece, Syria—were embraced as full members of the people of God. It was a great step forward. Ezra's achievement has sometimes been magnified out of all proportion, but such exaggeration is the result of sound motives. Judaism was now reconstituted in a form which was to last for centuries.

The problem of the comparative dates for Nehemiah and Ezra is difficult but not over-important: dates pale before the overriding impact of deeds. We might suggest that Nehemiah be placed in the reign of Artaxerxes I (465–423 B.C.) who, as governor, established a necessary social order. Since Ezra's religious reforms presuppose such a civil peace he may be placed under Artaxerxes II (404–358 B.C.)

Growth of Jewish communities abroad

Now, almost as it were out of deference to the growing pains of the new community, a curtain of silence falls. During the last hundred years of Persian rule almost nothing is known of Judah. However, during these years the Jewish communities abroad were growing both in size and in importance, imbibing new ideas as well as spreading their own. After so many years of stability the Jews must have viewed with alarm the sudden rise of Alexander the Great; but they could do nothing to turn aside the tide of history. Some time during the years 333-332 B.C. Palestine came into Alexander's power, and what is known as the Hellenistic period began.

In 323 B.C. Alexander died an untimely death, and almost immediately his empire began to disintegrate. Rival generals fought for control, and Palestine fell into the hands of Ptolemy Lagi who had seized power in Egypt. So far as it is known (records of this period are almost non-existent) any fears the Jews may have had were unfounded; for it appears that yet another hundred years passed by with the same privileges granted to them as they had enjoyed under Persian rule.

Meanwhile the Jewish community in Egypt grew out of all recognition; by this time there were more Jews living outside Palestine than there were living at home. It was not very long before the Jews of Egypt adopted Greek as their commercial language, and soon a generation grew up with a very hazy knowledge of Hebrew. Thus, during the third century B.C., a start was made on a translation of the Law of Moses, and later, of the other books, into Greek. It is this translation which is known as the Septuagint. Here indeed was a startling departure from previous attitudes. New opportunities were offered for the exchange of views between Jew and Gentile, new channels opened for the infiltration of Greek thought.

A SPLIT IN JEWISH SOCIETY

Such was the state of affairs until 223 B.C. when Antiochus III came to the throne of the Seleucid Kingdom, which ruled much of Asia Minor and some of Alexander's eastern provinces. After a long and bitter war which terminated in 198 B.C., Antiochus III wrested Palestine out of the hands of the Ptolemies, and once more the Jews had a new master. Antiochus showed the Jews the greatest consideration and in no way curbed the privileges which they had already enjoyed for three and a half centuries. Politically all was well. The danger lay elsewhere.

Slowly and insidiously, almost since the return of the Jews from exile, the policy of religious and cultural toleration had been breaking down old barriers. It was inevitable that the Jews of the Diaspora should become imbued with Greek thought; but the Jews of Palestine were not immune. Greek colonies dotted the countryside, and by the time Antiochus gained control of Palestine, a deep split was appearing in Jewish society. Some

THE HARBOR AT BYBLOS, *modern Jbeil, Lebanon*

favored Greek culture so much that they found their own laws an unbearable encumbrance. Others saw any form of Hellenization as a betrayal of their religious principles, and fought tooth and nail against any foreign innovation. An explosion was imminent.

REVOLT LED BY THE MACCABEES

Antiochus III was not always successful: he was unwise enough to fall foul of Rome. When Antiochus IV Epiphanes came to the throne in 175 B.C. after the twelve-year reign of Seleucus IV, it was all the Seleucid kingdom could do to find the money to pay the indemnity which had been imposed on it. With Antiochus Epiphanes desperate for money, a sordid situation grew up in Jerusalem. Various aspirants began to vie for the high priesthood: the legitimate holder was ousted, and the office went to the highest bidder. As the various parties stooped lower and lower to gain preferment, arguments and rioting broke out. In 169 B.C. the temple was plundered with the high priest's connivance and a Seleucid commissioner established in Jerusalem in an effort to keep order, and force through a policy of Hellenization.

Such was the opposition that in 168 B.C. Antiochus Epiphanes sent his general Apollonius to Jerusalem with a sizable force. Many Jews were treacherously slaughtered, the city walls were razed, and a garrison installed. As if this were not enough, the cult of Zeus was established in the temple and swine's flesh offered up in sacrifice. The practice of Judaism was forbidden, and hundreds of loyal Jews were butchered for observing the Sabbath or having their children circumcised.

Antiochus Epiphanes had gone too far. Led by Mattathias, many Jews revolted, and later under the leadership of Judas Maccabeus, Mattathias' son, every enemy army which was sent out against them was defeated, but not without great loss of life. In 164 B.C. Judas entered Jerusalem in triumph, and cleansed and rededicated the temple. Once again the Jews had won religious independence.

The Law is Central

At this point historical questions can be set aside; for although the last century and a half before Christ was not without unrest and upheaval, by 164 B.C. Judaism, though it would develop further, had assumed the characteristic form which it bore for many years to come. The most obvious difference between pre-exilic Israel and post-exilic Judaism was their very basis for existence. Previously, to be a Jew was to belong to a complex national and cultic organization: by the time of Christ it was the keeping of the Law which marked off Jew from Gentile. Naturally, therefore, the Jews were greatly concerned to keep the Law accurately, for they saw the Exile as a punishment for previous failure to do so.

The Law was central: around it were clustered all other religious and cultural practices. Moreover this Law was a written Law. The completed Pentateuch, the first five books of the Old Testament, was known in Jerusalem soon after the time of Ezra's reforms: it was these books, called by the Jews *Torah,* (the Way to God), which constituted the Law proper, and which were accepted as fully authoritative. The canonization of the other books of the Old Testament followed later and was completed for the most part before the end of the Persian period. This offered the Jews something far more substantial, more authoritative than their counterparts in pre-exilic days had possessed. Here in black and white could be found God's will, God's commandments for all to consult. It is little wonder that the age of prophecy had come to an end: the prophet had lost his commission—the Law was sufficient.

Nonetheless cultic practices continued to flourish and were taken very seriously because they were specifically required by the Law. Over all the temple affairs was the high priest who claimed to trace his lineage back to Aaron through Zadok. However, once the Davidic dynasty ceased to play an active part in politics – that is, when Zerubbabel was removed from office by Darius – secular as well as spiritual power was concentrated more and more in the hands of the high priest.

With the passage of time the high priesthood became almost entirely a political office; because, although the cult flourished, the motive power behind it was now the Law, and spiritual power was vested in those who interpreted it. Therefore, it should not cause quite so much scandal as it tends to do, when we read of the depths of arrant worldliness to which men were willing to sink during Antiochus Epiphanes' reign, in an effort to be appointed high priest. The office was political. This should also be borne in mind when we read of Annas and Caiaphas in the Gospels: their duplicity and hypocrisy should not be taken as a yardstick to measure contemporary Judaism.

Scribes

Spiritual power had been transferred elsewhere. The all-pervading importance of the Law demanded some human authority to interpret it and explain any difficult passages or contradictions. This need was filled by a class of people called the Scribes, who spent their time studying the Law and passing on their findings to the people through their disciples. Their origin is obscure. They looked back to Ezra as their founder, and certainly it was sometime after his death that they came to the fore. Their importance doubtless grew in direct proportion to the increasing influence of the Law, and by the time of the Maccabees they had, for all practical purposes, usurped the spiritual primacy once held by the priestly aristocracy.

Wisdom teachers

Side by side with the emergence of the Scribes, there grew up a group of people called wisdom teachers; these were not a separate class – Ben Sirach, the writer of Ecclesiasticus, was a Scribe – but they were different in their function. Wisdom literature, whose origins can be found in pre-exilic writings, borrowed a great deal from parallel literature in the other Near Eastern countries. Its purpose was practical; for it attempted to show how a pious Jew would put the Law into practice in his daily life. The criterion for a good life, which was the end-product of wisdom, was the observance of the Law. This, of course, was the basic difference between the wisdom literature of the Jews and the wisdom literature of other countries. In the Old Testament the book of Proverbs, some of the later Psalms, Job, the book of Wisdom, the Song of Songs, Ecclesiasticus and Ecclesiastes are all examples of wisdom literature. For the study of development in Jewish thought they are of inestimable value, and yet at the same time they are the most neglected books in the Bible.

The Law, then, was not, at least for a long time, an end in itself. Its purpose was ethical – to teach the acquirement of those virtues pleasing to God. But the very practice of interpretation of the Law had intrinsic dangers: it sowed the seeds which gave rise to that concentration on outward conformity which was so prevalent in the days of Christ.

Theological Developments

Before the Exile the tendency had been to look upon Israel as a nation set apart: there was at times unhealthy introspection. After the Exile this exclusiveness was attacked and something almost amounting to a missionary spirit was kindled in the hearts of many Jews: the author of Jonah has a most convincing universal vision. Even when Judaism was forced to look in upon itself with the infiltration of foreign culture, there were still many who believed that the Gentiles would eventually turn and acknowledge Yahweh as Lord. Certainly many converts were made: these proselytes,

SAMARITAN   CARRYING
TORAH

as they were called, are in ample evidence in the New Testament. Needless to say, there were still many who clung to the idea of election with grim determination.

In an age when traditional beliefs were being questioned, monotheism was never in danger. On the contrary the oneness and omnipotence of God were emphasized even more. The tendency, well-attested in pre-exilic days, to worship Yahweh as a God out of reach became exaggerated. By the third century B.C. the name Yahweh was no longer pronounced as a general rule: other titles were used—King of Heaven, Lord of Spirits, Head of Days and so forth. Sometimes Yahweh was called by one of his qualities—Divine Wisdom, Divine Word. It is interesting to note that these personifications are not Hellenistic but Palestinian in origin: how much they influenced the Christian doctrine of the Logos is hard to say.

As God's dealings with men became more remote, the part played by angels became more important. One hears of God's attendants long before the Exile, but post-exilic Judaism developed the concept considerably. There were seven archangels (we are familiar with three of them: Michael, Gabriel, and Raphael), and under them there was a hierarchy of countless other angels. The job they fulfilled was to act as God's agents in His dealings with men.

NEW APPROACH TO THE PROBLEM OF EVIL

However, the most spectacular advance in theological thinking during this period was the entirely new approach to the problem of evil. The traditional orthodox teaching, that the sinner is punished in this life and the upright blessed, had begun to wear thin. The humiliation and the degradation of the Exile could not be glibly explained: the book of Job makes it quite clear that men were beginning to think again.

One result of this intellectual struggle was an increasing role allotted to Satan and his angels. Going by various names (Mastema, Beliar, Belial) Satan, which in the Hebrew means "Adversary," seems to have originally been conceived as a member of the heavenly court whose function was to act as a prosecuting counsel (somewhat as the Devil's Advocate provides the opposition in the canonization process of today). Later he appears as head of the fallen angels who work in competition against God and tempt men to evil. Naturally, certain dualistic tendencies crept in—God and Satan were looked upon as two opposite and equal poles—perhaps as a result of influence from Iran; while this was frowned upon and appeared to die out, it never fully lost its influence.

RESURRECTION OF THE BODY

So far, the theology of post-exilic Judaism has been a logical development of teaching already to be found under the monarchy. Now, the dissatisfaction which Jews felt at the orthodox solution to the problem of evil gave rise to belief in the resurrection of the body. While there had always been vague teaching about the continued existence of a ghostly body after death in a gloomy and forbidding place called Sheol, it was not until the second century

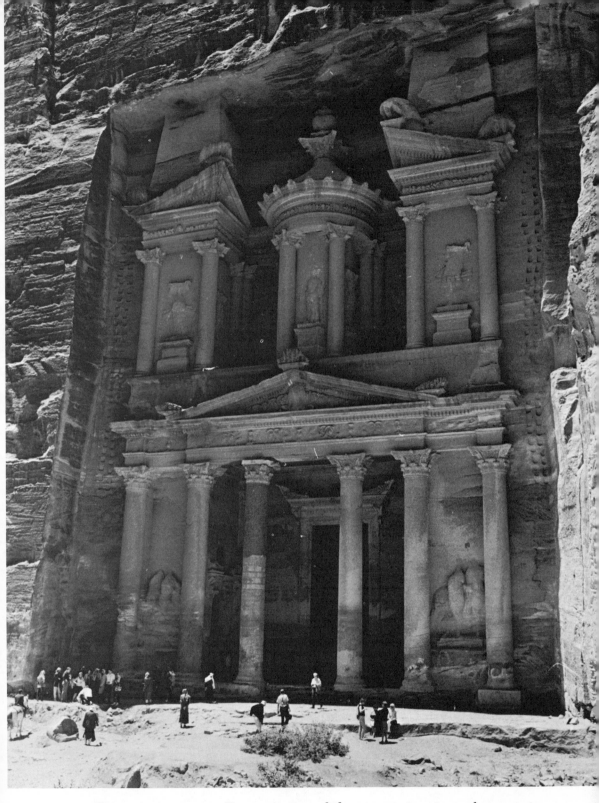

NABATEAN TOMB AT PETRA *is one of the many structures hewn out of the rock at this site*

B.C. that full-grown belief in the resurrection of the body was in any way accepted.

The fact that good men are often chastened in this world while the blatantly wicked go unpunished must have been evident to any thinking man for years: there had never been a real spur to goad people to acknowledge the facts of common experience. The necessity, however, of accepting resurrection was forced upon the Jews by the persecution under Antiochus Epiphanes. Men of the utmost integrity were being murdered for their righteous behavior in keeping the Law: surely there was some purpose in their martyrdom — otherwise, why bother? Yet the Old Testament affords scant evidence of a belief in the resurrection of the body.

The earliest witness to such a belief is Isaiah 26:19: "Your dead will come to life, their corpses will rise; awake, exult, all you who lie in the dust, for your dew is a radiant dew and the land of ghosts will give birth." This text, however, is difficult and cannot be used freely. Most probably based on this is Daniel 12:2-3: "Of those who lie sleeping in the dust of the earth many will awake, some to everlasting life, some to shame and everlasting disgrace." This represents a great advance on Isaiah, but the concept is still primitive.

The apocryphal literature, however, bears witness to a belief in the resurrection of the dead that eventually became general. Ethiopic Enoch (90:33; 91:10) suggests resurrection of the righteous only. Restricted belief in a *general* resurrection can be found in the Testaments of the Twelve Patriarchs: Simeon (6:7), Judah (25:1), Zebulon (10:2), Benjamin (10:6-8). Slavonic Enoch (1:2; 22:8; 65:6ff.) implies resurrection by talking of the blessed immortality of the just. See also Psalms of Solomon (3:12; 13:11; 14:3) and Apocalypse of Baruch (30:1; 42:7; 49:1-3). No book teaches *indubitably* a general resurrection of all mankind until IV Ezra (7:32-33; 8:53-54), but here we must allow for the possibility of Christian influence.

Summing up, then, the development of the doctrine of the resurrection of the dead is as follows: (1) righteous Israelites only;

SAMARITANS AT PRAYER ON MOUNT
GERIZIM

(2) righteous and wicked Israelites only; (3) righteous and wicked
everywhere.

SADDUCEES AND PHARISEES

As one might expect, the emergence of these new ideas caused
parties to form, for or against. The three sects most in evidence in
the New Testament are Scribes, Pharisees, and Sadducees.
Scribes have already been mentioned. They were doctors of the
Law, often with the honorific title of Rabbi; as such, they were not
a separate political or religious faction—they could and did join
any party they chose.

The Sadducees were in origin the priestly aristocracy which
down to the time of Antiochus Epiphanes had held the office of
high priest by right of their lineage. Although many of their number had been deeply involved in encouraging the spread of Hellenism, they were in religious matters dyed-in-the-wool conserva-

tives: the Torah alone was acceptable to them. Consequently all the oral law of the Scribes was offensive to the Sadducees and such new-fangled beliefs as immortality, resurrection, hierarchies of angels and devils were unthinkable. Their deep hatred of change, especially of a turbulent nature, not only explains their willingness to co-operate with foreign occupying forces, but also their mistrust of Jesus. They had too much to lose.

The Pharisees, on the other hand, followed in the footsteps of the Hasidim (Pious Ones), the Jews who had refused to flirt with Hellenism and had fought with Judas Maccabeus. They too were strict observers of the Law, but they considered the oral law, developed by the Scribes, as binding. Naturally, therefore, it was to this party that most of the Scribes belonged.

Being a moral rather than a political force in the country, the Pharisees were admired by the general populace and became the true spiritual leaders. They accepted wholeheartedly the recently formulated beliefs in such matters as the resurrection of the body. Nevertheless, by the time of Christ, they had fallen into the trap which the Law itself had set. They had become legalistic to a ludicrous degree, pondering at length whether a mother by dandling her child on her knee broke the law of the Sabbath. Such was their reverence of the Law, so strict their observance of it, that Jesus' claim to go beyond the Law repelled them. The liberals of one age had become the conservatives of the next.

The Dead Sea Scrolls

Nowadays a discussion of the last centuries before Christ would be unthinkable without some reference to the so-called Dead Sea Scrolls. The story of the discovery of these documents and the archeological investigations can be found in the many books written in all the principal languages. Here we can do no more than present some personal conclusions on this subject and its bearing on the organization of the early Christian church.

The independent archeological and paleographical evidence tends to show that there is a link between the cave scrolls and the buildings discovered nearby. The "People of the scrolls" were an organized group who lived at Qumran, a village northwest of the Dead Sea, from the second half of the second century B.C. to the year 68 A.D. This "end" date, strongly supported by Père de Vaux, O.P., has been challenged by other scholars. Indeed, very few statements made about the scrolls have gone unchallenged.

A study of the documents reveals a rigid communitarian system at Qumran (the Manual of Discipline), and a probably more lax organization for "mixed" (i.e., non-celibate) groups usually outside this center of the movement (the Damascus Document). The Manual of Discipline, a more fundamental document, shows traces of considerable addition. The original form could be the work of the Master of Justice (also called the Teacher of Righteousness) who may have led the group originally to the Judean desert as a protest against a usurping temple priesthood. (The first of the Maccabees, who exercised "illegally" the function of high priest in Jerusalem in the year 152 B.C., was Jonathan.)

THE ESSENES

Most authors still identify the Qumran community with at least a part of the general "Essene" way of life. Our accounts of the Essenes come from Philo (*ca.* 20 B.C.–A.D. *ca.* 50) and Josephus Flavius (A.D. 30–A.D. 90?). A comparison between the Essenes and the scrolls shows many similarities in rules of entry, organization, and discipline, even in the "strict" and "lax" way regarding celibacy. There are, however, some omissions: the concepts of covenant, and eschatological expectation, even the figure of the Master of Justice are not mentioned in our classical sources on the Essenes.

It may be that the classical authors left out ideas which would not be accepted or understood by Hellenized Jewish or Gentile readers. We should also take into account the difference in time

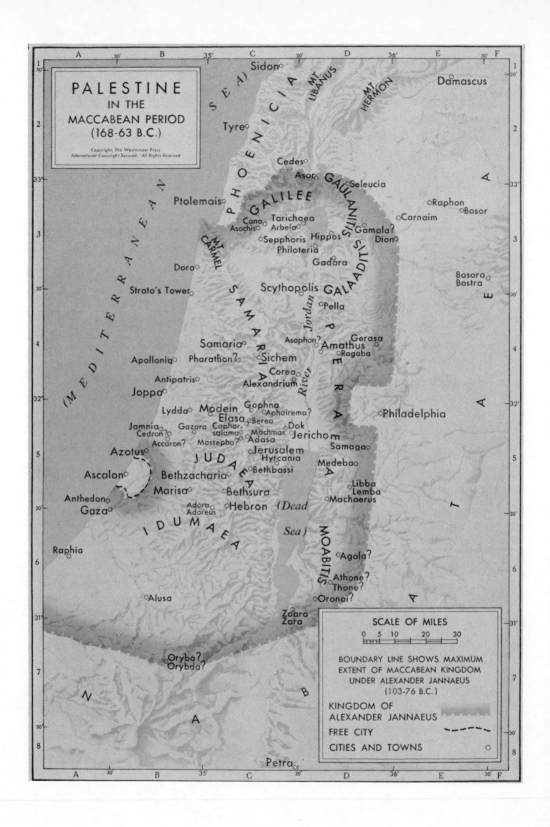

PALESTINE
IN THE
MACCABEAN PERIOD
(168-63 B.C.)

Copyright, The Westminster Press
International Copyright Secured. All Rights Reserved

MEDITERRANEAN

(SEA)

PHOENICIA

Sidon

Tyre

Cedes

Asor

Ptolemais

GALILEE

MT. LIBANUS

MT. HERMON

Damascus

Seleucia

Raphon
Bosor

Carnaim

GAULANITIS

Cana
Asochis
Tarichaea
Arbela
Sepphoris
Hippos
Philoteria
Gamala?
Dion

MT. CARMEL

Dora

Strato's Tower

Gadara

GALAADITIS

Bosora
Bostra

SAMARIA

Scythopolis

GALAADITIS

Pella

Jordan

Samaria
Apollonia
Pharathon?
Sichem
Asophon?
Amathus
Ragaba
Gerasa

P E R A E A

Antipatris

Joppa

Corea
Alexandrium

River

Lydda
Modein
Elasa
Gophna
Aphairema?
Berea

Jamnia
Cedron
Gazara Caphar-
salama
Accaron?
Massepha?
Machmas
Adasa
Dok
Jerichom

Philadelphia

Azotus

JUDAEA

Jerusalem
Hyrcania
Bethbassi

Samaga

Medeba

Ascalon

Bethzacharia

Marisa

Bethsura

Bethsura

Libba
Lemba
Machaerus

Anthedon
Gaza

Adora
Adoreus
Hebron

(Dead

IDUMAEA

Sea)

MOABITIS

Raphia

Agala?

Alusa

Athone?
Thone?
Oronai?

Zoara
Zara

N

A

Oryba?
Orybda?

B

Petra

between the original Qumran texts and the accounts given by Philo and Josephus; also the fact that Essenism consisted of a number of groups, not all of which seem to have been uniformly organized. Professor Frank Cross makes probably the most convincing point of all. The existence of an extensive library shows that the Qumran community was not a small ephemeral group. Josephus could not have passed them unnoticed. He constantly divides the Jewish sects into three: Pharisees, Sadducees, and Essenes. Cross also considers the Essene identification most likely though Professor Rabin of Jerusalem had already argued strongly for the Pharisees in 1957. We leave the hypothetical historical sketches of the group to the various books. One of the most fascinating is that written by an outstanding worker on the scrolls, Father J. T. Milik's *Ten Years of Discovery in the Wilderness of Judea.*

THE QUMRAN COMMUNITY AND THE PRIMITIVE CHURCH

Two fundamental points already outlined by Père de Vaux in 1956 seem to have become more widely accepted since then. Firstly, we have the fact that the Qumran community and the primitive church, the one and the other, are attached very closely to the Old Testament, and many of the resemblances can be explained by that common origin. Secondly, our Qumran discoveries have let us know in a privileged way one of the aspects of contemporary Judaism of the New Testament, but other baptist and community groups should be taken into account to appreciate justly the relationship between the primitive church and Qumran. There are certain parallels but no clear proof of borrowings. That the primitive church emerged from Qumran is certainly disproved from a consideration of the essential differences. We present now some particular conclusions.

In the matter of organizational offices, certain affinities have been found between the Qumran "overseer" (*mebaqqer*) and the Christian bishop (*episcopos*), in that the former was originally in charge of some form of economic and distributive activity. One can trace the growth of a monarchic idea in this office, parallel to the same development of the episcopate in the later part of the apostolic church. A parallelism is also possible between the "Supervisor of all the Camps," found in the Damascus Document, and Paul's "Regional Apostles," Timothy and Titus. However, we do not really know how widespread the former office was, or whether Paul would have been seriously influenced by it. There is really very little evidence for the existence at Qumran of any authoritative "Inner Council" to correspond with the position of the twelve apostles.

On the other hand, a striking similarity exists between the *Rabbim* ("Great Ones," "Initiated") of the Qumran Documents, and the *Pléthos* (full assembly of disciples) of the Acts of the Apostles. We have an interesting illustration as to how, in a Jewish environment, all the members of an organization could have a voice in deliberation. At least in the earlier stages, however, the *Rabbim* seem to have been far more powerful than any reference in Acts suggests for the Christian *Pléthos*.

The suggested "similarities" in the matter of organizational practices we consider to be, at the least, doubtful. Thus, the organized community of goods at Qumran is really in no way parallel to the free giving, on the part of some Christians, of a certain amount of their property for the needy. The latter activity is motivated by Christian charity, prompted by the Holy Spirit.

The "meal" and "baptisms" of Qumran are very poor in content when we compare them to the Christian sacraments of the eucharist and baptism. In the case of the eucharist, a parallel exists in the *agape*, but this can be traced to the general Jewish "common meal." As to baptism, we can find no proof at Qumran that there was any significant "washing" in the rite of initiation.

MESSAGE AND BAPTISM OF JOHN THE BAPTIST

We must now consider the message and baptism of John the Baptist, compared with Qumran. We are given a short account of John "that was called the Baptist" by Josephus (*Antiquities* 18, 5, 2). If we were to take this account alone, then we would have a similar idea behind John's baptism and that of Qumran. Josephus

JARS THAT HELD THE SCROLLS DIS-
COVERED IN THE DEAD SEA AREA

tells us that John exhorted the Jews to come to baptism, and to use it for the purification of the body, provided that the soul was thoroughly purified beforehand by righteousness. There are two elements, however, of prime importance which differentiate the baptism of John from the baptism(s) of Qumran.

Firstly, we have the urgent nature of John's mission. Even though the Qumranites at first might have prepared for a speedy deliverance, they settled into a community life as time went on, inhabiting well-constructed buildings, for the study of the Law. This study is their interpretation of Isaiah 40:3: "Hark! There is one who cries out in the wilderness, 'Prepare the way of the Lord, make straight in the desert a highway for our God.'" (cf. Manual of Discipline, 8, 12–16). The Baptist's interpretation is very different. "Even now the axe is laid to the root of the trees..." (Luke 3:9). His baptism was an urgent and unique ceremony. Judgment was at hand, and acceptance of baptism was part of the necessary conversion.

Secondly, John's message was for all, not merely for the Jews. The Qumran people on the other hand thought only in terms of their own narrow circle, striving to attain a greater degree of legal purity. Their way of life was quite separatist, avoiding contact not only with Gentiles, but also with their fellow Jews. They would have even less time than the Pharisees to spare for the untaught and negligent "people of the land." John's message, in the Gospel of Luke, delivered to multitudes, tax collectors, and soldiers, is totally different.

The Master of Justice and Jesus Christ

When we approach the question of the two "Founders," Jesus Christ and the vague figure of the Master of Justice, we find numerous and essential differences. Some authors built up originally an astonishing portrait of the Master of Justice, subsequently refuted by the textual evidence itself. Christ, in this view, a view that still strangely persists, would have been nothing more than a reincarnation of the Qumran Master. A study of the texts reveals the vast difference between the Christian's personal relationship with his Founder (through faith and baptism), and the Qumranite's following of the legal interpretation of his prophet.

The next point of difference lies in the concept of salvation. In Qumran, it is not the Master of Justice who saves, but God. There is no change from Old Testament theology. In our New Testament, while this idea is repeated, we have a new element: Jesus saves. Matthew defines Jesus' mission on earth thus: "You shall call his name Jesus, for he will save his people from their sins" (1:21). There is no counterpart for the salvific work of Jesus, the Christ, in the Qumran documents. For the Qumranites, their historical teacher was neither their priestly nor kingly messiah.

A third fundamental difference lies in the message of each. The Master of Justice guides his group to the desert to lead perfect lives according to the Law of Moses and the prophets, as interpreted by himself. These are the "sons of light," the "remnant of Israel," the predestined ones who, in the Final Period, will

PORTION OF A DEAD SEA SCROLL *that carries a commentary on the book of Habakkuk*

triumph over all others. Christ declares a new Pact with God, in which salvation is open to all: "Go therefore and make disciples of all nations, baptizing them..." (Matt. 28:19). Some will not respond to the teaching; this is the only limit to Christian predestination.

There are, however, some very positive elements in the message of the Master of Justice: (1) the need of a personal conversion through some form of new alliance, so that the predestined can draw near to God; (2) the foundation of a fraternal community, even though confined to the predestined, is more pleasing to God than any building of stone; (3) the internal praise of God is more important than any blood sacrifices.

A study of the Qumran psalms (*hodayot* — thanksgivings), perhaps written by the Master, also shows us a figure steeped in the Old Testament, but differing from Christ in his failure to pardon, and in his restriction of love and expiation to members of the community. When the community left Qumran, they still expected the Messiah. The followers of the way of Jesus knew that the Messiah had already come, and had perceived the universality of his message.

We can answer with Father Milik the question concerning the non-appearance of this movement in our New Testament documents: "The Essenes remained on the outskirts both of the life of the Jewish people at a time when it was undergoing the rapid transformation that was to result in the stabilization of Judaism that persists until today, and of that of the early Christians in their formative days."

CONCLUSION

The foregoing account, outlining the history of the Jews after the Exile and tracing the political and theological developments within Judaism during this period, is intended to help toward a better understanding of the world into which Jesus was born and of the situation in which Christianity had its roots. The triumphs and failures of early Christianity are understood in the light of post-exilic developments.

It should not be thought that Judaism was only a collection of warring sects. The faith was still held in common, observance of the Law was ranked high by all, and all in some way looked forward to a restoration of Israel. There were still some who upheld a violent nationalism as the means of bringing about Judah's greatness: such were the Zealots who instigated the fatal rebellion against Roman rule that resulted in the destruction of the temple in A.D. 70. We find an acceptance of the resurrection of the body, but a prejudice against changing, or at least reinterpreting the Law.

Again, it would be wrong to think of the Jews in terms of Scribes and Pharisees with their claim to work out salvation through their own legal observance, coupled with a forgetfulness that it is a free gift of God. The Old Covenant era cannot be a failure if its final product is the humble obedient "poor of Yahweh."

CAVES NEAR THE DEAD SEA WHERE THE SCROLLS WERE FOUND

These men and women, following the Old Testament prophets, expected the conversion of Gentiles and their sharing in the promises. Such people awaited enlightenment, and on them the church of Jesus was built.

Of these people the late Cardinal Bea wrote in his book *The Church and the Jewish People:*

> No one can take from the Jewish people the honor arising from the part played in the past in the preparatory stages of the work of redemption. In addition, it is indisputable that the church was grounded in this people and on individual members of it. Christ, the head of the church, was the pre-eminent descendant of Abraham. From Abraham's stock came also His blessed Mother, the apostles, who were the foundation of the church, and the first Jewish Christians who made up its earliest communities. True, the founding of the church constituted an entirely new beginning, wholly due to Jesus Christ who founded it on His apostles, chosen and taught by Him. This new start was manifested to the world by the descent of the Holy Spirit on the day of Pentecost. Nevertheless, this new commencement came from the people of the Old Testament . . .

Subject Index
and
Bible Reference Index

Subject Index

Bible Reference Index

This index lists all references to the Bible that appear in the book. The Bible references (chapter and verse) are printed in italic, and are followed by the page numbers where they are found.

Picture Credits

GOD SPEAKS TO US: 2—*Moses* by Michelangelo, Russ Busby; 6—*Semite with donkey,* wall painting, University of Chicago; 9—*Pastoral scene,* Russ Busby; 13—*Illumination from 16th-century manuscript,* Library of Congress; 15—*Camel trail to Sinai,* Matson Photo Service; 17—*Sixteenth-century woodcut,* Library of Congress, Lessing J. Rosenwald Collection; 20—*Samaritan priest,* Russ Busby; 22—*Ezekiel* by Michelangelo, Library of Congress; 23—*Cylinder of Cyrus,* British Museum; 25—*Bronze-age vessels,* Israel Office of Information; 30—*St. Jerome's preface to Pentateuch,* Library of Congress; 32—*Wilderness of Judea,* Matson Photo Service; 35—*Isaiah Scroll,* Professor John C. Trevor; 37—*Altar of Incense,* Library of Congress; 39—*Giant Bible of Mainz,* Library of Congress; 41—*St. Jerome with Sts. Paula and Eustochium* by Francisco de Zurbaran, National Gallery of Art, Samuel H. Kress Collection; 43—*Village of Judea,* Matson Photo Service; 45—*Model of Hypostyle Hall at Karnack,* Metropolitan Museum of Art; 47—*Joseph's Coat Brought to Jacob* by Giovanni A. de Ferrari, National Gallery of Art, Samuel H. Kress Collection; 49—*Madonna and Child* by Hans Memling, National Gallery of Art, Andrew Mellon Collection; 53—*Crowning with Thorns* by Titian, The Louvre, Alinari; 55—*Road between Bethlehem and Jerusalem,* Russ Busby; 57—*St. John the Evangelist,* Library of Congress.

LANGUAGE AND MENTALITY OF THE BIBLE WRITERS: 62—*Giant Bible of Mainz,* Library of Congress; 65—*Road from Jericho to Jerusalem,* Matson Photo Service; 68—*Cattle boats,* wall painting, University of Chicago; 70—*Arab drinking from "ibreek,"* Capital Baptist, Washington, D.C.; 75—*Picture of night sky,* Russ Busby; 77—*Arab plowing,* Israel Office of Information; 79—*Illumination from Bible of Nekcsei-Lipocz,* Library of Congress; 81—*Isaiah Scroll,* Israel Office of Information; 84—*Shepherd and his flock,* Library of Congress, Matson Photo Service; 86—*Adoration of Golden Calf* by Nicolas Poussin, M. H. de Young Memorial Museum, San Francisco, Samuel H. Kress Collection; 88—*Ruins of ancient Jericho,* Matson Photo Service; 91—*Isaiah* by Michelangelo, Library of Congress; 93—*Twilight scene,* Matson Photo Service; 96—*Cloud of locusts,* Matson Photo Service; 98—*Sea of Galilee,* Matson Photo Service.

THE INFLUENCE OF ISRAEL'S NEIGHBORS: 102—*The Great Sphinx of Gizeh,* Russ Busby; 105—*Archeologists with artifacts,* Israel Office of Information; 108—*The Euphrates,* Matson Photo Service; 110—*Bedouin dwelling,* Matson Photo Service; 113—*Relics of Canaanite temple,* Israel Office of Information; 115—*Map,* Westminster Press; 118—*Mount of Moses,* Russ Busby; 120—*Table of Showbread,* Library of Congress.

DEVELOPMENT OF DOCTRINE IN THE OLD TESTAMENT: 124—*Dead Sea Cave*, Russ Busby; 126—*Excavation at Tyre*, National Council of Tourism, Lebanon; 131—*Ezra Reading the Law*, Yale University; 133—*Samaritans showing Torah on Mount Gerizim*, Matson Photo Service; 135—*Bas-relief of Ark of the Covenant*, Israel Office of Information; 138—*Scholar with Dead Sea Scrolls*, Israel Office of Information; 141—*Mount Sinai in mist*, Matson Photo Service; 143—*The Euphrates*, Matson Photo Service; 145—*Hittite stele*, Library of Congress; 148—*Illuminated page of Nekcsei-Lipócz Bible*, Library of Congress; 151—*Bedouin home*, Russ Busby; 153—*Ruins on Mount Nebo*, Russ Busby; 157—*Elijah and the Raven* by Girolamo Savoldo, National Gallery of Art, Samuel H. Kress Collection; 159—*Assyrian boundary stone*, the Walters Art Gallery, Baltimore, Md.; 161—*The Archangel Gabriel* by Gérard David, Metropolitan Museum of Art; 163—*Dead Sea and mountains of Moab*, Matson Photo Service; 165—*Anathoth*, Matson Photo Service; 169—*Plain of the Law*, Matson Photo Service; 171—*Golden Menorah*, Library of Congress; 173—*Cedars of Lebanon*, Matson Photo Service; 175—*Ruins of synagogue at Capernaum*, Russ Busby.

THE GREAT THEOLOGIANS OF THE OLD TESTAMENT: 178—*Moses with the Tables of the Law* by Rembrandt, Staatliche Museum, Berlin; 182—*Sacrifice of Isaac* by Rembrandt, Library of Congress; 185—*Giant Bible of Mainz*, Library of Congress; 188—*Carrying offerings*, a wall painting, University of Chicago; 191—*Statue of Rameses II*, United Arab Republic; 193—*Cain and Abel*, Library of Congress; 195—*Pool of Solomon*, Russ Busby; 198—*The Wadi Hebron*, Matson Photo Service; 201—*Sumerian tablet*, the Walters Art Gallery, Baltimore, Md.; 203—*Road from Jerusalem to Jericho*, Matson Photo Service; 206—*Obelisk*, Russ Busby; 209—*Dead Sea from Mount Nebo*, Russ Busby; 213—*Assyrian winged genius*, the Walters Art Gallery, Baltimore, Md.; 215—*Sunrise over the Dead Sea*, Matson Photo Service; 217—*Reapers gather harvest*, Matson Photo Service; 219—*Articles used in Jewish religious observance*, Library of Congress; 221—*Boundary stone*, University of Pennsylvania Museum; 225—*Celebrating the Feast of Tabernacles*, Library of Congress; 227—*Noah's Sacrifice* by Bernardo Cavallino, Museum of Fine Arts of Houston, Samuel H. Kress Collection; 229—*Tickhill Psalter*, Library of Congress; 232—*Samaritan priest eating Passover*, Matson Photo Service; 235—*High Priest*, Library of Congress; 237—*The Euphrates*, Matson Photo Service; 240—*King David*, Cistercian Psalter, Library of Congress; 243—*The Jordan*, Matson Photo Service; 245—*Joseph Interpreting Pharaoh's Dream* by Lazzaro Bastiani, Columbia Museum of Art, S.C., Samuel H. Kress Collection; 247—*Bas-relief of Mede*, the Walters Art Gallery, Baltimore, Md.; 249—*Job and His friends*, Alinari; 251—*Jordan and Promised Land*, Library of Congress.

KINGDOM AND MESSIAH: 256—*King David* by Bernardo Ciuffagni, Library of Congress; 259—*Excavations at Ur*, University of Pennsylvania Museum; 262—*Code of Hammurabi*, University of Pennsylvania Museum; 264—*Samson Slaying the Philistine* by Bandinelli, National Gallery of Art, Widener Collection; 267—*Map*, Westminster Press; 269—*Wall of the Jebusites*, Matson Photo Service; 273—*Illumination from Greek Psalter*, Library of Congress; 275—*Solomon's stables*, Russ Busby; 279—*Map*, Westminster Press; 281—*Bethlehem*, Russ Busby; 282—*The Marriage of David*, Republic of Cyprus; 285—*Jeremiah* by Michelangelo, Library of Congress; 288—*Genealogy from the Book of Kells*, Library of Congress; 291—*Daniel in the Lions' Den*, Rubens, National Gallery of Art; 293—*Ruins of ancient Jericho*, Matson Photo Service; 296—*Dead Sea Scroll*, Israel Office of Information; 299—*Crucifixion* by Pietro Perugino, center panel of triptych, National Gallery of Art, Andrew Mellon Collection.

THE PSALMS: 302—*David Writing the Psalms*, Spanish miniature, National Gallery of Art, Lessing J. Rosenwald Collection; 305—*Dutch Psalter*, Library of Congress; 308—*Terra cotta plaque*, University of Chicago; 310—*Wadi Feiran at Sinai*, Matson Photo Service; 313—*David Playing the Harp for King Saul*, Rembrandt, Foundation Johann Maurits van Nassau, The Hague; 315—*Chant for Divine Office*, Library of Congress; 318—*Mount Sinai*, Library of Congress, Matson Photo Service; 320—*Pantocrator*, Alinari; 323—*Illumination from 14th-century Psalter*, Library of Congress; 324—*Samaritans praying at Passover*, Matson Photo Service; 328—*Moslem mother and child*, United Nations; 331—*St. John at the Foot of the Cross*, detail from *The Small Crucifixion* by Matthias Gruenewald, National Gallery of Art, Samuel H. Kress Collection; 334—*David's Tomb*, Russ Busby; 336—*Legend* "Come let us sing the Office"; 337—*Child praying*, Capital Baptist, Washington, D.C.

LAST CENTURIES BEFORE CHRIST: 340—*Ruins of the Temple of Jupiter at Baalbek*, Russ Busby; 343—*Moses Receiving Tables of the Law*, Raphael, Library of Congress; 346—*The Harbor at Byblos*, Lebanon Tourist Bureau; 351—*Samaritan carrying Torah*, Russ Busby; 353—*Nabatean tomb at Petra*, Russ Busby; 355—*Samaritans at prayer*, Matson Photo Service; 358—*Map*, Westminster Press; 361—*Jars that held Dead Sea Scrolls*, Russ Busby; 363—*Dead Sea Scroll*, Israel Office of Information; 365—*Caves near the Dead Sea where Scrolls were found*, Russ Busby.

THE HOLY LAND—Color photographs by Russ Busby and United Press International.